D1191744

Defining Humanity

Exploring Torah Insights Into Man and Morality

Rabbi Dov Berish Ganz

זה הספר מוקדש לזכר נשמת אבי מורי

הר"ר פסח צבי

בהר"ר משה דוד גאנץ ז"ל

This book is dedicated in memory of
my father

Mr. Herschel Ganz

of blessed memeory

Rabbi D. B. Ganz

In appreciation of

Mr. and Mrs. Sam Gershowitz

For their support of Torah education in

Suffolk County, Long Island

And for their sponsorship of this volume

In memory of

Mr. Abraham Horwitz

Mr. Irwin Horwitz

In loving memory of

Rivka Neugroschel

רבקה בת חיים ז"ל

Dr. and Mrs. Jonathan Turetsky

In memory of

Mrs. Betty Viders

חי׳ שבע רבקה בת ר׳   רפאל אדם ז״ל

Mr. and Mrs. Jay Viders

In loving memory of

Mr. Harold Goldman

חיים פלטיאל בן בנימין ז״ל

Dr. and Mrs. Max Rudansky

ACKNOWLEDGMENTS

Without the assistance rendered by the following individuals, I could not have produced this volume.

Much, if not most of the Torah I have merited to study is a direct consequence of the influence and teaching of my *rebbe*, R. *Alter Chanoch Henach Leibowitz, shlita*. Certainly the approach to *chochmas hamussar* to which I have attempted to adhere in this volume is almost entirely the result of his instruction. He and his *rebbetzin, tichyeh*, have also been a constant source of encouragement and guidance to both myself and my family.

From my early childhood on, my father, *z"l*, and mother, *yb"l*, did much to instill in me a belief in the primacy of Torah. I am an only son, yet, even before my bar mitzvah, I was sent to live in a different city in order to study Torah. I still derive benefit that decision on a daily basis.

My parents were models of generosity. Their example helped inspire my interest in teaching Torah to others. Furthermore, their financial assistance did much to facilitate my years spent in *yeshivah* and *kollel* and as a *marbitz Torah*. Without their generosity, these undertakings would have been infinitely more difficult.

Before writing each of the chapters, I desired that a *talmid chacham* and *baal mussar* of stature would concur that my basic idea was the *pshat* in the text. Rabbis Yoel Adelman, Dovid Baum and Avraham Semmel gave generously of their time and scholarship to review the ideas found in this volume. After the book's completion, it was given a final "once-over" by R. Eli Kaufman. In fact, several of the chapters had to be significantly altered (and in some cases completely omitted) because of their knowledgeable criticism. Their input was occasionally a time-consuming process, for, in some instances, fairly long discussions took place before the *pshat* was agreed upon.

I am neither trained nor experienced as a writer. As such, this book required major editing to enhance its clarity and elegance of language. Several individuals contributed many hours toward this task. I would like to especially recognize the assistance of Mrs. Barbara Bermanski, Mrs. Jill Rudansky, Mrs. Elaine Viders and Mr. Jared Viders. After dealing with their suggested corrections, the manuscript was then brought to Mrs. Judi Dick for a final edit. She added an expert professional touch, both in language and in the presentation of the ideas.

Finally, I would like to acknowledge my wife's role in this project. She, more than anyone else, provided editorial help; furthermore, she also offered profoundly insightful recommendations as to how many of the book's concepts should (or should not) be presented in print. She also graciously put up with the countless hours I spent working on the project, and was a constant source of encouragement and strength as well. She is largely responsible for this volume.

R. A.H. LEIBOWITZ *

Second day of *parashas Vayeishev,* 5759

My student, Rabbi Dov Berish Ganz, *shlita,* is one of the distinguished students of our *yeshivah,* outstanding in Torah and fear of *Hashem.* Aside from directing a *yeshivah* and occupying himself with his sacred work day and night with great sacrifice, he draws hearts close to Torah in the proper manner through pleasing classes built on our *mesorah* on the issues of *chochmas hamussar* and the principles of *daas,* which over the years have influenced many people to go in the path of Torah.

At present, my above mentioned student intends to bring to light some of the fruits of his labor, which are his teachings on the Book of *Bereishis,* to draw the hearts of the children of Israel in every land to our Father in Heaven.

In truth, it is of utmost importance in our generation to illuminate the darkness of the exile through the light of Torah, certainly for those who yearn for spiritual uplifting. This *sefer* could be of great benefit to those who delve into it.

Despite the fact that because of the burdens of the *yeshivah* I did not have time to sufficiently examine it as is needed, I bless him from the depth of my heart with love and affection that he should continue to benefit the public with his work in good health and with good fortune.

Closing with the blessings of Torah and those who study it,
Alter Chanoch Henach, son of my father and teacher,
Hagaon R. Chaim Dovid Hakohen Leibowitz, z"l

*Entirely translated from the Hebrew original

R. YAAKOV PERLOW

יום ד' כ"א שבט תשס"א

The great men of *Mussar* were unique in expounding the Torah in ways that challenge human behavior, and allow man to scrutinize his traits and refine his instincts. In having his work on *Bereishis* on the teachings of the *Alter* of *Slobodka*, Rabbi Berish Ganz has illuminated new depths of thought that will enrich seeking minds and deepen their understanding and appreciation of Torah values.

בברכת הצלחה וכל טוב
Yaakov Perlow

R. Mattisyahu Solomon

בס"ד

אור ליום ו' עש"ק וינש תש"ס

    I have seen a copy of the book *Within Bereishis** written by Rabbi Berish Ganz, שליט"א dean of the Hebrew Academy of Suffolk County, and I am very impressed by both its style and content.

    This book is a true example of the analytical approach of the *baalei mussar* of old to bring to light הנסטרות שבסיפורסמות, what is hidden in what is already well known, and to highlight the למעשה — the practical application of every דבר תורה.

על כן אברכו שיפוצו מעיינותיו חוצה
ויצליח בכל אשר יפנה
ממני הכו"ח לכבוד התורה

מתתיהו חיים סלימון

    * It was first planned that the book would be titled "Within Bereishis." The name was then changed to "Defining Humanity: Exploring Torah insights..."

R. NACHMAN BULMAN

To Whom It May Concern,

A striking Torah work has been brought to my attention. Its author is the distinguished Torah educator, R. Berish Ganz, who serves as dean of the Hebrew Academy of Suffolk County. The aforesaid work covers all the *sedros* of *Bereishis*. The author is an outstanding disciple of the great *Rosh Hayeshivah* and *mussar* mentor of *Yeshivas Chofetz Chayim* of Queens, New York, R. *Henach Leibowitz*.

What is unique about R. Leibowitz's *mussar* discourses is that, in content and style they are a pure representation of the *mussar* school of *Slobodka*.

R. Ganz's work is likewise a brilliant and penetrating exposition of *Slobodka mussar*. Every essay is based on accompanying sources from *Tanach*, Talmud, and *midrashim*, and is the fruit of painstaking analysis, and a lucid writing style.

Many will be grateful for R. Ganz's work, who otherwise might not have access to the treasures of *Slobodka*.

הכותב למען כבוד התורה לומדיה ומפיציה

נחמן בולמן
ישיבת אור שמח

R. ABRAHAM J. TWERSKI, M.D.

July 20, 1999

Which of many colors of a diamond is the true one? They are all true. The more perfect the diamond is, the more colors it reflects.

Torah is the wisdom of G-d. It is absolute perfection. It gives off many beautiful colors. All are true.

Rabbi Ganz has enabled us to see yet another dazzling color of this perfect diamond. Its brilliance can illuminate our way through life.

The Torah is not a historical text. Nor is it simply a manual of regulations. Every word of Torah is a teaching on how to conduct our lives. Throughout the ages, Torah scholars have been revealing the many ethical teachings contained in Torah.

All the teachings of Torah are eternal. However, each generation faces different challenges. We are certainly not bereft of serious challenges to ethical and moral behavior today. Torah addresses these as it addressed the problems of earlier times.

Rabbi Ganz's elucidation of Torah provides concepts for proper living in our turbulent times. His interpretation of Torah is another demonstration of its eternal truth.

R. BEREL WEIN

March 14, 1999

Dear Rabbi Ganz:

I thank you for sending me the manuscript to your work of insights on *Chumash Bereishis*. What makes this work particularly intriguing and valuable is its basis in the great thought pattern of *mussar* generally and *Slobodka mussar* particularly. In a time when much shallowness infects the Jewish world and even its Torah study methods, it is refreshing to see a work such as yours which combines depth of analysis, clarity of thought and faithfulness to the Torah text in its pages. I am certain that everyone that reads and studies this work will gain great mental and spiritual benefit from it, and I pray that this will be only a forerunner of many such works of yours in the future.

With Torah greetings and with blessings from Jerusalem, I remain,

Sincerely yours,

Rabbi Berel Wein

CONTENTS

PREFACE

There are several basic premises and approaches to Torah which form part of the basis for this volume. Therefore, to better communicate the book's ideas, a preface articulating many of these principles was included. It is my hope and prayer that I merit that this volume will be received favorably.

A) Identifying Piety

החסידות האמיתי הנרצה והנחמד רחוק מצייור שכלנו

הקדמה לספר מסילת ישרים

"True and desirable piety is remote from our conceptualization" [true piety is very different from what we would imagine it to be] — introduction to *Mesillas Yesharim*.

Our forefather *Avraham* was an exemplar of a supremely devout Jew. Though raised in a home and society committed to idolatry,

- by age three he recognized *Hashem*,
- he maintained his beliefs and practices in contradistinction to the entire world,

- he was saved by *Hashem* through a great miracle when he chose to be cast into a fiery furnace rather than adopt paganism and

- he converted many souls to monotheism.

Yet, the Torah only indirectly alludes to these great attestations of his faith. What the Torah does describe in relative detail are *Avraham's* various acts of kindness (see chapter 8). Why weren't the examples of *Avraham's* faith given equal coverage?

R. *Nosson Tzvi Finkel*, the *Alter* of *Slobodka* (*Or Hatzafun* I, section 2, *sichah* 8), addressed this question. He explained that what humans see of *Hashem* are consequences that He effects — life, death, sunshine, rainfall and so forth. However, the essence of *Hashem*, *kavyachol*, is utterly beyond the realm of human comprehension, even to one so knowledgeable G-dly as *Moshe*. All that *Moshe* could perceive of *Hashem* Himself were aspects of His traits of kindness, as observed through His interaction with the temporal world (*Shemos* 33:18-20). There is nothing else about *Hashem* that can be discerned by mankind. Accordingly, closeness to what humans can perceive of *Hashem* connotes emulating *Hashem's* goodness (see chapter 8 for further elaboration upon the kindness of *Avraham*; see also notes 2 and 4 ibid.). Thus, *the details of Avraham's hospitality described by the Torah are themselves the greatest testament to his closeness with Hashem.*

The Torah certainly requires the observance of its numerous and complex commands, and without observing these *mitzvos*, one cannot become consummately devoted to *Hashem*. However, many aspire to attain a lofty state of spirituality that surpasses what can be achieved by the unadorned performance of *mitzvos*. How can one recognize this exalted level? The *Alter* is teaching that the extent of a person's kindness toward others is the ultimate barometer of one's true *frumkeit* — his oneness with *Hashem*. In a sophisticated sense, it is such conduct toward others that can truthfully be termed "religious," "ultra-orthodox," "*chareidi*" or even "holy."

This idea of the *Alter* speaks volumes on the pursuit of true religiosity. To act with *Avraham*-like kindness toward others, one's own character traits (i.e., modesty, honesty, compassion, and so on) must first be perfected. To the extent that one is dishonest, unkind, egocentric, ungrateful, and the like, he will be incapable of heartfelt goodness toward others. Furthermore, truly helping others requires

• a penetrating understanding of human nature,

• a cognition of that person's particular needs and

• an academic knowledge of the Torah's teachings on ethics and character traits (see note 5).

As such, much of the pursuit of true, higher-level piety involves delving into the complexities of human nature and the definition of ethical platitudes.

Many of the *shmuessen* of the *Alter* investigated issues such as the primacy of Torah, the fear of *Hashem* and the placing of our trust in Him. But mostly, the *Alter's shmuessen* dealt with the human being and his relationships with others. Those *shmuessen* repeatedly remind one that the Torah is replete with profound insights and lofty ideals on ethical and human issues. Furthermore, exemplary conduct in these areas is central to one's closeness to *Hashem*.[1] This volume, as well, deals mostly

---

1.   R. *Dovid Liebowitz* also dealt with interpersonal issues in the majority of his *mussar shmuessen*. A student once asked why did he not address himself more often to the subject of being *frum*. R. *Leibowitz* answered by quoting "He who denies the good received from a friend will eventually deny the good received from *Hashem*" (*Midrash Tanchuma*, quoted by *Rabbeinu Bachya*, *Shemos* 1, 8).

with the Torah's precepts on human relationships.[1]

The Torah is providing a guarantee: deficient conduct toward others will undermine one's relationship to *Hashem*, even if one's spiritual devotion is otherwise exemplary. A similar concept can be found in *Midrash Rabbah, Koheles* 7:4, where it is written that "One who turns away from [the opportunity to perform] kindness is likened to one who turns away from *Hashem*." Avioding a chance to bestow kindness is comparable to avoiding *Hashem*.

1.   Throughout history there have been serious rabbinic disputes over various movements within Torah Judaism. It is axiomatic that these differences were normally over nuance rather than broader issues. For example, many wrongly assume that the original *Chassidim* and *Misnagdim* argued whether the service of *Hashem* was primarily an activity of fervor and joy, or one of Torah study only. In truth, the *Chassidic* movement produced some of the greatest Torah luminaries of the last 250 years, and a society that did not stress the supremacy of Torah study could not produce these individuals. Conversely, the Torah speaks of fervor (see chapter 30) and joy, and the *Misnagdim* could not oppose those principles of the Torah.

Rather, the issues of contention concerned the exact level to which these concepts should be stressed. Totally discounting the need for either Torah study or fervor and joy would be contrary to the classical tenets of both the *Chassidim* and the *Misnagdim*.

In a similar vein, the doctrine that interpersonal behavior is of supreme religious significance is not an invention of *Slobodka*, in particular, or the *mussar* movement in general. It resonates throughout the entire Torah. Great works of *mussar* (e.g., *Chovos Halvavos* and *Orchos Tzaddikim*) were written centuries before the lifetime of R. *Yisrael Salanter*. It is also mentioned in *halachah* (*Orach Chaim* 1, *Mishnah Brurah* 12 — *Orach Chaim*, end of 61 in *Rama*) that one should make a daily study of the works of *mussar*. Rather, because of certain specific problems besetting the Jewish people, the *mussar* movement arose and advocated an *additional* focus on the Torah's already existing ideals of ethical conduct.

B) Regarding Mesorah

The concept of *mesorah* denotes the study of Torah from a *rebbe*, who was a notable student of his *rebbe*, who was a notable student of his *rebbe*, and so forth. This continuity extends back to *Moshe*, who was the student of *Hashem*. There can thus be an uninterrupted link between the Torah studied today and the Torah taught by *Moshe*.

Although all Torah can be traced to the same source, differing legitimate approaches to Torah have existed for over two thousand years. Presently, there are major differences among Jews, such as *Sephardim/Ashkenazim* or *Chassidim/Misnagdim*. Furthermore, every major group consists of several primary divisions and yet further subdivisions.

It has often occurred that the same great *rebbe* had several eminent students who each carried on the tradition of their teacher in a somewhat different manner. There are numerous examples of this phenomenon, such as among the close disciples of R .*Yisrael Salanter*. There were significant differences in approach among his great students although all were righteous and faithful disciples of the same *rebbe*.

This volume is an attempt to deal with several texts in *Bereishis* in the style of *Slobodka mussar* taught by my *rebbe*, R. Alter Chanoch Henach Leibowitz.[3] He was the preeminent student of his father, R. *Dovid Leibowitz*, who was a close disciple, in *mussar*,

---

3. Two collections of my *rebbe's mussar shmuessen* have been published by his students. They are *Chiddushei Halev* in Hebrew and *Majesty of Man* in English. The material presented in those works is that of my *rebbe* and thus of an altogether higher caliber than what is found in this work. What this book contributes is a more explicit (and thus more lengthy) presentation of how ideas of this type are developed. This will hopefully assist the reader to better understand the style and content of this type of material.

of the *Alter* of *Slobodka*. In a private conversation I had with R. *Yaakov Kamenetsky* (who was himself one of the greatest students of *Slobodka*), he expressed the view that the ideas of *Slobodka mussar* are especially relevant to this generation.

The *Alter* had other great students who interpreted his teachings somewhat differently from R. *Dovid Leibowitz*; my *rebbe* was not his father's only disciple and I am but one of my *rebbe's* many students. I was also born after the Germans had destroyed *Slobodka* and the other great *yeshivos* of eastern Europe. Nonetheless, I feel that to a limited extent, through *mesorah*, I can lay claim to a connection to the approach of *Slobodka mussar*.

C) A Principle of Slobodka Mussar

The revealed Torah can be divided into two sections, *halachah* and *aggadah*. *Halachah*, which is based primarily on the Talmud and the *Shulchan Aruch,* is the law that defines the Torah's commandments. *Aggadah* is based on the incidents related in the Torah and their interpretation as found in the Talmud, *Midrash* and classical commentaries; *aggadah* forms the basis of the Torah's ethical teachings.

A typical question of *halachah* might concern whether a particular incident rendered a kitchen utensil not kosher. Obviously, a conscientious *rav* would never rule on the issue without positive proof from the Torah. The practice of deciding such matters based on personal intuition alone would surely give rise to regular violations of *kashrus*.

Slobodka mussar (as conveyed by my *rebbe*) taught that one's grasp of the Torah's definitions of proper behavior is also subject to personal bias, misrepresentation and error. Therefore, the principles and parameters of appropriate conduct should ideally be proven from the *aggadic* texts of the Torah just as if they were the *halachos* of kitchen utensils.

The *mussar shmuessen* of the *Alter* of *Slobodka* were generally academic and text-based. He would develop ideas from the Torah that were both novel in concept and also, provable from the text. It is often difficult to bring these two components together. Truly innovative humanistic insights are often not fully substantiated, while text-based ideas frequently lack sophistication. These *shmuessen* were normally delivered in a monotone as if to accentuate the scholarly rather than emotional nature of the material. Students reviewed and analyzed the material and its relation to source texts as they would other Torah dissertations of a *maggid shiur.* As the ideas were clarified, the numerous applications to everyday life would then become apparent.

Thus, it was my goal to be able to prove the idea – the basic concept of each chapter — from the quoted source texts of the Torah. Needless to say, I am limited by the extent of my ability to understand Torah, in general, and, in particular, to absorb this tradition from my *rebbe.*

D) An Illustration of That Principle

The following is a somewhat lengthy treatment of a particular text to illustrate how it might be approached by either utilizing or not utilizing the approach of Slobodka mussar. To those unfamiliar with Slobodka mussar, this section would likely be better appreciated after several of the book's chapters have been read.

When *Hashem* set out to create Adam, He addressed His Heavenly court, saying, "Let us make man" (*Bereishis* 1:26). *Rashi* explains that this provides non-believers with a unique opportunity. They could wrongly argue, based on these words, that *Hashem* was not the sole Creator. Nevertheless, the words "Let us" were utilized to teach a principle of respect and modesty: Before acting, one who is greater should deferentially consult with and ask permission of those who are of lesser stature.

How might one expound upon this *Rashi?* Following are

three possible approaches that will be compared:

1) *Hashem* taught His lesson on respect and modesty despite the possibly negative consequences for non-believers. *Hashem* thus demonstrated that one's Torah observance is of such supreme importance that he need not be concerned if that observance has a negative impact upon others. This idea is mirrored in *Hoshea*, 14:10, where it is written "The words of *Hashem* are just, and the *tzaddikim* will go in its ways, and the evildoers will stumble on its ways." One must do whatever is necessary to serve *Hashem*, for the same Torah that leads the righteous to greater spirituality, creates a stumbling block for the evil. If it is right one should do it, and he need not be mindful of how others will be impacted upon.

There is a hint to the relatedness of these two *pesukim*. The numeric value of the first Hebrew letters of the words of both phrases - ויאמר אלקים נעשה אדם בצלמינו כדמותינו   and כי ישרים דרכי י-ה וצדיקים ילכו בם ופושעים יכשלו בם equal eighty.

2) *Rashi* teaches the importance of respect and modesty. *Hashem* risked providing a rationale for non-believers in order to teach the importance of respect and modesty.

3) A great but unnamed *baal mussar* (quoted in *Maayano shel Torah*) explained that *Hashem*, by His example, was teaching a lesson of respect and modesty. *Hashem* was about to create man, the culmination and raison d'être of the entire creation. By the time He consulted His Heavenly court on whether to bring Adam into being, the other myriad and incredible aspects of the world had already been completed in preparation for humanity. If *Hashem* were advised not to make man, heeding that counsel would mean that all His previous creations were for naught.

In a somewhat equivalent human situation it would be

most difficult to sincerely consult with others at such late stages of a project. Can one truly objectively entertain a recommendation that entails discarding enormous efforts already invested? After committing so much toward a specific end, it is difficult to pause, to reflect and to contemplate a complete change of plans that would entail walking away from all of one's previous efforts.

The *baal mussar* explained that this text teaches the importance of being extremely flexible in one's decisions and thinking. One must always be open to the possibility of a complete about face from one's previous thinking and actions. And one's resolve to change courses should not be impeded by efforts and accomplishments already invested and attained in the pursuit of what is now being forsaken.

Approach 1 is, at the very least, not necessarily so, and probably downright wrong. Though eye-catching, that both phrases contain a numeric equivalent of eighty proves very little. Today's computers could probably find dozens of totally unconnected Torah phrases that somehow have the value of eighty. But approach 1 has a more serious problem.

The "proof" cited (by *Rashi*) from *Hoshea* is not a convincing substantiation if Rashi's intent was the first interpretation. It does not denote that one needn't be at all concerned over whether his Torah observance has a negative impact upon others. In fact, *Hoshea* 14:10 is applied by the Talmud (*Bava Basra* 89b) to a case where the only way at all that something proper could be done was by creating a possible temptation for others to err. Similarly, in this text, *Hashem* could only teach His lesson on modesty by creating this stumbling block – the possibility to misconstrue who indeed the Creator was.

Certainly, neither source indicates that, *as a general rule,*

one can be unmindful of the possibly negative impact of his
Torah observance upon others. Why should the factor of doing a *mitzvah* create an exemption from one's obligation to
avoid leading others astray? The fact that one is occupied with
personal Torah observance certainly does not create a dispensation to murder, to steal or to commit other sins. Logic dictates that unless the exemption is specifically mentioned in
Torah, none of Torah's guidelines can be trampled upon and
ignored just because one is involved with a *mitzvah*.[4]

Approach 2 may be true, but it says very little beyond the
obvious meaning of the text (which clearly states that respect
and modesty are most important). Approach 2 is also somewhat
vague because it does not clarify what particular aspect of

---

4.   In fact, there are numerous indications in the Torah that one
must be exceedingly careful of how his deeds will be viewed by
others (see chapter 3, section A). Following is a striking example:
Moshe knew that the plague of the firstborn would occur exactly at midnight. Yet, *Moshe* told Pharaoh that the plague
would take place around midnight. *Rashi* (*Shemos* 11:4) explains that *Moshe* feared that had he said "At midnight," Egyptian astronomers would wrongly calculate that the event did
not occur at exact midnight and that *Moshe* was therefore was
a liar. Due to this concern, *Moshe* said "Around midnight."

R. *Moshe Chait* pointed out that this illustrates the required
concern over the impact of one's actions on others. Saying "at
midnight" and having it happen at that exact second would have
been a greater Divine manifestation. Nevertheless, *Hashem's*
revelation was minimized to save idol-worshiping Egyptians from
wrongly criticizing *Moshe*. Certainly then, if possible, one is
obligated to be far more diligent in always taking ordinary
precautions that do not diminish *Hashem's* miracles to prevent Jews
from erring based on what one does.

modesty is of such importance. Is it the practice, the academic study, the striving to attain modesty or the teaching of the concept to students? Alternatively, *Rashi* may be teaching the need to publicize the virtue of modesty to the general public.[5]

Approach 3 is a sophisticated and more clearly delineated concept that has significant application. It teaches the importance of flexibility of thought; it teaches that, when needed, man must be willing to quickly abandon his previous ideas and plans, even after a major investment of emotions, finances and arduous work.[6]

---

5.   After writing this section, I saw that the *Alter* of *Slobodka* (quoted in Mishulchan Gavoha) derived something else entirely from this Rashi. *Hashem* said "Let us..." so that people would be taught that one should consult with and ask permission of those of lesser stature. This demonstrates how enormously vital it is that people make a *study* of the Torah's sophisticated definitions of character traits. *Hashem* was willing to risk abetting widespread apostasy in order to teach this one guideline of the Torah on respect.

This idea of the *Alter* also teaches that exemplary character traits are not merely the result of a good and righteous heart. It is absolutely vital that the Torah's parameters and definitions of these traits must also be studied.

6.   While on the subject of flexibility of thought, the following vignette is noteworthy. When World War II began, the Germans quickly overran Poland, France and the Low Countries, and many feared that they would soon conquer the entire world.

Hearing this view expressed, R. *Dovid Leibowitz* remarked that it would never happen, for "The Germans always lose the war." He explained that the Germans succeed only when operations go exactly according to blueprint. But the rigid German personality, however skilled and valiant in warfare, is largely incapable of recanting on previous plans and making midcourse changes. This is a fatal flaw in the conduct of warfare (as well as in almost

Once exposed, this third idea is evident in the text. Nevertheless, it is likely that only one extensively trained in *Slobodka*-style *mussar* (or something similar) would extract this third approach (as well as that found in note 5) from within *Rashi's* words.

E) The Source Texts of This Volume

This volume contains insights into *Bereishis*, as it is defined by the Talmud, the *Midrash* and the commentaries through the period of the *Rishonim* (roughly from the years 1,050 – 1,500 of the Common Era). This book also utilizes several well-known commentaries on *Rashi* such as the *Sifsei Chachamim* and other equally great but lesser-known commentaries on *Rashi* such as *Imrei Shefer, Maskil L'Dovid* and the like. It is only recently that several such works have become readily available in print.[7]

In general, as the Torah scholarship of successive generations diminishes, more textual support is required for original insights into Torah. Hence, the *Alter* of *Slobodka* might have presented a concept derived from a *Rashi* as *pshat*. Yet, someone of this generation might be unable to confidently posit the same idea as *pshat* without support from commentaries such as the *Taz, Nachalas Yaakov* and so on. For the most part, that is why I have made more extensive use of works of this type.

---

any other complex human endeavor).

7.   My *rebbe* taught that up to the end of the period of the *Rishonim*, a great commentator such as the *Ramban* could offer his own interpretation of a *pasuk* as *pshat*. The *Ramban's* explanation is considered *pshat*, despite the fact that the Talmud might interpret the same *pasuk* differently. Both are correct.

    Original interpretations of a *pasuk* by those who followed the *Rishonim* are viewed as *drash*. However, those of the post-*Rishonim* era can offer, as *pshat*, their original and differing interpretations of the same passage of Talmud, *Midrash* or of the *Rishonim*.

F) When Commentaries on Chumash Disagree

The Talmud is primarily a recording of the debates on matters of Torah between great rabbinic personalities. The Torah's approach is that though conflictual, both views are valid interpretations of the same words of Torah, since words of the Torah have multiple interpretations. "These and these are the words of the living G-d" (Talmud *Eruvin* 13b). The same text countenance, not just two, but numerous differing interpretations — as it is written, "There are seventy facets to the Torah" (*Midrash Rabbah, Naso* 13:15). Thus, traditional Torah learning involves the study of all sides of classical Tamudic dispute.

It is only in the realm of *halachah* that a choice between differing opinions is unavoidable. *Halachah*, by definition, can reflect only one opinion; a given food cannot be both kosher (in keeping with one opinion) and unkosher (according to the opposing view). A determination must be made.

As such, if the great commentaries disagree over the meaning of a *pasuk* (as in chapter 29) or a *Rashi* (as in chapter 15) there is no imperative to choose between them; the concepts themselves are not, by definition, mutually exclusive. The various interpretations can be analyzed, each for its distinctive idea and moral lesson. Accordingly, this volume contains several multi-section chapters where completely unconnected ideas are developed from differing classic interpretations of the same text.

G) The Great People of the Chumash and Their Errors

This volume is primarily a study of the words and deeds of the great people of the *Chumash*. The question is often raised: Were these people more G-d-like, or were they more human in nature? How should their "transgressions" be understood?

The following paradox has often been raised: The great people of the *Chumash* are the archetypal *tzaddikim* of all ages. Yet, the Torah occasionally describes their wrongdoing in terms suggestive of outright transgressions. For example, *Hashem* said to *Moshe* and *Ahron*, "You did not believe in Me" (*Bemidbar* 20:12). Can it be that *Moshe* and *Ahron* did not believe in *Hashem*? *Chalilah!*

Following is my rendering of my *rebbe's* approach to the issue, which reflects his *mesorah* from the *Alter* of *Slobodka*:

Certainly *Moshe, Ahron* and the other great people of the Torah were holy *tzaddikim* who were completely in step with *Hashem* and His dictates. By the standards of lesser people, all of their deeds (including those for which they were criticized) were utterly virtuous. It was only due to their exalted stature that various acts described in the *Chumash* were deemed improper at all. For example, see the introduction to chapter 1 quoted from *Or Hatzafun* regarding the minuteness of Adam's error.

The following may help illustrate the concept. The United States maintains an atomic clock in Fort Collins, Colorado that is accurate to one-ten-billionth of a second. A daily error of a billionth of a second would render that clock ten times more inaccurate than allowable; a daily error of a thousandth of a second is ten million times more inaccurate than what is expected. However, this standard is only germane to atomic clocks. A daily thousandth of a second inaccuracy is utterly irrelevant to even the costliest of everyday wristwatches.

The *tzaddikim* of the Torah were certainly human beings of flesh and blood. As such, upon the rarest of occasions, they may have erred. But they were criticized only because they were judged by standards that are totally inapplicable and incomprehensible to people of later ages. If, for example, *Moshe* and *Ahron* were described as "not believing," or if *Yosef's* brothers attempted to overturn *Hashem*'s decree (chapter 24, part II), that description is indeed factual. However, it was because of their great spirituality that they were criticized. However, relative to contemporary man, the actual wrongdoing described is as irrelevant as the wristwatch's thousandth of a second error.

Nonetheless, there is a universal and timeless quality to the Torah. Thus, the words "In the beginning *Hashem* created the heavens and the earth" (*Bereishis*, 1:1) are meaningful to a present day schoolchild on his level, as well as to the *Chofetz Chaim*, the *Rambam*, R. *Akiva* and *Dovid Hamelech*, each on their respective lofty levels. In a similar vein, there is eternal relevance to the Torah's descriptions of the "wrongdoing" of the biblical *tzaddikim*. However slight those errors were by our standards, the basic ethical issues and lessons are eternally pertinent.

H) Ideas Discussed by the Chumash

This volume contains chapters based on the groundless accusation of a raven (chapter 3), the remarks of a dove (chapter 4), what "people" might say about *Avraham* (chapter 10) and Pharaoh's suspicions of *Yosef* (chapter 31). Certainly what someone such as *Yaakov* said or did is instructive for all ages. But can truth be deduced from study of the responses of Pharaoh, the general public or a bird?

My *rebbe* explained that the Torah does not describe or even refute arguments that are absurd. Almost everything that Pharaoh said during his lifetime is not related in the Torah. However, if Pharaoh's suspicion of *Yosef* was permanently included as part of the Torah, it must be at least theoretically possible that *Yosef* could have reacted as Pharaoh suspected. The same is true of the statements of the raven, the dove, and so forth.[8]

8.   In fact, there are numerous instances of the Torah's precepts
being derived from less than exemplary personalities. For example, the Torah deduces from the conduct of *Bilam* that an
important person should only embark upon a journey with
two attendants (*Bemidbar* 22:22). *Bilam* himself was indeed a
rasha, but his conduct at that moment was nevertheless noted
and utilized to teach an eternal truth of the Torah.

FOREWORD

I. The chapters of the book consist of four components: the text (and overview of the text), the idea, the possible applications and the notes.

- *The text* is an excerpt from the Torah's classical commentaries upon which the idea is based; the overview presents a brief sketch of the general story and my understanding of the quoted text.

- The second component is *the idea*. This is the main component of each chapter. It is an original insight that I also attempt to substantiate from the words of the text.

- The third section is *possible applications*, which present instances of the idea's potential relevance to everyday situations.

- Finally, there are *notes*, which deal with somewhat peripheral issues, not necessarily critical to the basic concept. Some of the notes are essays in and of themselves.

There are chapters divided into sections A, B, and so forth; each of these subsections consists of a completely independent idea. They are joined in the same chapter because they are based on the same text. Creating separate chapters would require a repetition of the text and overview. If a chapter contains the headings part I, part II and so on, it is to indicate different aspects of the same general concept.

II. Exhaustive efforts were expended at attempting to make certain that the idea in every chapter is *pshat* — proven from the source text (see preface, section C). To better appreciate this process, it might be helpful, before reading a section, to first analyze the text in search of ideas embedded in the words. Upon completion of that analysis, one can better understand and/or question the author's insight into the source material.

The applications of the ideas and insights derived from the *pshat*, however, are only *possible* applications. That is because there can be numerous mitigating factors that render virtually every application "not necessarily so." For example: Chapter 8 might discuss the importance of hospitality. Nevertheless, there may be any number of reasons why a particular guest should not be invited at a certain time.[1] Judgment and care must first be exercised before applications are made. It is also true that countless applications exist that are not enumerated in the book.

The possible applications were included to demonstrate how there can be a seamless link between a text, an idea and everyday human situations. It is also true that applications often help clarify the basic idea.

III. Following is a discussion of several language-related issues

---

1. In a similar vein, the *Maggid Mishnah* on the *Rambam* (end of *Hilchos Shecheinim*) wrote that the Torah does not contain hard and fast *halachos* on ethical conduct as in other areas such as the laws of *tefillin*. That is because the laws of *tefillin* are standardized for all people. However, although the principles of proper conduct are universal, their application can change according to the subjective situations and individuals.

that pertain to this volume.

The American, English-speaking, *yeshivah*-educated community has developed a vernacular in which certain Hebrew and Yiddish words are freely included as part of the English vocabulary. For example, in those circles one hears the English words *Avraham, Yitzchak* and *Yaakov,* but almost never "Abraham," "Isaac" and "Jacob." On the other hand, one who never interacted with the *yeshivah*-educated population may not even be aware that *Avraham, Yitzchak* and *Yaakov* are Hebrew words for Abraham, Isaac and Jacob.

Which usage to utilize in this book became problematic. The decision made was to (1) make some use of but to italicize all words that are a Hebrew/Yiddish part of the "new English" and (2) to translate these "new words" in a separate glossary. Thus, for example, Adam appears in roman type for that is both English and "new English" for the same word; *Chavah,* (Eve), however, is italicized, for it is not a proper English word.

Another language problem had to do with titles. There are several different deferential titles in Hebrew and Aramaic as well as in English that have been used in different periods, such as *Rabban, Rabi, Rabbeinu, Rav, Reb, Rabbi.* I chose to avoid erring in these distinctions by always using as a preface the letter R followed by a period.

Another language-related issue concerns gender. It is apparent that in-depth study of *mussar*-type concepts was intended for women as well as men. R. *Yisrael Salanter*'s student, R. *Yitzchak Blazer,* wrote in *Shaarei Or,* 5 in the name of R. *Yonason Eibeschutz* that *mussar* should be studied by women as well as men. R. *Yisrael Salanter*'s third letter in *Or Yisrael* indicates as well that *mussar* study as self-improvement of character and fear of *Hashem* is equally incumbent upon women. My *rebbe* has also stated that many of the *mussar*-style insights into the human being can be understood more deeply by women as a result of the fact that "*Hashem* granted additional understanding to women — more than to men" (Talmud *Niddah* 45b). Indeed, there were several women of previous generations who were notable *baalei mussar* in their own right, including the wife of R. *Simcha Zisel* of Kelm (see ArtScroll Press, *The Fire Within* by R. Hillel Goldberg). R. *Akiva Eiger* wrote that he would often conduct lengthy discussions with his wife on the subject of the fear of *Hashem* until the middle of the night (*Iggros Sofrim*, p. 65).

As such, almost all of the concepts of this volume are germane to both men and women. Although the book's mention of gender is almost exclusively in the masculine, that was done as a matter of style and convenience. The intention was to avoid the constant use of phrases such as "his/hers" and "he/she."

Each chapter begins with a a translation of the source text being analyzed. Much of this book hinges upon careful analysis of these texts, and very often even the slight alteration of a word can dramatically change the implied meaning. The book therefore utilizes a fairly precise English translation of the original Hebrew texts, in both word meaning and sentence syntax, despite the frequent awkwardness of language.

IV. There are many facets to each incident described in the Torah. Generally, the chapters of this volume focus on one aspect of an event without making an attempt to explain the entire matter. For example, the overview to chapter 24 begins with a description of *Yosef*'s rise to power in Egypt. Pharaoh had dreamt, and the interpretations offered by his court experts were considered unacceptable. *Yosef's* interpretation, however, was accepted. *Yosef* was then released from jail and elevated to the second most powerful position in Egypt.

One might ask, How did Pharaoh know that *Yosef's* interpretation was more accurate? In fact, although that question may have always been problematic, it is not connected to the ideas of chapter 24, and it should not interfere with the study of that chapter.

The following example is illustrative. A medical student was attending a lecture on the heart valve. Suddenly, he was most troubled by how the blood arrives at the heart in the first place. If thinking about that question distracts his concentration from the lecture on the valve, he is doing himself a great disservice. The two issues can and should be compartmentalized. The student should focus on the lecture, and if he chooses, he can later research his problem on the blood movement.

In a similar vein, the reader is advised to put aside incidental questions unrelated to the chapter itself and to proceed with the basic idea. Those other questions can be explored at a subsequent time.

CHAPTER 1

בראשית, בראשית ג:ב-ה

ב. ותאמר האשה אל־הנחש מפרי עץ־הגן נאכל.

ג. ומפרי העץ אשר בתוך־הגן אמר אלהים לא תאכלו ממנו ולא תגעו בו פן תמתון.

ד. ויאמר הנחש אל־האשה לא־מות תמתון.

ה. כי ידע אלהים כי ביום אכלכם ממנו ונפקחו עיניכם והייתם כאלהים ידעי טוב ורע.

שמות יט:ג

ומשה עלה אל־האלהים ויקרא אליו יהוה מן־ההר לאמר כה תאמר לבית יעקב ותגיד לבני ישראל.

מדרש רבה שמות כח:ב

אמר רבי תחליפ' דקיסרין אמר הקדוש ברוך הוא כשבראתי את העולם לא צויתי אלא לאדם הראשון ואחר כך נצטוית חוה ועברה וקלקלה את העולם עכשיו אם איני קורא לנשים תחלה הן מבטלות את התורה לכך נאמר כה תאמר לבית יעקב.

יפה תואר הארוך על מדרש רבה

אם איני קורא לנשים תחלה: תימא מה טעם תחלה וסוף וכי
מפני שלא נצטוית חוה תחלה עברה הא לא משמע שעברה אלא
מפני פתוי הנחש כמו שאדם גם הוא עבר מפני פתויה אע"פ שנצטוה
תחלה. ושמא י"ל דס"ל שהאשה לא חששה כ"כ בעביר' שחשבה
שעיקר הקפד' ה' על אדם שציוהו תחל' אבל בה אין כ"כ קפידה
וכמו שעכשיו הנשי' פטורו' מכמה מצו' ולא ציו' אות' אלא על צד
היות' טוב לפי שהיא משותפת לאדם ולזה לא חשבה שתמות
באכילה... וכן במתן תורה אלו לא יצטוו אלא באחרונה יחשבו כי
אין קפידה בהן כ"כ וכ"ש בראותן פטורן מ"ת וכמה מצו' ותרפינ'
ידיהן ויטו לב הבעלים אחריהן לכן ציון תחלה להראות כי ה'
מקפיד בקיום מצותיהן כמו האנשים.

BEREISHIS, BEREISHIS 3:2-5

2. And the woman said to the serpent: Of the fruit of the trees of the garden you may eat.
3. But of the fruit of the tree that is in the midst of the garden, Hashem has said: You should not eat of it and you should not touch it, lest you die.
4. And the serpent said to the woman: You will not surely die.
5. For Hashem knows that on the day you eat thereof, then your eyes will be opened and you shall be as Hashem, knowing good and evil.

SHEMOS 19:3

Moshe went up to Hashem, and Hashem called to him out of the mountain, saying: So shall you say to the House of Yaakov [the women] and tell to the children of Israel [the men].

MIDRASH RABBAH SHEMOS 28:2

So shall you say to the House of Yaakov: This refers to the women. Why did He command the women first? ... R. Tahlifa of Caesarea said, Hashem said: "When I created the world, I only commanded Adam, and afterward Chavah was commanded, and she [therefore] transgressed and ruined the world. If I do not now call out to the women first, they will disaffirm the Torah." Thus it says, "So shall you say to the House of Yaakov."

YEFE TOAR HAARUCH on the Midrash Rabbah

If I do not now call out to the women first: [This] is difficult [to understand]. What is the reason for [Hashem's speaking of] first and last? Was it because Chavah was not commanded first that she violated [Hashem's word]? Is it not indicated that she sinned because of the inducement of the snake, just as Adam transgressed because Chavah induced him to do so, although he was commanded first?

And one can perhaps answer that the woman was not so mindful of the transgression, for she thought Hashem's stricture applied mainly to man, who was commanded first – but not such a firm demand was made on her, just as now women are absolved from many mitzvos. And [Chavah assumed that] He commanded her only as a function of her being joined to Adam, and she therefore assumed that she would not die from eating [of the Tree of Knowledge].

And so too with the giving of the Torah. If the women were commanded only at the end, they [the women] would think that there is not so serious a demand placed upon them [by Hashem], and certainly when they saw themselves absolved from Torah study and many mitzvos. And they would [therefore] be weakened [in their Torah observance], and they would turn the heart of their husbands after them. Therefore, He first saw fit to show [the women] that Hashem demands the fulfillment of their mitzvos, just as those of man.

OVERVIEW OF TEXT

When *Hashem* forbade eating from the Tree of Knowledge in the Garden of Eden, Adam was admonished first. *Chavah* was commanded later. The *Midrash* explains that as a result of this sequence, *Chavah* sinned by eating of the forbidden fruit and then induced Adam to do the same.

When the Jews arrived at Mount Sinai after leaving Egypt, they were addressed in a very specific order on the subject of the Torah that would soon be revealed by *Hashem*. *Hashem* instructed *Moshe* to first speak to the women regarding the receiving of the Torah. Afterward he spoke to the men. *Hashem* feared that if the women were spoken to second, their Torah observance would falter just as *Chavah* faltered as a result of her being commanded second.

The *Yefe Toar Haaruch* raises a problem. The *Chumash* clearly indicates that *Chavah* sinned because of the serpent's persuasion (see chapter 2, note 1) rather than as a result of her being commanded second; her transgression was similar to that of Adam who, despite being commanded first, sinned as a result of persuasion. This seemingly contradicts the *Midrash* that attributes *Chavah's* sin to the factor of her being commanded subsequent to Adam.

The *Yefe Toar Haaruch* answers that *Chavah's* sin was indeed caused by the serpent. However, there was a special factor that made her vulnerable to the serpent's argument: *Chavah* made an incorrect assumption. She wrongly assumed that *Hashem* was mostly adamant that Adam should abstain from forbidden fruit, but He was not as exceedingly demanding upon her. Her "proof" was from the fact that she was only commanded second.

HaShem thus recognized what could transpire if the women were addressed after the men regarding the Torah.

They might wrongly assume that *HaShem*'s primary demand was that the males should observe the Torah. And that assumption would be further augmented by the fact that women are absolved from Torah study and numerous other *mitzvos*. This would result in a weakening of their observance and they would then sway their husbands as well. Moshe therefore spoke to the women first.

INTRODUCTION TO THE IDEAS

Adam and *Chavah* were endowed with a lofty and G-dly stature. To illustrate [though perhaps hard to comprehend] the ministering angels assumed Adam to be a deity; they wished to recite praises to Adam that were customarily directed to *Hashem* (*Midrash Yalkut Shimoni, Bereishis* 23). *Chavah* too was endowed with comparable greatness. In a sense, *Chavah's* greatness and wisdom even exceeded that of Adam (*Or Hatzafun* I, 4:2). Yet, despite their greatness, Adam and *Chavah* violated *Hashem's* command almost immediately after their creation. The following provides an approach to the understanding of these errors:

The *Alter* of *Slobodka* (*Or Hatzafun* I, 4:2) explained that the sinful character of the serpent's proposal was far from self-evident. The serpent's suggestion touched upon subtle and profound concepts that even the Heavenly angels could not fathom. Proof of this is that the angels questioned why Adam and *Chavah* were punished. Although they clearly ate from the tree, the angels could not recognize any wrongdoing. Adam and *Chavah* no doubt pondered their course of action with great sincerity, wisdom and holiness and acted only after feeling that they were correct.

Why then were Adam and *Chavah* punished? The *Alter* clarified that it was because their wisdom exceeded that of the angels. They, unlike the angels, were able to grasp the theoretical evil of the serpent's proposal. That is why they were held accountable. The "wrongdoing" was their failure to exert their intellect to such an extent that their wisdom would surpass that of the angels. Had they applied their minds to that degree, they would have discerned the sinful character of the serpent's idea.

SECOND PLACE   51

A) SECOND PLACE

Adam was admonished concerning the Tree of Knowledge before *Chavah* was created; *Chavah's* warning came later.
That is what led to her mistake. *Chavah* wrongly assumed that
being commanded second meant that *Hashem* was less adamant about *Chava* not eating from the tree than He was about
Adam doing the same.[1] In truth, *Hashem* forbade the tree
equally to both Adam and Chavah.

How did *Chavah*, (whose wisdom exceeded that of the
Heavenly angels, *Or Hatzafun* I, 4:2), erroneously conclude that
being spoken to second indicated that the command, once issued, was less binding upon her?

Chavah's reaction can perhaps be understood through the
following comparison: In a fighting army, the importance and

---

1.   Based on the fact that she was commanded second regarding
      the tree, *Chava* wrongly assumed that her observance of
      mitzvos was less critical to *Hashem* than that of Adam. The *Yefe
      Tar Haaruch* adds that contemporary women might arrive at
      the same error based on the fact that the Torah requires fewer
      mitzvos of them.

      It should however be noted that *Chava* never assumed that
      that a woman's overall spiritual potential was less than that of
      a man. She understood that a woman can equal or surpass her
      male counterpart's ultimate closeness to *Hashem*. This can be
      observed from *Rashi* on *Bereishis* 21,12 who writes that Sarah's
      level of prophecy was greater than that of her husband
      Avraham.

responsibilities of the individual soldiers tend to rise in tandem with their rank. Accordingly, the performance of a general is certainly more critical to the army than that of a single private.

In *"HaShem's* army" *lehavdil*, it could perhaps be said that the great and righteous scholars of Torah occupy the highest rank (see *Pirkei Avos* 6:6). However, *HaShem's* army is different. It is a basic tenet of faith that *HaShem* can achieve His objectives without even the most righteous human assistance. People only work to accomplish sacred goals such as teaching Torah because such is *HaShem's* dictate. But if it is *HaShem's* will that Torah be taught, it will be accomplished, regardless of whether any given person undertakes that task.

What the Torah does command is that each and every person should realize his distinct potential. It thus follows that to *HaShem*, since the end product or result will be the same anyway, all those who fail to accomplish what they are capable of, are equally guilty. A young man with the capacity to become the *gadol hador* will be brought to task if he falls short of that; however, another person who could have become a knowledgeable layman may face *HaShem's* equally intense disapproval if he likewise fails to maximize his ability.[2]

However, there is a tendency to gauge the importance of one's service of *HaShem* by "concrete" results as if it was service in a secular army – what did he accomplish globally, relative to others? If that standard is employed, one who has minimal Torah knowledge could make a terrible mistake. He might wrongly imagine that his Torah, *davening, chessed,* abstention from sin, etc., are of diminished significance; and he

---

2.   In a similar vein, R. *Yisroel Salanter* reputedly said that in heaven, he will not be asked why he did not become the *Vilna Gaon* (who far exceeded R. *Yisroel*). But he will be asked why he did not become R. *Yisroel Salanter.*

will then posit further that *HaShem* will be less critical of his failure to maximize his potential than he is of the *tzaddikim*.

It was this type of thought process that caused *Chava* to sin. *Chava* wrongly assumed that being commanded second denoted that her compliance with *Hashem's* edict was correspondingly less important than Adam's. That, in turn, led her to err in thinking that *HaShem* would criticize her less than He would Adam if either ate from the tree.[3]

In truth, every Jew is equally obligated to observe the Torah. One's position in Torah society's hierarchy does not determine the exactitude of *HaShem's* demands upon the said individual to fulfill the Torah to the fullest extent of his capability.

POSSIBLE APPLICATIONS

This story of *Chavah* speaks to one's approach to the *mitzvos* incumbent upon women. It is true that men are given more *mitzvos*. Furthermore, the *Yefe Toar* clearly writes that the factor of being given fewer *mitzvos* could beget in womankind a *Chava*-type response, "It is more permissible for us to sin - *Hashem* cares less than He does when men violate the same." In fact, women must remember that the *mitzvos* they are required to observe are as obligatory upon women as men. Ac-

---

3. There is a powerful temptation to reason thusly. To illustrate: The mission of the *yetzer hara* is to cause man to sin and thereby be toppled from his lofty and spiritual perch. Adam and Chava were then at the most exalted level attainable by man (see Introduction). As such, the *yetzer hara* no doubt marshalled the most potent weapon in his arsenal to ensnare them in sin. What was the weapon chosen? It was the idea implanted in *Chava's* mind that being commanded second proved that *Hashem* would be less critical if she sinned and ate from the tree than He would be had Adam done the same.

cordingly, women and men are equally responsible to be knowledgeable of the myriad *halachos* of *Shabbos* and *berachos* as needed to observe these areas properly; the same holds true regarding the intensity and proper observance of the prayers of women.[4] In fact, the *Yefe Toar Haaruch* clearly states "Therefore

---

4.   The following illustrates the importance and the impact of the prayers of women. In II *Melachim* 22:14 it is related that an omen that portended evil for the Jews and the First Temple was brought before the Jewish king. A messenger was then dispatched to the prophetess *Chulda* to apprise her of the omen. The Talmud (*Megillah* 14b) asks: Why was word of the omen sent to *Chulda* and not to the prophet *Yirmeyahu* who lived at the same time?

One answer given by the Talmud is that women are more compassionate than men. The *Maharsha* explains this to mean that because women are capable of deeper emotions than are men, it was hoped that *Chulda*'s more deeply felt prayers for the Temple would ward off the impending tragedy while the prayers of *Yirmeyahu* might not. Her prayers could have accomplished more than the prayers of *Yirmeyahu*.

Though on a different subject from this chapter, the following is most worthy of note.

My *rebbe* once discussed this *Maharsha* in a *mussar shmuess* and said something akin to the following: *Yirmeyahu*'s very essence was devoted to averting the impending tragedy of the Temple's destruction. Had *Yirmeyahu* prayed in response to the new omen, he would have done so with every fiber of his exalted and prophetic being, both intellectually and emotionally. The reason that *Chulda*'s prayers might have been more effective was because of the extra measure of emotion that a male simply cannot attain. Yet, it was theoretically possible that *Chulda*'s prayers' additional dimension of intensity could have been the deciding factor that prevented the Temple from being destroyed. *Such can be the enormous practical result of even a*

He first saw fit to show [the women] that *Hashem* demands the fulfillment of their *mitzvos*, just as those of man."

.   .   .   .

This general concept has broad application beyond the *mitzvos* of women. Many people erroneously assume that *Hashem* is less exacting with those who do not occupy the most outwardly prominent positions of society. They think that whether or not their potential is fulfilled is less critical to *Hashem* and to the world as a whole. This is not true! To *Hashem*, the efforts of all to fulfill their requirements are equally important.

In fact, the world would be entirely different if all people saw their endeavors as being supremely meaningful. Even a job at a secular workplace can become a sacred endeavor.[5] Certainly, if a third grade *rebbe* believed that the level of his job performance was as vital to *Hashem* and to the universe as that

---

slightly greater emotional input into the prayers of but one person.

5.   A former student once approached my *rebbe* with the following quandary: Though he had studied Torah for several years after high school, he felt incapable of being either a synagogue rabbi or a teacher of Torah. He was employed in industry, but he was troubled by the nagging feeling that his daily work was fundamentally devoid of higher meaning.

My *rebbe's* answer was that all Jews, including those in the workplace, bear the responsibility to sanctify *Hashem's* Name and to spread *Torah*. Fulfilling that obligation to the greatest possible extent is fulfilling what *Hashem* asks of them; their Heavenly reward may then equal that of great and famous rabbis. He advised the young man to always distinguish himself by absolute integrity in his job performance and by the dignity of his manner. People will then laud and respect the Torah whose study produced an employee of such sterling character. The fellow later acknowledged that in his presence, the other employees automatically speak with far less profanity. My *rebbe* cited that as an example of a significant and ongoing *kiddush Hashem*.

of the *gadol hador*, then his third grade would be very special. The consequences could affect generations.

This idea can also effect one's original decision on whether to become a third grade *rebbe*. If *Hashem* is primarily concerned with the future *gadol hador*, then whether or not one teaches Torah to third graders would seem to be of little import. If, however, one understands the significance of contributing whatever he can, then he would be more likely to undertake that sacred task. As it is written (Talmud *Shabbos* 119b), "We do not disturb the children who are studying Torah with their *rebbe*, even for the purpose of building the Temple." [6]

---

6.   In discussing this general idea, my *rebbe* mentioned the story of R. *Yochanan ben Zakai*. The great *Hillel* had eighty students. At the very bottom of the group was R. *Yochanan ben Zakai* who ranked number eighty (Talmud *Bava Basra* 134a). R. *Yochanan ben Zakai* no doubt expended every ounce of his potential to raise his standing — and he failed, not even progressing to number seventy-nine. He could have then easily abandoned his Torah study altogether by rationalizing that whether or not he strove mightily to maintain his lowest rung status hardly mattered, either to *Hashem* or to mankind.

R. *Yochanan ben Zakai* did not fall prey to these demoralizing and mistaken thoughts and the resultant temptation to quit. Though only capable of eightieth place, R. *Yochanan ben Zakai* recognized his obligation to strive to maintain that position as if it were number one. The consequences were historic. Despite where he stood relative to his peers, R. *Yochanan ben Zakai* nevertheless developed into a *talmid chacham* of enormous distinction (ibid.). Furthermore, he ultimately became the savior of the Jewish nation. When the Second Temple faced destruction, R. *Yochanan ben Zakai* stood at the helm of the Torah faithful in Jerusalem. It was his wisdom and decisive leadership that assured the continuity of Torah (Talmud *Gittin* 56). Where would the Jewish nation now be without R.

B) HASHEM'S DEMANDS AND DECISION MAKING

The *Yefe Toar Haaruch* explains that because *Chavah* underestimated *Hashem's* demands upon her, she was won over by the serpent's logic. She therefore sinned, induced Adam to the same and brought death to the world.

The words of the *Yefe Toar Haaruch* require further clarification. What is meant by "*Hashem's* stricture applied mainly to man?" Did *Chavah* see herself as exhorted against eating from the tree or did she not? *In pasuk* 3, *Chavah* clearly told the serpent that if she ate from the tree she would die. Evidently, *Chavah* acknowledged that *Hashem* had commanded her as well. What then did *Chavah* mean in that she saw herself as not being "fully admonished" against eating from the fruit?

What is so fascinating is that aparrentĺy, if commanded first, Chava would have realized that both herself and the one commanded second could not eat from the tree. It was her being commanded second that somehow caused her to see the matter differently. How can this be?   How did being commanded second cause this change of thought?

Yochanan ben Zakai's accomplishments?

This story illustrates the enormous benefit that can accrue to the world when a person understands the significance and responsibilities of even number eighty out of eighty and then functions at the peak of his capacity to maintain that status.

Section A of this chapter discusses how being commanded second led *Chava* to believe that *Hashem* was less demanding upon her than He was upon Adam. If so, the following is true: Being commanded first would have given rise to a more immediate and more profound sense of fear and awe of *Hashem* - a deeper feeling that *Hashem* was before her and commanding her regarding the tree.

It was the diminished awareness of *Hashem* and His demands upon her that ultimately altered her conclusion. It must be that there is a correlation between the depth of one's awareness of *Hashem* and the outcome of his complex decision making. A stronger feeling of *Hashem*'s agenda for humanity exerts a subtle but meaningful influence over one's thought process. The ability to reason correctly and to discern truth is upgraded as one feels the immediacy of *Hashem*'s expectations and edicts.

This phenomenon can perhaps be through the example of a dinner guest whose level of conversation is unusually thoughtful. For that visitor, any issue raised becomes an object of careful analysis. The host may suddenly find himself contemplating his dinnertime conversation as never before. Simply spending time with the visitor automatically upgrades the host's thinking. This subtle change can beget a practical outcome. A decision made by the host while in that more thoughtful state of mind might result in a different and more accurate conclusion.

Similarly, the logic of a person who feels the immediacy of *Hashem*'s expectations will be upgraded; he reflexively adjusts his thought process to be more in tune with *Hashem*'s ultimate truth. As one's awareness and fear of *Hashem* grows, his wisdom will correspondingly increase. That enhancement of the thought process can beget more correct decisions.

When that cognition of *Hashem*'s demands is lessened

(even minutely, as with *Chavah*), its beneficial effect may diminish, sincerity and/or intelligence notwithstanding. Misjudgments on even life-threatening issues may result. *Chavah's* slightly diminished feeling of *Hashem's* demands affected her thought process, and she erred. Tragic consequences ensued.[7]

---

7.   People occasionally face a dilemma where no matter how much an issue is pondered, it is almost impossible to discern what is right and what is wrong. R. *Yisrael Salanter* advised that when facing this quandary, one should imagine that it is at the time of *Neilah*. How would he decide during that moment when he is most in touch with his accountability to *Hashem*?

R. *Yisrael Salanter's* words reflect the general relationship between accurate judgments and the feeling of being accountable to *Hashem* at that moment. This text illustrates the extent of this influence. Even a slight difference in fearing or awareness of *Hashem* can sway a life-or-death decision that impacts upon the entire world (such as the decision faced by *Chavah*) — even where the most righteous and brilliant of people are deciding. How much more then are average people at the mercy of these influences during ordinary decision making!

My *rebbe* developed a similar point from the *Midrash Rabbah,* in *Devarim* 4:1, where it is written: *Hashem* said, "It was not for their [the Jews'] detriment that I gave them blessings [for exemplary conduct] and admonitions [the promise of punishments for sinful conduct]. It was but to *inform them of which is the proper path* they should choose so that they could secure reward."

The indication is that without the system of *Hashem's* rewards and punishments, people would simply be incapable of discerning right from wrong – sin could appear as a great *mitzvah* and vice versa. The awareness of *Hashem's* rewards and punishments expands the absolute outer limits of one's capacity to discern good from evil.

POSSIBLE APPLICATIONS

One of the classical tenets of the *mussar* movement involves the need for a person to remind himself constantly of his accountability and judgment before *Hashem*. That ongoing reminder forms a powerful inducement to avoid sin. This text provides yet a different benefit from this type of reminder: One's judgment and his ability to discern truth will be upgraded. Had *Chavah* had a slightly deeper cognition of *Hashem's* demands upon her, she would have decided differently and the course of the world would have been changed.

CHAPTER 2

בראשית, בראשית ג:יד

ויאמר יהוה אלהים אל־הנחש כי עשית זאת ארור אתה מכל־הבהמה
ומכל חית השדה על־גחנך תלך ועפר תאכל כל־ימי חייך:

רש״י

כי עשית זאת: מכאן שאין מהפכים בזכותו של מסית, שאילו
שאלו למה עשית זאת, היה לו להשיב דברי הרב ודברי התלמיד
דברי מי שומעין (סנהדרין כט.):

תוספות סנהדרין כט:א

דברי הרב ודברי התלמיד: וא״ת א״כ כל מסית יפטור עצמו
באותה טענה וי״ל דדוקא נחש שלא נצטוה שלא להסית ולא נענש
אלא לפי שבאת תקלה על ידו אבל מסית שנצטוה שלא להסית
נמצא כשמסית עובר:

משכיל לדוד על רש״י

...ולדידי לק״מ דשאני הכא דאכתי לא ניתן בו באדם יצה״ר עד
האידנא שנתלבש היצר בנחש להסיתו ויכול היה לומר שעשה כן
לטובתו של אדם כדי שלא ישמע את דבריו ויקבל שכר דאל״כ אלא

שאין לו יצה"ר אינו כדאי לקבל שכר ולכך א"ל כן ואיהו הוא
דאטעי אנשפי' דהול"ל דברי הרב וכו' אבל מסית דעלמא אינו יכול
לטעון כן דהא בל"ז יש לו יצה"ר באדם ומאי אהני ליה איהו הילכך
לא מצי לטעון כן אבל נחש אה"נ דהו"מ לטעון כן אלא שלא רצה
הקב"ה להניחו שיטעון ללמד הא גופה דאין טוענין למסית:

BEREISHIS, BEREISHIS 3:14 [1]

*And Hashem, G-d said to the serpent,[2] "Because you have done
this, you shall be more cursed than all of the animals and all of the
beasts of the field; on your belly you shall go, and dust you shall eat
all the days of your life."*

RASHI, Sanhedrin 29a

Because you have done this: *From here [we can learn] that we do
not intercede [to find merit] for the benefit of a masis [one who in-
stigates others to sin], for had Hashem asked him [the serpent],
"Why have you done this?" he could have answered, "The words of
the rebbe and the words of the student, whose words does one follow?"*

TOSAFOS, Sanhedrin 29a

The words of the rebbe and the words of the student: *And if you
will ask, If so, every masis can exonerate himself with this argument,
one can answer that only the serpent, who was not forbidden from
being a masis [could have defended himself this way]; and he was*

---

1.   See chapter 10, note 3
2.   In his work *Emes L'Yaakov*, R. Yaakov Kamenetsky explains the
status of the original serpent, based on the Talmud (*Sanhedrin*
59b). That serpent was a walking and talking being with intelligence comparable to man's. It was created to be a servant that
would provide for all human needs. Every person would have
had two such creatures at his disposal at all times. This would
have allowed man to concentrate entirely on spiritual matters.
After Adam and *Chavah* sinned, all of this was revoked.

punished only because misfortune came through his [the serpent's] hand. But a [present-day] masis was commanded not to mislead others, and from the moment he is a masis, he is in violation.

MASKIL L'DOVID on Rashi

[The Maskil L'Dovid begins by asking the question of Tosafos.] And to me, this [question] is not difficult at all. For it is different here, for man had not yet been given a yetzer hara. The yetzer hara cloaked himself in [the form of] a snake to incite him. And he [the serpent] could have said that he did so for man's benefit so that he should not heed his [the serpent's] words and [thereby] receive reward. For if not so [without the serpent's enticement], and if man would be left without a yetzer hara, he [man] would not deserve to receive reward. Therefore, he [the serpent] spoke to him such [enticing him to violate Hashem's command].

And he [the serpent] was the one that tripped himself up, for he could have said, "The words of the rebbe," and so on. But a typical [present-day] masis cannot argue so, for without this [additional enticement], man has the yetzer hara, and how is he [the masis] helping him? Therefore, we cannot argue such ["The words of the rebbe" and so forth]. But the serpent truthfully could have argued so. But Hashem did not wish to allow [assist] him to speak thus to teach this itself, that we do not intercede on behalf of a masis.

OVERVIEW OF TEXT

The serpent was punished for causing Adam and Chavah to sin, thereby bringing great misfortune upon the world. Rashi explains that, in fact, a valid defense was available. The serpent could have contended that "The words of the rebbe and the words of the student, whose words does one follow?" The serpent (the "student") advocated eating from the tree, an act that Hashem (the "rebbe") specifically forbade. As such, Adam and Chavah bore the guilt, for they should have chosen to listen to the *rebbe* rather than to the student. But the serpent did not realize that presenting this argument on its own behalf would have lead to an acquittal.

But the serpent was not informed of this way of defending itself. That is because normally, in capital cases, if the accused is unaware of a valid plea, the *beis din* provides him with the information. However, the court does not help a *masis* formulate his own rejoinder.[3] Therefore, *Hashem* did not assist the serpent by advising that this argument ("The words of the *rebbe...*") would have been an acceptable defense.

Tosafos in *Sanhedrin* and several other commentaries ask the following:

How can this reasoning ("The words of the *rebbe...*") constitute a valid defense? If it is valid, any *masis* can always argue that the person he led astray should have elected to listen to *Hashem* (the *rebbe*) rather than to the *masis* (the student). Why then is any *masis* ever guilty?

---

3.   Why the court does not argue on behalf of a *masis* is explained by the *Iyun Yaakov*. The normal practice of helping defendants is based on "Open your mouth to [on behalf of] one who cannot speak" (*Mishlei* 31:8). If one cannot speak in his own defense, the court speaks [argues] for him. A *masis* is presumed to be clever and crafty by dint of the fact that he was able to ensnare others. As such, he cannot be classified as one who "cannot speak." Therefore, the court does not argue on his behalf.

One might nonetheless question how *Hashem*, with His ultimate knowledge of truth, would punish the serpent if an acceptable defense was indeed available. That may be an issue of Torah philosophy that this author is unequipped to deal with. Perhaps this unusual harshness is based on "You should not have compassion over him" (*Devarim* 13:9, quoted in *Sanhedrin* 29a) which deals with a *masis*.

Tosafos answers that there are two punishable aspects to being a *masis*.

- *Halachah* forbids attempting to lead others astray. The attempt itself is a technical violation of Torah law even if the transgression never actually occurred. This prohibition, however, only became binding after Sinai. Therefore, it was irrelevant to the incident of the serpent in *Gan Eden*.

- Another aspect to the offense of a *masis* is the more general ethical transgression of having brought misfortune upon others. This second factor was viewed as a punishable moral wrongdoing even before Sinai.

It was the second offense that the serpent was found guilty of. However, were the argument "The words of the *rebbe*..." presented, it would have absolved the serpent of sin. The serpent would have been judged innocent, while those led astray would have borne the guilt. The serpent, however, did not realize that he could so defend himself. And *Hashem* did not apprise him of this valid defense, due to the nature of the crime.

The *Maskil L'Dovid* offers the following answer to the question of *Tosafos*: Normally, *Hashem* rewards observance of His commandments only when effort is involved. An angel, who automatically fulfills *Hashem's* will, cannot earn merit. Adam and *Chavah* were created free of the *yetzer hara*, like angels. As such, despite their sublime natures, they would not have received Heavenly recompense for their praiseworthy actions.

The serpent could have argued that there was no moral wrongdoing associated with inciting Adam and *Chavah* to sin. To the contrary, enormous benefit could have evolved from this enticement. Adam and *Chavah* were suddenly tested by the choice between the words of the *"rebbe"* and the words and enticement of the "student," and they could then exercise correct moral judgment.

The serpent thus provided them with a unique opportunity. They could serve *Hashem* by overcoming temptation in order to fulfill His *mitzvah* of not eating from the tree. They could thereby merit Heavenly reward that was otherwise unattainable. That argument, if used, would have been the valid defense against the charge of *masis*.

This explanation answers the question of *Tosafos*. The serpent who was in *Gan Eden* could have been absolved from being a *masis* by this claim. But that defense is no longer available to a *masis*. Since the banishment from *Gan Eden*, a part of mankind's everyday existence is the *yetzer hara*. That *yetzer hara* provides all of the challenges necessary for man to be rewarded for *mitzvos*. As such, a *masis* does not provide an "indispensable service" with his enticement, and he cannot thereby be absolved.

A) RESPONSIBILITY AND BLAME

The serpent initiated a vicious and highly sophisticated attempt to ensnare Adam and *Chavah*. Although Adam and *Chavah* were tremendous *tzaddikim*, they succumbed to the serpent's lethal enticement (see Introduction to the Ideas, Chapter 1). As such, the serpent was seemingly the party most responsible for their sin.

Nevertheless, *Tosafos* writes that Adam and *Chavah* bore the real guilt. The serpent had the valid defense (if argued) that Adam and *Chavah* should have chosen instead to heed *Hashem*. Why would this argument exonerate the serpent?

The following may help clarify the problem: If persons A and B are involved in an auto accident, an investigation is typically held to determine the extent of each party's liability. If A is held to be 35 percent of the cause and B 65 percent, they are then each liable in that proportion. If A or B damage each other, B can collect 35 percent of his damage from A, and A 65 percent from B. A third party with a $1,000 accident-related claim against both A and B collects $350 from A and $650 from B.

Following this legal system, the serpent perhaps bore 99 percent of the guilt. It launched a malicious attempt to destroy others. (*Rashi* on *Bereishis* 3:15 explains that the serpent was hoping Adam would be killed because of the sin, and he would then marry *Chavah*)

Adam and *Chavah*, on the other hand, were supremely righteous. Seemingly, their error, which the Heavenly angels couldn't even discern, was relatively minor. When analyzing the serpent's proposal, they failed to exert their intellect to a level that surpassed even that of the angels. Their guilt should perhaps be one percent. Yet, only Adam and *Chavah* would have been punished had the serpent properly defended itself.

Tosafos is revealing a fundamental insight into the accountability for one's own actions. The serpent had indeed caused 99 percent of the problem. However, it was Adam and *Chavah*, and not the serpent, who had to ultimately decide on whether or not to eat from the tree. The one who must act bears the overwhelming responsibility for the deed.

Generally speaking, provocation to sin by others is not an acceptable excuse for wrongdoing. The primary guilt does not reside with those others. Rather, if one has the ability, he must rise above these inducements and abide by the Torah. As such, Adam and *Chavah* were held liable, and they could not lay the blame on the serpent.

POSSIBLE APPLICATIONS

The de-emphasis of individual responsibility for one's failings is a phenomenon of modern times. Western society often excuses even depraved wrongdoing as being an unavoidable function of one's society, family background or personality type. Some even glibly attribute their shortcomings to injustices perpetrated upon their ancestors centuries ago.

Tosafos's concept stands in sharp contradistinction to this mind-set. Adam and *Chavah* could not absolve themselves of guilt by laying the blame upon the serpent. As a rule, if man is capable of proper behavior, the Torah expects it of him. Even an overpowering urge or a powerful external inducement to sin will likely not excuse iniquity. Rather, man is called upon to rise to challenges and to act properly.

B) DIFFICULT MITZVOS

Since the expulsion from *Gan Eden*, man coexists with the *yetzer hara* which constantly attempts to undermine the performance of *mitzvos*. By resisting the inducements of the *yetzer hara*, one earns Divine merit and a resultant reward.

Adam and *Chavah* lived in pre-*yetzer hara* times, a world with neither temptation to sin nor Heavenly recompense. The serpent offered Adam and *Chavah* a "benefit," a one-time enticement to disobey a commandment of *Hashem*...therefore, an opportunity to earn *Hashem's* reward if they were able to withstand the temptation.

Was this really assistance? Indeed, the serpent could have ultimately helped Adam and *Chavah*, had they resisted the serpent's temptation and earned Heavenly reward. However, it also created an enormous peril. If they failed, all humanity would bear the burden for eternity. And that, in fact, is exactly what happened! Because of the serpent's "favor," mankind was banished from *Gan Eden*; death and suffering became an everlasting part of the human condition. Nevertheless, the argument that it was providing a service could have exonerated the serpent. (Irrespective of what its motives were, the serpent could have rightly claimed that it was providing a benefit.)

This underscores the incredible significance of performing a *mitzvah* in the face of adversity. That Adam and *Chavah* capitulated was tragic. It resulted in their (and our) downfall. However, they weren't coerced into sin; the enticement could have been resisted. It was worth risking eternal suffering and death for all of mankind to provide Adam and *Chava* an opportunity to overcome difficulty in order to observe a single command of *Hashem*. Such is the incredible consequence of a *mitzvah* done in the face of overwhelming adversity.

POSSIBLE APPLICATIONS

Certain *mitzvos* can only be performed with considerable hardship. Some people instinctively react by concentrating instead on those *mitzvos* that are easier to observe. Alternatively, many are inspired by the words "According to the suffering is the reward" (*Avos* 5:26); the greater the suffering when doing a *mitzvah*, the greater the reward. Some may thus even rejoice when faced with a difficult *mitzvah*.

In *Avos D'R. Nosson* 31:2 it is written that a person performing one *mitzvah* sustains an entire world. It is further written (ibid. 3:6) "One thing [*mitzvah*] with pain is better for man than one hundred with comfort." As such, if an "everyday" *mitzvah* sustains an entire world, a *mitzvah* performed with difficulty upholds at least one hundred worlds.

Many assume such statements to be either exaggerations or a metaphoric description of the great reward for a difficult *mitzvah*. The *Maskil L'Dovid* demonstrates just how literally the words of *Avos D'R. Nosson* must be taken. Being tempted to eat from the tree meant that Adam and *Chavah* could be catapulted to an entirely different level of heeding *Hashem's* commands. For one opportunity to first overcome temptation in order to perform one *mitzvah*, it was worth jeopardizing this entire world; mankind could face death forever after.

Such is the significance of heeding even one *mitzvah* with great hardship.

CHAPTER 3

בראשית, נח ח:ז,ח,י,יא

ז. וישלח את־הערב ויצא יצוא ושוב עד־יבשת המים מעל הארץ:
ח. וישלח את־היונה מאתו לראות הקלו המים מעל פני האדמה
י. ויחל עוד שבעת ימים אחרים ויסף שלח את־היונה מן־התבה:
יא. ותבא אליו היונה לעת ערב והנה עלה־זית טרף בפיה וידע נח
כי־קלו המים מעל הארץ:

רש"י

ז. **יצוא ושוב:** הולך ומקיף סביבות התיבה ולא הלך בשליחותו
שהיה חושדו על בת זוגו.
יא. **טרף בפיה:** אומר אני שזכר היה.

שפתי חכמים על רש"י יא

והא דשלח את הזכר והלא יש לחוש שלא יחשדוהו כמו שחשדו
העורב וי"ל כל הפוסל במומו פוסל והעורב שימש בתיבה מש"ה
חשדו אבל נח כוונתו היה לגלות זה לכל שהרי היונה ג"כ זכר היה
והלך בשליחותו מפני שהיונה ג"כ לא שימש בתיבה מש"ה לא
יחשוד גם את נח שישמש עם בת זוגו.

סנהדרין פרק אחד עשר קח ב

והנה עלה זית טרף בפיה:

א״ר אלעזר אמרה יונה לפני הקב״ה רבש״ע יהיו מזונותי מרורים
כזית ומסורים בידך ואל יהיו מתוקים כדבש ומסורים ביד בשר
ודם.

מהרש״א על סנהדרין קח ב

והענין מבואר כמ״ש [א] המצפה לשלחן חברו חייו אינם חיים ואנו
מבקשים בברכת המזון ונא אל צצריכינו ה' אלהינו לא לידי מתנת
בשר ודם וכו' כי אם לידך המלאה וכו' וסיים שלא נבוש ולא נכלם
וכו' שהוא המונע ממתנת בשר ודם... ורמז זה בעלה זית... שיסתפק
האדם במועט משל הקב״ה ולא ילך אחר הפרי והמותר משל בשר
ודם למ״ש חז״ל [ג] עשה שבתך חול ואל תצטרך לבריות:

ביצה פרק רביעי לב ב

ואמר רב נתן בר אבא אמר רב כל המצפה לשלחן חברו העולם חשך
בעדו... רב חסדא אמר אף חייו אינן חיים. תנו רבנן ג' חייהם אינן
חיים אלו הן המצפה לשלחן חברו ומי שאשתו מושלת עליו ומי
שיסורין מושלין בגופו.

BEREISHIS, NOACH 8:7, 8, 10, 11

7. And he [Noach] sent forth the raven, and it kept going and returning until the waters were dried from upon the earth.

8. And he [Noach] sent forth the dove from him, to see whether the waters had subsided from the face of the ground.

10. And he [Noach] waited another seven days and he again sent out the dove from the Ark.

11. And the dove came back to him in the evening – and behold! It had plucked an olive leaf with its bill! And Noach knew that the waters had subsided from upon the earth.

RASHI

7. Going and returning: *It continued to circle the ark and it did not go on its mission, for it [the raven] was suspicious of him [Noach] concerning its [the raven's] mate...*

11. Plucked...with its bill: *I say that it [the dove] was a male...*

SIFSEI CHACHAMIM on Rashi

And [if you will ask why was it] that he sent the male [dove], he should have taken precautions so that they would not suspect him in the same way that the raven suspected him. One can answer "Anyone who faults [accuses] others, does so with his own failing" [Talmud Kiddushin 70a]. And the raven [itself] cohabited in the ark [even though it was forbidden]. Therefore it suspected him [Noach, of similarly licentious and sinful behavior]. But Noach's intention was to reveal this to all, for the dove was also a male and [nevertheless] he did go on his mission, [and the reason was] because the dove also [like Noach] did not cohabit in the ark. It, therefore, would not suspect that Noach would cohabit with its mate..

TALMUD SANHEDRIN 108b

And, behold! It had plucked an olive leaf with its bill: R. Elazar said, The dove said before Hashem, Master of the universe, let my food be bitter like the olive and placed in Your hands and let it not be sweet like honey and given over to the hands of flesh and blood.

MAHARSHA on Sanhedrin 108b

And the issue is explained [understood] by what is written [in Talmud Beitzah 32b]: "Anyone who hopes for the table of his friend [one who seeks to be fed by his friend], his life is not [considered] living." And we ask [in benching], "And please, Hashem our G-d, do not make me dependent on others for gifts..." and it [that section of benching] concludes "So that we should not be embarrassed..." For this [the shame] is what prevents people from [seeking] the presents of others ...

The olive branch...implies that a person should be sated by the small amount from Hashem and not seek the "fruit" and the excess from others, as the Rabbis wrote "Make your Shabbos like weekdays [make due with less on Shabbos] and do not require the help of others" (Talmud Shabbos 118a).

TALMUD BEITZAH 32b

(Quoted by the Maharsha in his explanation of Sanhedrin 108b)
R. Nosson bar R. Abba said in the name of Rav: Anyone who hopes for the table of his friend [one who looks to the table of his friend as a place from where he will be fed], the world is black for him...R. Chisda said, even his life is not [considered] living...

The Rabbis taught, there are three whose life is not [considered] living; these are:
- *one who hopes for the table of his friend,*
- *one whose wife rules over him and*
- *one with physical suffering that dominates his body.*

OVERVIEW OF TEXT

When the waters of the flood began to recede, *Noach* sent forth a raven from the ark to search for dry land. The raven, however, feared that while it was away, *Noach* would copulate with its mate.[1] Therefore, it did not pursue its mission but instead circled the ark so that it could keep a suspicious and

---

1.   It may be difficult to understand how the reactions of a bird can be portrayed as humanlike emotions. It also seems difficult to even imagine the physical reality of *Noach* sinning with a bird. In fact, the *Tzeidah Laderech* explains that the sin was technically doable, and theoretically, *Noach* was not beyond suspicion.

This chapter deals with the moral/psychological issues behind the raven's conjecture and its mistrust of *Noach*. For these purposes, the fact of the raven's humanlike response is taken as a given simply because such is written in the Torah. There are perhaps other works that explain how these realities existed (see foreword, part IV).

watchful eye trained on *Noach*.

Noach's second scout was a dove, and *Rashi* explains that there too, a male dove was deliberately chosen for the task. The *Sifsei Chachamim* asks, Why didn't *Noach* fear that dispatching a male might prompt a repeat of the raven's vilification? He answers that the raven's wariness of *Noach* must be understood in light of the Talmudic dictum, "Anyone who faults [accuses] another does so with his own failing" (Talmud *Kiddushin* 70a). People project their own shortcomings on to others. The raven itself had sinned by improperly cohabiting in the ark. Being immoral itself, the raven assumed *Noach* to be prone to a similar form of sin.

Noach understood the source of the raven's suspicion. *Noach* therefore set out to defend his honor by deliberately sending a male dove (that could similarly distrust *Noach* for the same reasons as the raven) rather than a female. Being personally honorable and chaste, the dove would entertain no such suspicions of *Noach*. That would demonstrate to all that it was the raven rather than *Noach* who was depraved. *Noach's* purity would be thus publicly confirmed.

The first time the dove was sent to scout for land it returned empty-handed. The second time, it returned with a branch from an olive tree and declared that it would prefer bitter food provided directly by Hashem rather than more sumptuous fare provided by others (in this case, *Noach*).

The *Maharsha* explains the dove's reasoning. It was based on the Talmudic concept (*Beitzah* 32b) that one who seeks to be fed by someone else is compared to one who has no life; the Talmud (ibid.) further equates this suffering to that of one whose body is racked by pain.

A) UPHOLDING ONE'S REPUTATION

Noach was the greatest and most noble person of his time; he is referred to in the Torah as a *tzaddik* (*Bereishis* 6:9). Furthermore, the raven was personally aware of *Noach's* great piety. While in the ark, he and all of the other animals were cared for by *Noach* with great dedication and kindness (see Talmud *Sanhedrin* 108b).

Though all of the earth's beings were then residing in the ark, it was only the raven that suspected *Noach*. And that was only because it wrongly projected its own personal immorality on to *Noach*.

Nevertheless, *Noach* took steps to have his innocence publicly vindicated by choosing a male dove for the next mission. One might argue that it is inappropriate to respond when such obvious calumny is leveled at the *gadol hador*, the greatest person alive. It dignifies and lends credence to a positively scurrilous charge. Furthermore, will anyone who might believe such unfounded lies be interested in the truth at all?

Apparently, there are times when untrue slander should not be allowed to stand unchallenged. It should instead be publicly contravened, notwithstanding the truth that may seem painfully obvious.[2] This remains true even in cases where one of the most disreputable of individuals is foolishly and wrongly blaspheming the undisputed *gadol hador*.

2. The Talmud (*Sanhedrin* 108b) relates that *Noach* spoke very sharply to the raven and repudiated its suspicions. However, in defending his honor before others, *Noach* chose not to dispute the raven openly. Rather, in a clever and indirect fashion, *Noach* saw to it that others (i.e., the dove) would disavow the charge. This is often a model of how one should deal with false charges and/or rumors of this type.

B) PERCEIVING REALITY

There is a valuable insight into human psychology that can be gleaned from this same text. The *Sifsei Chachamim* explains that it was the raven's own immorality that caused it to see *Noach* as a potential adulterer. That is because accusations of others tend to reflect the failings of the accuser.

This Torah concept can be explored further. What is the usual mind-set of one who falsely libels others with falsehoods that are true of the attacker himself? Does he or does he not actually believe his own canard? Perhaps the story is only fabricated to delude others. But the aggressor is aware that the target of his smear is innocent of the charge. Alternatively, it may be that the slanderer actually believes what he is saying. Something more psychologically complex than name-calling is taking place. He is unconsciously redefining humanity; his new worldview is that many others share his own personal failings; he actually believes his own lie.

The text supports the latter interpretation. *Rashi's* language "for it [the raven] was suspicious of him [*Noach*] concerning its mate..." indicates that it sincerely believed that *Noach* had licentious designs. Yet, from the commentary of the *Sifsei Chachamim* we know that the raven's distrust was not rational; rather, it emanated from its own immorality. Apparently, the raven's own personal wrongdoing gave rise to a genuine reinterpretation of reality.

This concept yields an interesting insight into the human psyche. If one commits a certain praiseworthy deed, one who is righteous may recognize the act for what it is. A conceited person, however, may ascribe an arrogant motive to that action. Someone who is personally immoral may see immorality in the same deed. A fourth man who is lazy assumes it to be a function of laziness. Each of the four different people (all of whom may be intelligent and basically well adjusted) attribute entirely different motives to the same behavior.

Apparently, even the unquestioned greatness and piety of a *gadol hador* (such as *Noach*) is not immune to this form of warped thinking. A person who has lowered himself to the level of stealing from others may observe the most righteous of people and believe him to be a thief. How much stronger then is the tendency to project one's own inadequacies onto others who are less than the greatest people of their age (see chapter 32, note 4).

(*R. Eli Kaufman* added the following: Copulation in the ark was forbidden [Talmud *Sanhedrin* 108b] because such is inappropriate when the world is in a state of pain and destruction [*Midrash Tanchuma, Noach* 11]. Thus, the raven's promiscuity with its own mate while in the ark was improper because it demonstrated callousness to the suffering of others. Yet, that transgression itself led the raven to suspect *Noach* of sinning with a different species – a capital offense — a sin far greater than that of the raven. This proves that the psychic mechanism of projecting one's failings onto others, and believing them as well, can entail the projecting of failings that are far greater than those of the accuser.)

POSSIBLE APPLICATIONS

Were the raven more upstanding, it would have recognized *Noach*'s greatness rather than viewing him in light of its own unsavory ways. This highlights an additional benefit of improving one's character. Every slight refinement in one's character will result in a correspondingly more accurate and wholesome view of humanity. It is the most righteous individuals who are most capable of a truthful and unobstructed assessment of others.

C) TAKING FROM OTHERS

Part I

My *rebbe* developed and explained the following:

The dove willingly chose being self-sustaining and modest over being lavishly supported by *Noach*. How can this preference be understood? One possible explanation is that, rightly or wrongly, an exceedingly generous donor could eventually develop a somewhat begrudging attitude. And a resentful patron can transform an otherwise delicious meal into a loathsome experience. It was the provider rather than the provision that was unacceptable.

However, the dove was choosing between minimal self-sustenance and the meals served by *Noach* in the ark. *Noach* acted with enormous dedication and magnanimity. To cite an example, animals that before the flood customarily ate at night were fed at night; those that had eaten by day were fed during the daytime (Talmud *Sanhedrin* 108b). If the pain associated with taking from others is a function of an ungracious provider, this was certainly not the case with *Noach* who was certainly a most benevolent host.

One must therefore conclude that the inner discomfort associated with receiving largesse is not a consequence of the donor's goodness, or lack thereof. Even if the provider acts with unrivaled magnanimity and geniality, somehow, one's internal dignity is offended by being on the take, and he sustains mental anguish. If the suffering is not conscious (as with a recipient who believes that he is getting away with something), then it may be subconscious.

I do not believe that my *rebbe* mentioned this point, but it should also be noted that there was another factor that, seemingly, should have lessened the dove's discomfort over taking personally from *Noach*. This was not a typical case of a generous person voluntarily providing for a recipient who is then on the taking end of another individual's personal largesse. Primarily, *Noach* fed the animals in the ark because *Hashem* commanded him to do so. Nevertheless, the dove sought to avoid being the recipient of even this human kindness.[3] [4]

---

3.   A certain measure of common sense and understanding must be exercised when applying this idea. The reaction of the dove would not prove, for example, that one's inner dignity has somehow been profoundly defiled if a friend drives him home from *shul* on a rainy day or if an uncle treats him to dinner at a restaurant.

The ride home is hardly a gift at all, for favors of this character are generally reciprocal. In the second case, the uncle's treat was a single act of kindness, rather than an ongoing program of support (which is what the dove had been receiving from *Noach*).

If, however, the man was constantly receiving benefit from his friends and relatives without ever reciprocating, then indeed he could be compromising his dignity. This would remain true even if the providers were most gracious in their kindness.

4.   The *Ralbag* in *Vayetzei* articulates a similar idea. *Yaakov* went to *Charan* where he met *Rachel* at a well. Upon hearing that she had met *Yaakov*, who was a cousin, her father *Lavan* invited *Yaakov* into their house. To repay the gratis hospitality, *Yaakov* immediately began to work for *Lavan* without wages.

The *Ralbag* (*Toeles* 6 and 7) explains that *Lavan's* invitation was issued in keeping with an ethical code: Relatives should be hospitable to each other in order to maintain intra-family love. Yet, although *Lavan* felt morally obliged to host family members, *Yaakov* nonetheless chose to work, for it allowed him to remain

Part II

The Talmud in *Beitzah* (quoted by the *Maharsha* to explain the response of the dove) lists three types of people who are considered as having no life. Two of those are (1) one who looks to another for his sustenance and (2) one whose body is wracked by severe physical pain. The Talmud's grouping them both together as people without a life indicates that the degree of suffering in examples (1) and (2) is somewhat comparable.

What type of individual that looks to another for his sustenance is the Talmud describing in such stark terms (one who has no life — similar to one whose body is overcome by pain)? The Talmud could be referring to:

a) one who is utterly indigent. He must entreat others for his food or face starvation; his survival is thus dependent upon human generosity; he lacks the autonomy to live his own independent life, or

b) one capable of supporting himself who nonetheless willingly takes from others. Rather than "paying his own way," he chooses instead to subsist at someone else's expense.

At first glance it might appear that it is probably the person described in (a) who has no life. His existence is dependent upon the whims and the mercy of others. But can the same be said of the person described in (b)? He is not truly reliant on others, for he can sustain himself without them.

The dove was in category (b), for two choices were available: being supported generously by others (*Noach*) or directly by *Hashem* (which is akin to being self-sustaining). The *Maharsha* explains that the dove understood that being supported by someone else meant that its world would be "black"; it would have

---

in *Lavan's* house without shame. The *Ralbag* is clearly stating that the shame of taking from others is present even among family and/or where the donor views his own generosity as obligatory.

no life. Evidently, even a category (b) type who chooses to be supported by others [5] will have no life. This remains true even

---

5.   The concept of studying in a *kollel* has gained wide acceptance among Torah-observant Jews. Yet, study in a *kollel* generally entails being supported by public moneys. This begs the question — isn't this modus vivendi rendered inadvisable by the attitude expressed by the dove? And it is further contradicted by statements such as "Make your *Shabbos* like weekdays and do not require the help of others" (Talmud *Shabbos* 118a); "Do not make them [the words of Torah] a hoe to dig with [do not use the Torah as a means of earning money]" (*Avos* 4:5), or "He who hates gifts will live" (*Mishlei* 15:27).

I cannot speak for the many great students of today's *kollelim* and their even greater *roshei yeshivah*. However, I believe that the following reflects some of my *rebbe's* thinking on the issue.

In truth, the *kollel* lifestyle (as we know it) was not a part of earlier and greater generations. The famed *Kovno kollel*, probably the first of this type, was formed in 1877 out of necessity. It was a response to what was then a new problem: the level of Torah learning at the highest levels was in decline. It became apparent that the Torah study taking place before marriage was often inadequate to attain the highest levels of Torah leadership. *Kollel* was a finishing school for future leaders and thus open only to those who were already highly accomplished Torah scholars in their own right.

Members of the original and select *Slobodka kollel* included R. *Yaakov Kamenetsky* and R. *Dovid Leibowitz*. That *kollel* had a maximum attendance period of five years, and its members pledged to serve afterward as *rabbanim* or teachers of Torah. That was because the need for qualified *talmidei chachamim* to fill those positions was so great that they felt it improper to absolve themselves from that sacred task for more than five years (see *Reb Yaakov* by ArtScroll Press, pp. 89-95).

Presently, Torah scholarship is infinitely weaker than in prewar Europe. As such, the years of *kollel* study are now vital for a far greater segment of *yeshivah* students. My *rebbe* had often

when a *tzaddik* of *Noach's* caliber is the most willing provider. This reveals the extent of the inner hurt that one inflicts upon himself by habitually taking from others. His agony is likened to excruciating and unremitting physical pain; this torment remains despite the fact that he voluntarily chose the lifestyle of taking.

To summarize, part I makes the point that the pain of taking from others is also present in the case of a most generous provider; part II illustrates the intense degree of internal suffering that even voluntarily being on the take can engender.

POSSIBLE APPLICATIONS

Institutions must occasionally deal with individuals who endeavor to avoid paying for services provided. There are those who regularly attend a *shul* or register their children in a *yeshivah* and expend every effort to get away with paying as little as possible. They seek the proverbial free ride. This is not a criticism of those who truly cannot afford to pay. The beleaguered administrators of these institutions may find themselves struggling with these attitudes and their real and practical implications. It may seem like a conflict between "us and them."

On a deeper level, it is more a case of "them against them." The institutions are deprived of money. But those who successfully beat the system sustain far greater damage than they inflict; their entire sense of well-being is compromised — their internal psychic discomfort will grow to the pain-level of one whose body is tormented by intense physical suffering. It is always in one's selfish self-interest to fully pay his fair share, for the ultimate suffering of not paying far eclipses the "agony" of paying.

---

said that even an *aleph-beis* teacher will be far more effective if he has spent additional years of study in *kollel*.

It is the urgent ongoing need for the *talmidei chachamim* that can be produced by *kollel* that outweighs other considerations (such as the reluctance to take from others).

D) CONSCIOUS/SUBCONSCIOUS DISPARITY

According to the Talmud in *Beitzah*, one who looks to another for his sustenance has no life. The Talmud further likens his suffering to one whose body is wracked by severe physical pain. Severe physical pain can totally dominate almost all other conscious thoughts. For example, the excruciating agony of an abscessed tooth in need of a root canal can block one's ability to think of almost anything else. The Talmud is teaching that taking from others promotes comparable inner pain.

Why is the person described in category b (see section C, part II) so pained by being 'on the take'? Though capable of being self-sustaining, he opted for the support of others. His decision was a product of his free will, so he would seemingly rejoice when others provide for him.

Apparently, a duality is being played out within his personality. On a deeper, perhaps subconscious level, one who is supported by others sustains an unrecognized but profound psychic wound; his sense of independence, self-respect and *tzelem Elokim* is ravaged. This suffering will occur even when the donor has the exemplary and generous character of *Noach*. Furthermore, this pain is even greater than terribly severe physical suffering (section C, parts I and II). Yet, while this inner torment is occurring, he is outwardly delighted when people step forward to sustain him. Simultaneously, he is outwardly happy and inwardly miserable.

This illustrates the enormous disparity that can exist between one's conscious and subconscious responses to the same activity.

This phenomenon can be viewed through the following example: A person succumbed to alcoholism, and his life began to deteriorate. He soon lost his job and family, and ended up living on the street, begging for money to buy food and spirits. On one hand, in his lucid moments he is doubtlessly saddened when contemplating his ruined life. Yet, on the other hand, nothing would gladden his heart like a year's supply of his favorite spirits.

The simplistic understanding is that he is almost always focused on alcohol; it is only during infrequent episodes of lucid thought that he suffers from what became of him. According to the idea of this section, the alcoholic could even be suffering during his most "joyful" moments of sating his habit. As he rejoices outwardly while imbibing, he is also inflicting terrible anguish upon his inner being with each and every drink.

POSSIBLE APPLICATIONS

Very often, people decide on whether they should pursue a given activity based on whether it feels good or right. In particular, secular mental health professionals (especially those with Freudian leanings) are often automatically biased against restrictive behaviors that promote even temporary discomfort.

Based on the idea of this section, an obvious rejoinder to that notion is that the sensation of outward comfort is not necessarily indicative of a corresponding inner contentment. Activities that seemingly promote the most ecstatic and pleasurable of sensations may in fact be devastating the well-being of one's inner soul. Conversely, outwardly painful activities may in fact envelop one's entire personality with a profound sense of inner contentment.

. . . .

In a very general sense, this duality is often a feature of one's pursuit of Torah study and *mitzvos*. For example, it is written, "Torah will only endure in one who [figuratively] kills himself over it" (Talmud *Berachos* 63b). Yet, when one is in mourning (such as on *Tisha B'Av* or when sitting *shiva*), it is forbidden to study Torah, for it is written "The commands of *Hashem* are just; they rejoice the heart" (*Tehillim* 19:9). Which is it? Is Torah study painful or is it joyous? Evidently, both are true. On one level, there may often be real suffering associated with Torah study. Yet, it remains true that in a deeper sense, "The commands of *Hashem*...rejoice the heart."[6]

---

6.   My *rebbe* brought out a similar idea pertaining the subject of modesty. *Tosafos* (*Sanhedrin* 20a) writes that a Jewish woman is shamed when men gaze upon her. Yet, many women expend great energy on their appearance in the hope of attracting male attention; thus, when such occurs, they presumably rejoice. Evidently, while on one hand the male stares may be a source of conscious joy to those women, their inner (perhaps subconscious) feeling of well-being is being simultaneously ravaged by those same stares.

CHAPTER 4

בראשית, נח יא:כח

ויּמת הרן על פני־תרח אביו בארץ מולדתו באור כשדים:

רש"י

...ובמדרש אגדה י"א שע"י אביו מת שקבל תרח על אברם בנו לפני
נמרוד על שכתת את צלמיו והשליכו לכבשן האש והרן יושב ואומר
בלבו אם אברם נוצח אני משלו ואם נמרוד נוצח אני משלו וכשניצל
אברם אמרו לו להרן משל מי אתה אמר להם הרן משל אברם אני
השליכוהו לכבשן האש ונשרף...

משכיל לדוד

...זה כי היה פוסח על שתי סעפים.

BEREISHIS, NOACH 11:28

And Haran died in the presence of Terach his father in the land of
his birth, in Ur Kasdim.

RASHI

There is an interpretation in the Midrash that [the pasuk means that] it was through his father that he died; that [was because] Terach complained to Nimrod about Avraham his son over the fact that he [Avraham] destroyed his idols. And he [Nimrod] threw him [Avraham] into a fiery furnace. And Haran was sitting [observing] and said in his heart: "If Avraham is victorious, then I am one of his. And when Avraham was saved they said to Haran, "Of which group are you?" He said to them, "I am of Avraham." They threw him into a fiery furnace and he was burned...

MASKIL L'DOVID on Rashi

...this [Haran's death in Nimrod's furnace] was because he was a poseach al shtei s'iffim [one who vacillates and does not make a commitment to either side of a given idea or course of action].

OVERVIEW OF TEXT

According to the *Midrash*, *Avraham*'s brother *Haran* died because of *Terach*. As a youth, *Avraham* avidly opposed the idolatry of his father *Terach*. Eventually, *Terach* reported *Avraham* to their king, *Nimrod*. *Nimrod* then attempted to deal with the situation by having *Avraham* thrown into a furnace. However, a miracle occurred and *Avraham* emerged from the furnace unscathed.

As these events were unfolding, *Avraham*'s brother *Haran* resolved to join with whomever prevailed. If *Avraham* would be saved, he would cast his lot with *Avraham*; if *Avraham* perished, he would adopt *Nimrod*'s belief system.

Haran's loyalty was then challenged, and he was interrogated as to where his sympathies lay. Upon rejecting *Nimrod*, he too was cast into a furnace, but he did not survive. The *Maskil L'Dovid* explains that *Haran* did not merit *Avraham*'s miraculous salvation because he was a *poseach al shtei s'iffim*, he was hedging his bets.

CONDITIONAL FAITH

The term *poseach al shtei s'iffim* describes one who equivocates between alternative choices. The connotation is not always negative, but it frequently is. The term typically describes one who, when faced with a choice, tarries until it becomes apparent which side will prove most expedient.

According to the *Maskil L'Dovid, poseach al shtei s'iffim* (in its negative context) is the epithet that described *Haran. Haran* delayed his decision on idolatry pending the outcome of the confrontation between *Avraham* and *Nimrod.* He planned to then jump on the bandwagon of whomever triumphed. After beholding the great miracle, *Haran* declared his allegiance to *Avraham.*

Seemingly, one is no longer a *poseach al shtei s'iffim* after making a decision; the resolution indicates a clear choice. If so, why was the term applied to *Haran* to explain his death? He had just unequivocally embraced *Avraham's* faith, even in the face of being cast into *Nimrod's* furnace. Can a person so utterly dedicated to *Hashem* be described this way?

Answering this question necessitates a deeper look at the decision of a person who was initially a *poseach al shtei s'iffim.* It may be that his choice indicates that his new determination is steadfast. However, at other times, that may not be the case.

Let us imagine a person forced to choose between ideology A or B who chose A because it appeared to be more personally beneficial. Is he truly dedicated to option A? In truth, he may hardly be committed to A at all! His choice is only a function of seeing A as being more advantageous. If B would suddenly show itself to be more gainful, he might glibly change courses in midstream and opt for B. Actually, that person may be a consummate example of a *poseach al shtei s'iffim*, both before and even after his decision to adopt A. His only creed is to attain the greatest personal benefit.

This explains how the *Maskil L'Dovid* could say that *Haran* perished because he was a *poseach al shtei s'iffim*. *Haran* no doubt assumed that he too would be saved from the furnace like *Avraham*. *Haran* never embraced an ideological doctrine. Rather, he only joined with *Avraham* for he saw it as the most expedient choice. Accordingly, his new belief would have been readily deserted if doing so suddenly became most opportune.

Consequently, *Haran* did not merit the miracle of salvation, for he was a *poseach al shtei s'iffim*. He was one who had never declared his fealty to *Hashem* at all. *Haran* failed to see that *Avraham* was saved because of his true and unconditional faith in *Hashem*; *Avraham* was willing to enter the furnace even if he were not saved.

This demonstrates that even a seemingly passionate devotion to an individual, an idea, or, *lehavdil*, to *Hashem* may in fact be no commitment at all. There may have never been any allegiance from the very start.

A related point worthy of mention is that an outwardly righteous *poseach al shtei s'iffim* may be totally unaware that his faith in *Hashem* is all but meaningless. The proof is from *Haran*. Seemingly, *Haran* saw himself as a supremely devoted believer in *Hashem*. Otherwise he would not have lept into the furnace with the confidence that *Hashem* would miraculouly save him.

POSSIBLE APPLICATIONS

The focus of this chapter calls upon man to honestly reexamine his presumed attachment to much of what he holds most sacred. For example, one's outwardly intense faith in *Hashem* as well as his love of friends and family may in fact regrettably be the *poseach al shtei s'iffim* of *Haran*, to a greater or lesser degree. If so, these relationships would be correspondingly tenuous and in need of significant overhaul and rededication.

. . . .

It is probably true that ignorance of what the term *poseach al shtei s'iffim* really means lies behind many divorces and subsequent broken families. Although *Haran* was devoted to *Hashem* to the extent of leaping into a furnace, he was deemed a *poseach al shtei s'iffim*, one who was not committed to anything other than what was best for *Haran* himself.

The same holds true when love of a spouse is predicated, whether consciously or subconsciously, upon self-indulgence. That is not love of another. Rather, it is more akin to the type of "love" one has for a favorite food. He does not love the food itself at all; he loves the sensations it affords him. Once that food no longer provides adequate gratification, some other dish will then become his favorite. So too, marriage for the pursuit of pleasure will tend to more quickly unravel when the rapture wanes or when other opportunities for greater ecstasy present themselves.[1]

My *rebbe* recently mentioned this type of idea in a related context. He was conducting a question-and-answer session with the junior high school girls in an out-of-town coed yeshivah day school. The following issue was raised: The boys and girls are together in class every day, and they know each other well. If, theoretically, they refrain from activities that are specifically forbidden by *halachah*, why is it wrong for the girls to develop close personal friendships with the boys?

He responded by saying that such camaraderie would likely

eventually result in less fulfilling marriages. He explained that their present friendships with boys are primarily motivated by the drive for personal pleasure. Self-indulgence may easily then become their overriding criterion for judging future male/female relationships. This mind-set will tend to endure, and one's choice of a marriage partner might then be determined by which male offers the absolute very most in personal satisfaction.

He then continued by saying that eventually, this recipe for marital bliss may easily beget a state of diminished happiness. The very foundations of the marriage may be threatened as soon as the mutual self-gratification wanes, ever so slightly.

---

1.   This raises an intriguing question. Many people make the decision to enter marriage, in part, because of feelings of personal pleasure experienced when interacting with the other party. Does this mean that this aspect of their mutual attraction is nothing more meaningful than *Haran's poseach al shtei s'iffim?*

This topic is too complex for this note. However, the following is one thought on the subject: It is one's primary motive for pursuing the marriage that is most critical.

When the expectation of personal pleasure is the primary mover behind entering marriage, one's fidelity will likely resemble that of *Haran* to *Avraham's* belief system; and that union may eventually be headed for trouble. However, marriage pursued first and foremost because of an overall sense of responsibility and *mitzvah* is different. Then, the ecstatic feelings of attraction and well-being typical of courtship, engagement and the first stages of marriage will likely forever enhance the relationship. Such commitment bears little resemblance to that of *Haran.*

CHAPTER 5

בראשית, לך לך יב:יג

יג. אמרי נא אחתי את למען ייטב־לי בעבורך וחיתה נפשי בגללך:

רש"י
יג. למען ייטב לי בעבורך: יתנו לי מתנות.

שפתי חכמים על רש"י

וא"ת דמשמע שאברהם רצה במתנות, והא לקמן גבי מלך סדום אמר (יד כג) אם מחוט ועד שרוך נעל לא אקח, אף על פי שמן הדין היה שלו שהרי נטלו מן המלכים אפילו הכי לא רצה במתנות, כל שכן במתנות חנם שאינו רוצה דכתיב משלי (טו כז) שונא מתנות יחיה... ועוד י"ל דעכשיו לא היה לו עושר לכך היה נוטל מתנות כמו שפירש רש"י לקמן (יג ג) בפסוק וילך למסעיו, לפרוע הקפותיו, אבל גבי מלך סדום היה לו עושר משום הכי אפילו מה שהיה מן הדין ליטול לא נטל משום שונא מתנות וחיה:

BEREISHIS, LECH LECHA 12:13

Please say that you are my sister so that it will be good for me because of you, so that I will live because of you.

RASHI

So that it will be good for me because of you: They will give me gifts.

SIFSEI CHACHAMIM on Rashi

And if you will ask that it appears that Avraham wanted gifts; but later [in the incident] with the King of Sodom, he [Avraham] said, "Whether a thread or a shoelace, I will not take" [Bereishis 14:23] even though halachically it was his, for he took it from the kings [that he defeated]. Nevertheless, he did not want gifts. [If so,] certainly, outright gifts [such as the gifts from the Egyptians] he would not want, as it is written, "He who hates gifts will live" (Mishlei 15:27).

... Another answer is that now he did not have wealth. Therefore, he took gifts, as Rashi explains later on the pasuk (Bereishis 13:3) "And he went on his journey": to pay his debts [this proves that he was not wealthy]. But [at the time of the incident] with the king of Sodom, he had wealth. Therefore, even that which was his halachically to take, he did not take because of "He who hates gifts will live."

OVERVIEW OF TEXT

Avraham and his wife Sarah were traveling to Egypt because of a famine raging in *Eretz Yisrael*. Sarah was extraordinarily beautiful.[1] *Avraham* thus feared that she would be seized at the Egyptian border to be taken to Pharaoh as a potential concubine or wife. A component of that dreaded Egyptian

---

1.   The Talmud (*Megillah* 15a) lists Sarah as one of history's four women who were singled out for their beauty.

practice was the summary murder of the husband of the woman kidnapped (see the commentary of *Ramban*). *Avraham* therefore asked Sarah to state that she was his sister. This lie was permissible and unavoidable because of the immediate danger to life.

Having been forced to lie anyway, *Avraham* then hoped that the misrepresentation would yield an ancillary benefit. *Avraham* looked forward to the Egyptians showering him with presents as the brother of Pharaoh's (concubine or) wife-to-be.

The *Sifsei Chachamim* poses two questions:

- Avoiding gifts from others is an accepted ethic of the Torah, as it is written, "He who hates gifts will live" (*Mishlei* 15:27). If so, why did *Avraham* eagerly anticipate being given gifts?

- In a later situation, *Avraham* acted very differently. He refused his rightful booty from the war with Sodom, declaring that he wanted only what came directly from *Hashem* and not what came from others. That response was very different from *Avraham's* behavior when entering Egypt.

One answer offered by the *Sifsei Chachamim* is that when *Avraham* approached Egypt he was in debt and in need of money; he needed presents. However, by the time of his war with Sodom, Avraham had become wealthy; he therefore refused what came from others.

INTRODUCTION TO THE IDEAS

According to the *Sifsei Chachamim, Avraham* adopted two overtly conflicting forms of behavior. As the consummate *tzaddik*, his basic inclination was no doubt in keeping with "He who hates gifts will live" (*Mishlei* 15:27); he abhorred gifts. It was in that spirit that he refused the spoils of the war with Sodom. Yet, when his financial situation demanded it, he was capable of an about-face. He was able to accept willingly, and even eagerly, being helped by others.[2] (There is another entirely different instance of an about-face in this incident. *Avraham* no doubt understood the significance of honesty (see chapter 17, section A). Yet, because there was danger to his life, he instructed Sarah to falsely state that *Avraham* was her brother.)

Obviously, the Torah's concepts and directives are not contradictory. Rather, different circumstances may call for differing responses. Man is called upon to understand what the Torah deems appropriate for every situation and to act accordingly.

---

2.   A similar paradox can be found in *Orchos Tzaddikim* (*Shaar Tzikanus*), where it is written that one's attitude to spending money must countenance opposite extremes, depending on the circumstances. The example given is *Yaakov*, who was able to act with unrivaled magnanimity when parting with his money. He freely gave *Eisav* all that he earned in twenty years of working for *Lavan* in order to purchase the one remaining burial place in the cave of *Machpelah* (*Rashi, Bereishis* 50:5). However, *Yaakov* was also extemely frugal. In the midst of preparations for a life-or-death conflict with *Eisav*, *Yaakov* took the time to retrieve a few inexpensive objects (see chapter 20, section A).

A) CONFLICTING DIRECTIVES

Basic physical drives (such as the urge to eat) are vital for the maintenance of the body. However, if these same drives are left uncontrolled, they can become excessive and highly destructive. For example, the *Ramban* (*Vayikra* 19:2) articulates that even permissible activities involving human desire should be pursued only in moderation, but not to an extreme. Though technically not sinful, one who continually cohabits with his wife and constantly indulges himself with food and drink is referred to by the *Ramban* as "one who is abominable within legal confines of the Torah."

This text illustrates that it is not only physical lusts that can proceed onward to negative or destructive patterns and behaviors. Even the generally commendable human virtues (e.g., modesty, kindness and the like) must have boundaries and lines of demarcation. If not, they may at times find expression in behavior that is excessive, inappropriate or even sinful.[3] *Avraham's* virtue of avoidance of gifts would have been deemed deficient and improper had it been exercised when he arrived in Egypt.

There are at least two factors that can make this type of emotional changeover most painful:

---

3.   A striking example of this phenomenon can be found in *Bereishis* 19:8. *Lot* first welcomed his guests with the kindness reminiscent of *Avraham* and then protected them from danger with great dedication. However, *Lot's* enormous concern for his guests then led him to attempt protecting them in a manner that was consummately evil (*Ramban*, ibid.).

- It is often emotionally difficult to refrain from what was always one's normal form of behavior.

- Aside from character tendencies, there is oftentimes an issue of philosophy. One who continually lives by and believes in a given virtue may feel, intellectually, that this applies to almost all circumstances. Thus, he may have trouble recognizing a situation when such is ill-advised.[4]

Nevertheless, the Torah calls upon man to exert control over spontaneous emotions so that he can desist, as needed, from inappropriate conduct. [The applications of this idea are most numerous. There are times when virtually every normally praiseworthy human trait must be bottled up and ignored. For example, it is true that, generally, one should act with kindness toward others (see chapter 8). Yet, in certain situations, one must desist from those same behaviors. Parents, for instance, should normally nurture and protect their children. However, there are times when they must step back and allow their children to take some of life's hard knocks.]

What *Avraham* did was especially reflective of greatness. *Avraham* didn't merely reign in his normal tendency as needed; *Avraham* affected a complete changeover when such became proper. Although he lived by the virtue of avoiding being the object of others' largesse (as witnessed later when he refused booty from the war with Sodom), *Avraham* then

---

4.   Inflexibility of thought is especially apparent on the societal and political levels. For example, secular political thinkers and ideologues tend to be either categorically conservative or liberal. Typically, they are incapable of realizing that one social issue may call for a liberal type of response, while another situation demands a solidly conservative approach. The tendency is to embrace one belief system and then to negate and dismiss the other ideology (see preface, section D and note 6).

yearned to be the recipient of gifts. This (as was the case with *Yaakov*; see note 2) was a complete transition from one appropriate extreme to another — intellectually, behaviorally and emotionally. It might seem difficult for one healthy and integrated personality to embrace diametrically opposed approaches to seemingly parallel situations.

But in truth, nothing about *Avraham's* (or *Yaakov's*) change of course was contradictory. All of the Torah is the unified and consistent wisdom of *Hashem*. Thus, although the same Torah may first call for one course of action and then expect something radically different in another situation, these responses only appear to be contradictory. As one's maturity, piety and understanding of Torah grow, he will more clearly see consistency of thought where others see conflicting ideas.

This idea can be understood through viewing an everyday phenomenon. A young child may see his parents as people who change — they are "good" parents that provide presents and entertainment at one moment, and then "bad" parents that demand completion of homework. As the child matures, he increasingly perceives that the parental behavior is not at all contradictory. Rather, both responses are logical and compatible; both emanate from the same fountainhead of adult wisdom and parental love.

Similarly, greater Torah knowledge and spiritual growth beget a correspondingly deeper insight into the reasoning of the Torah.[5] The inherent symmetry in outwardly conflicting

---

5.   My father-in-law, R. *Shlomo Twerski, z"l,* once remarked that Jews who were not *yeshivah*-educated must typically overcome an inherent obstacle to their acceptance of the Torah's concepts. That is because the basic thinking process of Western man is still based upon the principles of Greek philosophy. In that system, the highest form of "'objective" truth is that which can be arrived at

dictates then becomes more evident.[6]

---

through the process of empirical reasoning; if man's logic sees
a concept as being truthful, then that becomes his ultimate
truth.

In Torah thinking, *lehavdil*, an initial premise is that of *naaseh
v'nishmah* (*Shemos*, 4:7). We first accept the entire Torah without reservation, for it is the word of *Hashem*, and thus absolutely
truthful. It is only in the aftermath of that recognition that we
undertake the study of the Torah's principles to the extent of our
abilities.

When faced (as *Avraham* and *Yaakov* were) with the Torah's
seemingly opposing dictates, a typical Western thinker might
react by saying "It doesn't make sense! I'll have to be convinced
of that one!" The Torah thinker, *lehavdil*, might ask, "Why did
the Torah first indicate this response and then the other?" He
would then delve into the matter more deeply in search of the
underlying and unified logic.

6.   The following incident is related in *Moreshes Avos* (*Pekudei*).
The *Alter* of *Slobodka* was walking with R. *Shraga Feivel Frank*,
an individual who was known as a great *baal tzedakah*. A beggar approached R. *Frank* asking for funds and was turned away.
The *Alter* realized that, for certain reasons, it was improper to
contribute to that particular individual. The supplicant repeatedly beseeched R. *Frank* who steadfastly refused to be moved
by the heartrending pleas for charity.

After each refusal of R. *Frank*, the *Alter* was heard muttering to
himself, "He is such a great *baal tzedakah; he is even a greater baal
tzedakah* than I realized." The *Alter* was later asked how refusing
to contribute was testament to R. *Frank's* great *tzedakah* giving.
Seemingly, it was a demonstration of insensitivity and/or possible cruelty.

The *Alter* explained that at that moment givng *tzedakah* was considered inadvisable according to the Torah. It was for that reason
that R. *Frank*, who normally was so compassionate, refused the
pleas of the beggar. He was able to act most "uncharitably,"

B) RUNAWAY PIETY

A craving to act in accordance with the Torah's model is generally viewed as a righteous expression of the *neshamah*. Thus, the urge to avoid presents is normally a sacred emotion. However, that drive cannot be one's only determinant of what is a commendable activity. That is because instinct alone is generally incapable of accurately discerning the precise line of demarcation between right and wrong.

The Torah's behavioral guidelines are what define and de-lineate the correct expression of praiseworthy personality traits. *Avraham's* story illustrates that while at one moment the Torah may call for avoiding gifts, at another moment an opposite reaction may be called for. If one is incapable of these "flip-flops," it is all but guaranteed that lines of demarcation will be overlooked. A person will see himself as acting in ac-cordance with the Torah, when in fact the opposite is true.

This leads to an interesting paradox. That same previ-ously righteous impulse becomes an urge for wrongdoing if the Torah's mandate for an about-face is not heeded. The same drive to avoid presents is detrimental and almost sinful at a moment when one should be eagerly seeking out gifts. When

---

personal feelings notwithstanding. If it was only a naturally gener-ous personality that had always prompted R. *Frank's* charity, he would have melted before those requests. The adamant refusals were thus proof-positive of the exalted nature of R. *Frank's* mo-tives. They were congruent with the hallowed *mitzvah* of *tzedakah* — *Hashem's* definition of such.

approaching Egypt, *Avraham* was hoping for gifts since, at that moment, such was proper according to the Torah. Had he then been unequal to this contrary imperative, *Avraham's* virtuous trait of avoiding gifts would have itself been the impetus for disobeying the Torah's call to acquire gifts at that time.

Without a thorough knowledge of the Torah's precise ethical guidelines and a deep commitment to their fulfillment, any one of man's most praiseworthy attributes can potentially become the very force driving one to sin. This is most insidious, for the violation of Torah is then being motivated by ostensibly laudable and even sacred motives.[7]

To summarize: Section A makes the point that at times it is necessary for otherwise commendable traits to be constrained. Section B points out that if not properly restricted, a once sacred urge may itself become a drive for wrongdoing.

POSSIBLE APPLICATIONS(sections A and B)

A fervent secular idealist does not have the Torah's checks and balances to temper the pursuit of his high-minded goals. He is therefore, by definition, potentially dangerous. To cite some contemporary examples:

• In the name of establishing a "worker's paradise,"

---

7.   R. *Yisrael Salanter* once remarked that the deadliest *yetzer hara* is the one that cloaks itself in holiness. There are at least two contributory factors that make this *yetzer hara* so especially devastating: (1) When the *yetzer hara* speaks in terms of the sublime, the sinful nature of the activity is harder to detect. (2) To a greater extent, the sinning will tend to be without inhibition. The perpetrator has convinced himself that his work is for a higher cause, and he therefore justifies acting (sinning) without restraint.

twentieth-century Communist governments committed many more murders than the Nazis. Furthermore, while the Germans murdered Jews and other "undesirables," while the Communists did almost all of their killing among their own brethren.

• The pro-life movement in the United States has, of late, become increasingly violent. Abortion clinics have been bombed, and people working in these institutions have been killed. My *rebbe* once remarked that America's politically active religious right poses a deadly threat to all Americans. However gentle-sounding those people may appear, many are potential murderers, albeit in the name of G-d.

Lehavdil, the same tendency can poison the pursuit of *Yiddishkeit*. For example, some contemporary instances of *chillul Hashem* have occurred when a sincerely righteous drive to support a *yeshivah*[8] leads individuals to perpetrate fraud for this exalted purpose.[9] Even thinking about helping a *yeshivah*

---

8. R. *Dovid Leibowitz* once remarked: "If you see an unlearned Jew with an absolutely burning passion to accomplish for *Yiddishkeit* - watch out! He presumably meant that sincerity notwithstanding, ignorance of Torah is a red flag that warns of that person's unawareness of the Torah's checks and balances. As such, that very same initially righteous desire is in great peril of evolving into a driving force for wrongdoing.

In a somewhat similar vein, the Talmud (*Shabbos* 63a) writes, "If an *am haaretz* is a *chassid*, do not live in his neighborhood." If one is ignorant of Torah, he should not adopt the ultrareligious conduct of a *chassid*. Amazingly, the Talmud is saying that *even one am haaretz acting as a chassid renders an entire neighborhood unfit for habitation.*

9. While speaking at the inauguration of a new yeshivah, the *Alter* of *Slobodka* remarked that "one may open a *yeshivah* only if, when necessary, he is willing to close the yeshivah."

can at times be improper. While one is *davening*, thoughts of how to help a *yeshivah* are entirely inappropriate.

There is an expression that was prevalent in the *yeshivos* of eastern Europe. "The world is a very narrow bridge, and the main thing is not to fear at all." This chapter makes that expression more easily understood.

In virtually every human activity, even in the case of a praiseworthy *mitzvah*, there is a constant peril of error, either in one direction or the other. One can easily fall off the proverbial bridge by doing too little of the *mitzvah* or by doing too much. A person who sees this potential hazard in virtually every human activity might be overcome by a reaction of reticence, of fear and of holding back –"I'll never get it right!" Yet, "the main thing is not to fear at all." One must nevertheless pursue righteousness with confidence and enthusiasm.

Presumably, the *Alter* was saying that opening a *yeshivah* unleashes a sacred and potent force within the Jewish heart — the desire to maintain that institution of Torah at all costs. However, the credo of "at all costs" can engender acting improperly if that is needed to keep the doors open. Thus, the *yeshivah* would be better left unopened unless there is a commitment to close it when such becomes proper.

CHAPTER 6

בראשית, לך לך יד:ח,ט

ח. ויצא מלך סדם ומלך עמרה ומלך אדמה ומלך צביים ומלך בלע הוא־צער ויערכו אתם מלחמה בעמק השדים: ט. את כדרלעמר מלך עילם ותדעל מלך גוים ואמרפל מלך שנער ואריוך מלך אלסר ארבעה מלכים את החמשה:

רש"י

ט. ארבעה מלכים וגו': ואעפ"כ נצחו המועטים להודיעך שגבורים היו ואעפ"כ לא נמנע אברהם מלרדוף אחריהם:

נחלת יעקב על רש"י

דהוקשה להרב מניינא למה לו פשיטא דאלו הם ארבעה ואלו הם חמשה ועל זה תירץ שבא הכתו' להודיענו הבטחון של אברהם.

BEREISHIS, LECH LECHA 14:8,9

8. And the king of Sodom went out and the king of Gomorrah, the king of Admah, the king of Tzevoyim and the king of Bela, which is Tzoar, and engaged them in battle in the valley of Siddim.
9. Against Kedorlaomer, the king of Eilam, Sidal, the king of Goyim,

Amraphel, the king of Shinar and Aryoch, the king of Elasar, four kings against five.

RASHI

9. Four kings: *And even so, those who were fewer were victorious, [and this is] to inform you that they [the four kings] were mighty, and even so, Avraham did not refrain from pursuing them.*

NACHALAS YAAKOV on Rashi

... The Rav [Rashi] had a difficulty with the following: Why was a counting [of the number of kings] necessary? And to this he answered that the pasuk came to teach us the bitachon of Avraham.

OVERVIEW OF TEXT

During *Avraham's* lifetime, a conflict erupted that involved nine warring kingdoms. Five of the kingdoms battled the other four, and it was the second group that emerged victorious. One of the hostages taken by the victors was *Avraham's* nephew *Lot*. *Avraham* with only his servant *Eliezer* (*Rashi, Bereishis* 14:14) then set out to attack the four kings in order to rescue *Lot*.

Rashi explains that the armies of the four kings were especially capable warriors, for they defeated the army of five nations, a numerically superior foe. *Rashi* continues that this factor demonstrates the greatness of *Avraham*. Although the four kings were especially adept at warfare, *Avraham* nevertheless waged war against them in order to save *Lot*.

Explaining *Rashi*, the *Nachalas Yaakov* writes that the Torah's praise of *Avraham's* especially miraculous victory makes a special point. It demonstrates the extent of *Avraham's bitachon* - his trust in *Hashem*.

LEVELS OF TRUSTING HASHEM

Part I

Avraham undertook this conflict accompanied only by his servant *Eliezer.* Yet, he persevered against the four mighty kings and emerged victorious. The *Nachalas Yaakov* explains that this was a function of the exalted degree of *Avraham's bitachon.*

This incident teaches an elementary principle of faith in *Hashem*: as one's level of *bitachon* grows, he can expect ever greater assistance from *Hashem.* For one person, the expectation of Heavenly support at a certain level may be a legitimate and sacred exercise of closeness to *Hashem.* Yet, that very same practice might be considered recklessness for another person of lesser faith. It was due to *Avraham's* great *bitachon* that he was able to responsibly go to war with only *Eliezer* at his side against such overwhelming odds.[1][2]

---

1.   A similar idea can be found in the Talmud (*Berachos* 35b). The Talmud quotes the opinion of R. *Shimon bar Yochai* that one should study Torah continuously while leaving the problem of providing for his needs entirely to *Hashem.* The Talmud continues that "Many attempted to do as R. *Shimon bar Yochai* but they did not succeed."

The *Maharsha* explains that the others did not merit being supported by miracles because their piety and *bitachon* did not equal that of R. *Shimon bar Yochai.* My rebbe added that presumably, some of the other spiritual giants of the time also attempted emulating R. *Shimon bar Yochai.* However, despite their greatness, their level of *bitachon* did not quite equal that of R. *Shimon bar Yochai.*

Part II

A deeper exploration of this same text yields an additional aspect of the trait of *bitachon*.

The Torah is pointing out that *Avraham*'s war against these four kings was especially indicative of an extreme level of faith. *Avraham* not only had the *bitachon* to attack an ordinary army fielded by four nations; he even had the *bitachon* to overcome a four-nation army that was an especially formidable fighting unit — one that was capable of defeating a larger force of five kings.

It is hard to ascertain the size of the armies that *Avraham* fought. For argument's sake, let us say that each nation's army consisted of only a thousand soldiers. By that count, the army faced by *Avraham* consisted of four thousand especially adept

---

Therefore, their attempts to emulate R. *Shimon bar Yochai* failed.

2.   There are numerous stories that depict the *bitachon* of the great *tzaddikim* of yesteryear. One story of the *Chofetz Chaim* comes to mind. During much of his adult life, he was supported by the income from a grocery store that was run primarily by his wife. His daily practice was to close the store when enough income for the day was generated. His rationale was that *Hashem*, through the intermediary of the store, had given them what they required for one day. Accordingly, there was no need to be bothered by the further pursuit of money. If *Hashem* would desire to help them similarly on the next day, He would again send the sustenance through His messengers.

While this routine was appropriate for the *Chofetz Chaim*, it would likely be highly inadvisable for one of lesser faith. For such a person, the same practice might be considered a reckless disregard for his own vital needs. At the very least, it could engender a great deal of tension and unhappiness. A sacrifice for the service of *Hashem* could be one person's source of joy. Yet, for another individual of lesser faith, the same sacrifice could be a cause of anguish and sorrow (see chapter 15, note 5).

soldiers. The Torah is thus making the following point: not only did *Avraham* (with one assistant) have the *bitachon* to defeat four thousand regular fighters, he even had the faith to persevere against four thousand outstanding fighters.

How much *bitachon* would *Avraham* have needed to overcome four thousand ordinary fighters? Seemingly, the victory by two individuals over that force could have only been accomplished by an outright miracle that completely transcended all pragmatic realities.

As such, it seems difficult to understand how this particular incident demonstrated additional evidence of *Avraham's bitachon*. Why should the greater skill of the troops be of any consequence? To *Hashem*, the proficiency of the soldiers was certainly immaterial. As for *Avraham*, if he was able to rely on Heavenly assistance to defeat an ordinary army of four thousand, what difference was there if the warriors were particularly skillful? Either way, *Avraham's* victory would require *Hashem's* performing an out-and-out miracle.

Nevertheless, there is an infinitesimal difference in the level of the supernatural occurrence as the skill of the troops changes. A victory by two over four thousand average soldiers is a minutely lesser revalation than a victory over four thousand extraordinary soldiers. Accordingly, possessing the *bitachon* to rely on one incredible miracle does not mean that one can necessarily rely on the occurrence of another miracle that is even minutely greater.

Avraham was lauded for possessing the requisite *bitachon* to even prevail over the more formidable force. Had *Avraham* "only" attained the absolutely incredible faith needed to wage war against four thousand ordinary troops, his attacking four superior armies might have been considered an irresponsible or reckless venture that could have ended tragically.

These infinitesimal and seemingly esoteric differences in miracles are relevant to the pragmatic exercise of *bitachon*. Even the smallest of circumstances could alter one's right to rely on *bitachon*, and one's plans may be required to change accordingly. Certainly, if a level of practical reliance on *bitachon* is totally beyond one's spiritual reach, then acting upon that *bitachon* is unquestionably considered inadvisable by the Torah.

There is a corollary to this idea, but in a positive context. It was the minutely greater dimension of *bitachon* attained by *Avraham* that enabled him to wage war with Sodom to save his nephew *Lot*. This demonstrates that increasing one's *bitachon*, even minutely, can beget significant pragmatic results. Major undertakings that were once impractical and hence inadvisable may suddenly become realistic and doable due to a person's heightened *bitachon*.

POSSIBLE APPLICATIONS

One of the obligations of *halachah* is that of daily Torah study. As a rule, that study comes at the expense of some other activity. Moreover, as more time is spent in study, greater sacrifice of other activities is required. When study interferes with one's ability to earn a livelihood, a question frequently arises concerning the extent to which one can have *bitachon* that his finances will be somehow taken care of by *Hashem*.

Obviously, each case is different. However, one must realize that a simplistic approach that blindly invokes *bitachon* may be improper. It is at times extremely difficult to know whether or not *bitachon* is appropriate for a given individual at a given time. Even the most minute differences in one's *bitachon* can be enormously significant. Those slight differences alone can determine whether or not *bitachon* is reasonable or inappropriate.[3]

---

3.   The *Steipler Gaon* once responded to a question in a manner that is reminiscent of this idea. A *kollel* student in an American *yeshivah* approached the *Steipler Gaon* asking whether he should emigrate to Israel. He felt that his Torah studies would benefit from the move. After examining various aspects of the matter, it became apparent that the young man's finances in America didn't make sense. He never really had the realistic expectation of making ends meet, but yet, somehow, he always managed. However, the discussion also revealed that living in Israel would be even more impractical.

The *Steipler Gaon* strongly advised against the move. His opinion was that it was indeed *bitachon* that had miraculously enabled the young man to live in America without incurring long-term debt. However, that did not mean that that same *bitachon* could also compensate for the somewhat larger shortfall that could be anticipated if he lived in Israel. Those words of the *Steipler Gaon* teach that proper *bitacon* consists of far more than mere fervor; it requires wisdom and judgement. What is yet further evident from this chapter is the incredible and precise Torah understanding that may at times be required simply to differentiate between ennobling *bitacon* and irresponsible and self-destructive recklessness.

CHAPTER 7

בראשית, לך לך טז:ב,ג

ב. ותאמר שרי אל-אברם הנה-נא עצרני יהוה מלדת בא-נא אל-
שפחתי אולי אבנה ממנה וישמע אברם לקול שרי:
ג.ותקח שרי אשת אברם את-הגר המצרית שפחתה מקץ עשר שנים
לשבת אברם בארץ כנען ותתן אתה לאברם אישה לו לאשה:

רש"י

ב. **אולי אבנה ממנה:** בזכות שאכניס צרתי לתוך ביתי:
ג. **ותקח שרי:** לקחתה בדברים אשריך שזכית לידבק בגוף קדוש
כזה:

באר מים חיים על רש"י ב

פי' בזכות שנתנה היא את צרתה בחיק בעלה כדי שיוליד הוא
ממנה, ואע"פ שהיה לה בזה צער גדול לכך נענית היא ג"כ עמה,
שכל המתפלל על חבירו והוא צריך לאותו דבר הוא נענה תחילה,
במדה שאדם מודד מודדין לו.

ד:יפה תואר הארוך על מ"ר ע"ב

ומה צורך לשרה לפייס את שפחתה כי למה תמאן בדבריה, ושמא
להיותה בת מלך תמאן להזקק לזקן ותקוה להיות לאיש שכמותה.

BEREISHIS, LECH LECHA 16:2,3

2. And Sarai said to Avram: Behold, Hashem has prevented me from bearing; please come to my maidservant, perhaps I will be built up through her; and Avram listened to the voice of Sarai.

3. And Sarai, the wife of Avram, took Hagar, the Egyptian, her maidservant, at the end of ten years of Avram's living in the land of Canaan, and she gave her to Avram her husband to be his wife.

RASHI

2. **I will be built through her:** Through the marriage, that I will bring my rival [associate wife] into my house.

3. **And Sarai, the wife of Avram, took Hagar:** She took her with words [persuading her by saying], "Fortunate are you that you merited to be joined with a holy body such as this" (Midrash Rabbah 45:4).

BE'ER MAYIM CHAIM on Rashi 2

[Rashi means to say] that in the merit of the fact that she gave her associate wife [maidservant] over to him so that he should have off-spring from her, even though she had great pain from this, therefore she [would be] also answered with her, for "Anyone who prays for his friend when he [the person who is praying] is in need of that thing [being prayed for], he is answered first (Talmud Bava Kama 92a)...In the manner that a person measures out [to others] They [in Heaven] measure out to him "(Talmud Megillah 12b).

YEFE TOAR HAARUCH on Midrash Rabbah 42:4

....Why was it necessary for Sarah to persuade her maidservant, for why would she [Hagar] refuse her words [proposal]? And perhaps [one could answer] that due to her being the daughter of a king, she *would refuse to be joined with an old man and she would hope for a man like herself...*

OVERVIEW OF TEXT

The Talmud (*Yevamos* 64a) writes that if a married couple lived together in *Eretz Yisrael* for ten years without producing children, they should consider an extreme alternative such as divorce. Perhaps it was ordained that they should not bear offspring together. After ten years of childless marriage while living in *Eretz Yisrael*, *Avraham* and Sarah[1] realized that something radical must be done in order for them to conceive.

Sarah suggested that *Avraham* take *Hagar*[2] as a concubine, saying, "Perhaps I will be built up through her." The *Midrash* (quoted by *Rashi*) explains that Sarah hoped that perhaps she too would conceive in the merit of advocating *Avraham's* marriage to *Hagar*.

How would promoting *Hagar's* marriage to *Avraham* cause Sarah to conceive herself? The *Be'er Mayim Chaim* explains that Sarah's motive was based on an idea found in the Talmud

1.   The original names of *Avraham* and Sarah were *Avram* and *Sarai*. *Hashem* then changed their names to *Avraham* and Sarah. At this point in the *Chumash* they were still *Avram* and *Sarai*. Nevertheless, many commentaries already refer to them as *Avraham* and Sarah. Therefore this text uses *Avraham* and Sarah as well.

2.   *Hagar* was the daughter of Pharaoh the king of Egypt and herself a person of great spirituality. In the beginning of *Lech Lecha* the *Torah* describes Pharaoh's abduction of Sarah and her salvation through *Hashem's* miracles. Upon witnessing this manifest G-dliness, Pharaoh stated that *Hagar* would be better off as a servant in the house of *Avraham* than as a princess elsewhere (*Rashi, Bereishis*16:1). There is no indication that *Hagar* disagreed with her father's value judgment. A further indication of her greatness can be found in the *Sforno* (16:7), who clearly states that *Hagar* was worthy of prophecy.

(*Bava Kama* 92a). The Talmud there teaches that when person A beseeches *Hashem* to grant something to person B, if it is an item that person A requires himself, the request is granted to person A first. By bringing *Hagar* into her home, Sarah was providing *Avraham* with a new opportunity to sire children. Sarah understood that facilitating *Avraham's* ability to procreate would earn Heavenly merit and possibly arouse *Hashem's* mercy to grant her the ability to bear children.

. . . .

Hagar did not immediately consent to the change from maidservant to concubine/wife; she had to first be convinced. Sarah won her over by arguing that it was a great privilege to be joined in marriage with a person of the stature and holiness of *Avraham*.

The *Yefe Toar Haaruch* questions why *Hagar* was at first reluctant to marry *Avraham*. *Hagar* was a great *tzaddekes* (note 2) who forsook her royal status and embraced slavery in order to draw close to *Avraham's* holiness. Without a doubt, the proposed marriage would provide far greater access to the greatness of *Avraham*. Why then did *Hagar* have to be convinced?

The *Yefe Toar Haaruch* answers that, as the daughter of a king, *Hagar* felt entitled to be wed to someone closer to her age. As such, she was reluctant to marry *Avraham* who was much older than she was.

A) HASHEM'S MEASURE FOR MEASURE

Part I

The Talmud (*Bava Kama* 92a) teaches that if one beseeches *Hashem* to grant others something that he himself requires, he is answered before the person for whom he is praying. An interesting question of interpretation can be posed: Perhaps it is only prayer on behalf of another that can somehow effect the Heavenly reciprocation? Or alternatively, perhaps the Talmud's mention of prayer was not exclusionary. The same reciprocity may apply to any attempt at helping another individual, whether through prayer or any other means; *Hashem* first rewards the initiator of the kindness (if needed), measure for measure.

The *Be'er Mayim Chaim's* commentary validates the second, broader application. The Torah does not relate that Sarah prayed that *Avraham* should conceive a child. Rather, she provided *Avraham* with an additional opportunity to father children. It was in the merit of that act of kindness (rather than prayer) that Sarah hoped to merit conception herself. Apparently, *Hashem's* "measure for measure" is activated by any attempt to benefit others. The initiator of the kindness will be granted that same assistance first (if he requires it).

Part II

The Heavenly reciprocity mentioned in the Talmud (*Bava Kama* 92a) is certainly activated on behalf of one who innocently helps another, with no expectation of recompense. What if an individual is aware of this Talmudic idea and sets out to help others in order to activate the Heavenly "measure for measure" on his own behalf? One could perhaps argue that he is hardly setting out to help the other person at all — the motor driving him is the desire to help himself. Will he also merit that response from *Hashem*?

It is evident from the *Be'er Mayim Chaim* that the answer is a resounding "Yes." Sarah set out to help *Avraham* beget children by proposing his marriage to *Hagar*. Yet, Sarah's unabashedly expressed motive was the hope that *Hashem* would grant her children of her own. Apparently, assisting others with this personal ulterior motive in mind can bring about Heavenly assistance on behalf of the helper.[3] (And it does not seem that Sarah was in any way faulted for this act and its underlying motive.)

Obviously, although the ultimate intention may be that of personal gain, at the very least, one must sincerely desire to assist the other individual.

---

3.   A most unusual story was recently related that resonates with this second concept gleaned from the *Be'er Mayim Chaim*. An American woman had been childless for many years, and all her attempts at medical intervention were unsuccessful. She approached an Israeli rabbi and asked for a blessing that she would conceive. The rabbi demurred, saying that he was not a great enough *tzaddik* for his blessing to impact upon so intractable a matter.

But the woman refused to take "No" for an answer. The rabbi finally broke down and related that he himself had a married daughter of a similar age who was being tormented by the almost identical predicament. He quoted the Talmud in *Bava Kama* 92a and proposed the following: The woman before him should pray daily for his daughter living in Israel, and his daughter would do the same for the American woman. Both women agreed to the arrangement. Two years later, both women gave birth on the very same day.

POSSIBLE APPPLICATIONS

Parts I and II reveal an entirely different dimension to helping others. A perfectly legitimate vehicle to obtain a personal requirement is to endeavor to afford the same benefit to others. Any kindness performed might elicit *Hashem's* response of bestowing the same goodness, if needed, upon the one who enacted the original kindness.

If one works to help others get married, there will be greater Heavenly assistance in the marriage of himself or his loved ones; helping others establish themselves financially elicits *Hashem's* financial assistance on behalf of the helper; one wishing to merit scholarship of Torah can be assisted from Heaven by making it possible for others to study Torah. The applications of this idea are as numerous as human needs.

In a similar vein, the daily *davening* contains requests people make for virtually everything in life. Almost all of those prayers are written in the plural. We say in *Shemoneh Esreh* "Cure us and we will be cured" rather than "Cure me." A person who is gravely ill might articulate the words "Cure us," while what he really means to say is "Cure me." He may feel that his personal need is too pressing to distract himself in order to focus on the recovery of others.

Based on this chapter, a way to insure that *Hashem* will more likely heed his prayers of "Cure me" is if the supplicant sincerely beseeches Him to "Cure us." This remains true even if one's motive to concentrate on the words "Cure us" is solely to effect a Divine personal intervention so that one's personal recovery will be granted.

B) CONSISTENCY AND INCONSISTENCY

It is perhaps understandable that a young woman would be reluctant to marry a much older man. Certain natural physical considerations could make him unavoidably undesirable. This normal tendency might explain *Hagar's* hesitation to marry *Avraham*, however righteous she may have been.

However, the *Yefe Toar* does not mention this factor as the cause for *Hagar's* reluctance. Apparently, on a personal level, *Hagar* would have gladly married *Avraham*. Rather, it was her royal background that posed an impediment to the marriage. *Hagar* felt that, as the daughter of a king, she was entitled to wed someone closer to her own age.

There is hardly a greater departure from the august position of a princess than becoming a slave. Yet, *Hagar* accepted slavery as her permanent lot in order to be in the sacred household of *Avraham*. She understood that by the standards of absolute truth, even *Avraham's* household servant occupied a more exalted status than a princess elsewhere. ("Better to be the tail of a lion than the head of a fox" [*Avos* 4:15].)

This begs the question: If *Hagar's* royalty did not prevent her acceptance of slavery, why then would it lead her to insist on marrying someone closer to her own age? It is especially difficult to understand when one considers that the marriage would additionally alleviate her slave status and also draw her closer to the spirituality of *Avraham*.

This paradox gives rise to the following conclusion: It is

at times true that inconsistent behavior is unacceptable. For example, it is normally hypocritical to preach one thing to others and then personally act in an opposite manner. However, there are types of outwardly inconsistent behaviors that are perfectly justifiable.

Individuals with great strengths in area A may be severely challenged by the difficulties in area B; other people who easily negotiate the second area may have serious trouble with the first. Because personal differences can be so uniquely individual, how can one say: "If you excel in area A, why is your behavior less exemplary in area B?"

Whatever the reason may be, *Hagar* was far more capable of the sacrifice of accepting slavery than that of marrying someone less befitting her royal status. Seemingly, if *Hagar* accepted the comedown of slavery, she should have certainly accepted a far lesser indignity - a marriage to the greatest person alive who, however, was not her own age. Pertaining to the circumstances of her own marriage, *Hagar* may have harbored a unique personal sensitivity to entering a married state with someone who did not meet a certain description appropriate to royalty. The *Yefe Toar Haaruch* is teaching that such behavior is not necessarily condemnable.

POSSIBLE APPLICATIONS

R. *Akiva* taught that the *mitzvah* to love a fellow Jew as one loves himself is a fundamental principle of the Torah — one that affects many other areas (*Yerushalmi, Nedarim* 9:4). It is thus a sad and significant occurrence when the warmth between Jews is diminished.

One factor that can cool the affection between people, so lauded by R. *Akiva*, is unmet expectations. For example: A wife may feel let down by an otherwise considerate husband who constantly forgets to clean up after himself; the husband may react similarly to a normally obliging wife who frequently keeps him waiting when they go someplace together. In each case, it is the consideration shown in one area which heightens the disappointment in the second — "If you are so good about this, why can't you do that?"

The husband and wife must understand that the logic behind the expectation may be unfair. One may be marvelously considerate in a general sense, but characterologically challenged in certain specific areas. Keeping things orderly may be an inborn problem for the husband's nature, while the wife may have an inherent weakness in matters of time management. As such, even an outpouring of one form of kindness need not imply that another form of consideration can be automatically expected to follow.[4]

---

4. Obviously, both the husband and wife are obligated to attempt improving upon whatever it is that the other may find irritating. However, the point being made is that one cannot assume that if one is the recipient of one type of kindness, another can be automatically expected or demanded.

CHAPTER 8[1]

בראשית, וירא יח: א-ה,כז

א. וירא אליו יהוה באלני ממרא והוא ישב פתח־האהל כחם היום:
ב. וישא עיניו וירא והנה שלשה אנשים נצבים עליו וירא וירץ
לקראתם מפתח האהל וישתחו ארצה:
ג. ויאמר אדני אם נא מצאתי חן בעיניך אל־נא תעבר מעל עבדך:
ד. יקח־נא מעט־מים ורחצו רגליכם והשענו תחת העץ:
ה. ואקחה פת־לחם וסעדו לבכם אחר תעברו כי־על־כן עברתם על־
עבדכם ויאמרו כן תעשה כאשר דברת:
כז. ויען אברהם ויאמר הנה־נא הואלתי לדבר אל־אדני ואנכי עפר
ועפר:

רש"י

א. **וירא אליו**: לבקר את החולה אמר רבי חמא בר חנינא: - יום
שלישי למילתו היה ובא הקב"ה ושאל בשלומו (ב"מ פ"ו):
פתח האהל: לראות אם יש עובר ושב ויכניסם בביתו:
כחם היום: הוציא הקב"ה חמה מנרתיקה, שלא להטריחו

---

1. This chapter presents several insights into the virtues of hospi-
    tality and kindness that can be observed from the conduct of
    Avraham. Some of the ideas (especially parts III and IV) are in-
    spired by, if not directly taken from, the talks of the *Alter* of
    Slobodka as they appear in *Or Hatzafun,* vol. 1.

באורחים, ולפי שראהו מצטער, שלא היו אורחים באים, הביא
המלאכים עליו בדמות אנשים (ב"מ פ"ו):
ג. דבר אחר: קודש הוא והיה אומר להקב"ה להמתין לו עד שירוץ
ויכניס את האורחים.
ד. ורחצו רגליכם: כסבור שהם ערביים שמשתחוים לאבק רגליהם
והקפיד שלא להכניס ע"ז לביתו (ב"מ פ"ו):
ה. וסעדו לבכם: אמר ר' חמא: 'לבבכם' אין כתיב כאן, אלא
'לבכם', מגיד שאין יצר הרע שולט במלאכים (ב"ר):

מדרש רבה
בראשית מט:יא

ויען אברהם ויאמר הנה נא הואלתי: אמר אלו הרגני אמרפל לא
הייתי עפר ואי שרפני נמרוד לא הייתי אפר.

מהרז"ו

וכוונתו כאשר גמלת אתי חסד זה כך תעשה עם סדום.

גור אריה

שאין יצר הרע כו': ואם תאמר והלא אברהם לא ידע שהיו
מלאכים, ולמה אמר "לבבכם", ונראה לי שכך פירושו - שאברהם היה
מכוין לדבר לשון כבוד לאורחים - ואמר "לבכם", אף על גב דשני
לבבות לאדם (ב"ב יב:) - קראן לשון כבוד שיצר טוב הוא העיקר
בכם, דומה למלאכים שאין בהם רק יצר טוב לגמרי.

נחלת יעקב על רש"י ה

ועל שני בני אדם שייך לומר לבבכם לפי שאין דעותיהם שווה
כדאיתא בסנהדרין דף לח ע"א, והטעם מפני הגזלנים והחמסנים
והיינו היצה"ר ששולט באדם, אבל המלאכים אין להם יצה"ר א"כ
שוים הם בדעותיהם שייך לומר לבכם.

BEREISHIS, VAYERA 18:1-5,27

1. *And Hashem appeared to him [Avraham] in the plains of Mamreh, as he sat at the entrance of the tent in the heat of the day.*
2. *And he lifted up his eyes, and looked, and, behold, three men were standing over him; and he saw [them], and he ran to meet them from the entrance of the tent, and bowed down to the earth.*
3. *And he said [to the leader of the three men]: My lord, if now I have found favor in your eyes, please pass not away from your servant.*
4. *Let now a little water be fetched, and wash your feet, and recline [yourselves] under a tree.*
5. *And I will fetch a morsel of bread, and sustain your heart; after that you shall go on, for such you have come to your servant. And they said: So do, as you have said.*
27. *And Avraham responded and he said: Behold I have desired to speak to my G-d and I am dust and ashes.*

RASHI

1. And [Hashem] appeared unto him: To visit the sick. R. Hama, the son of Hanina said: It was the third day of his [Avraham's] circumcision, and the Holy One Blessed Be He came and inquired about his welfare (Bava Metzia 86b).

At the entrance of the tent: To see if there was a passerby whom he might invite into his house.

In the heat of the day: The Holy One Blessed Be He took out the sun from its container, so as not to burden him with guests. But *since He saw him grieved because there were no guests coming, He brought the angels to him in the form of humans (Bava Metzia 86b).*

3. ... Another interpretation is: *My Lord [is referring to Hashem], and [Avraham] was beseeching the Holy One Blessed Be He to wait for him until he would run and bring in the guests.*

4. And wash your feet: *He [Avraham] assumed them to be Arabs who bow down to the dust of their feet, and he was scrupulous about not bringing idol worship into his house.*

5. And sustain your heart: *R. Hama said, "'Your hearts' is not written here, but 'your heart,' as if to indicate that the yetzer hara does not rule over angels."*

NACHALAS YAAKOV on Rashi 5

When referring to two people it is appropriate to say "your hearts" [plural], for their opinions [desires and philosophies of life] are not the same... And this [usage of "hearts"] is because of the thieves [and various other types of sinners]. And this [disparity between the direction in the lives of different people] is due to the yetzer hara which rules them. However, the angels do not have a yetzer hara, and they are thus of a common heart. If so, it is appropriate to say of them "your heart" [singular].

GUR ARYEH

If you will ask, but Avraham did not know that they were angels, so why did he say "your heart" [singular]? And it appears to me that this is its explanation: That Avraham intended to speak to them in a language of [giving] honor to guests. And he said "your heart" [singular], even though man has two hearts [the inclinations for evil and good]. He addressed them with a language of honor [using "heart" as if to indicate] that the yetzer tov was dominant in them, like angels who have only the yetzer tov...

MIDRASH RABBAH BEREISHIS 49:11

And Avraham responded and he said: Behold I have desired ....He said: If Amrafel had killed me, would I not have been dust, and if Nimrod had burned me, would I not have been ashes?

MAHARZU

And his [Avraham's] intent was: Just as You bestowed this kindness upon me, so too should You do with Sodom.

OVERVIEW OF TEXT

It was the third day after *Avraham* had circumcised himself at age ninety-nine, and the postsurgical pain was at its most intense. In this weakened condition, *Avraham's* usual practice of caring for guests would have been exceedingly difficult. *Hashem* sought to spare him this travail and therefore made the day unusually hot. The extreme heat would discourage wayfarers and potential guests from travel. *Avraham*, however, was distraught over the inability to extend hospitality, and he sat at the entrance to his tent, looking for guests. *Hashem* then appeared before *Avraham* to fulfill the fundamental kindness of visiting the sick.

Hashem had determined that three Heavenly angels would call on *Avraham*, each with a specific mission. One angel was to announce that Sarah would have a baby, one was sent to destroy the city of Sodom and the third came to cure *Avraham*. They would have appeared in their true ethereal form. However, in order to accommodate *Avraham's* desire to help others, *Hashem* sent the angels disguised as idol-worshiping humans.

Assuming the three to be passing travelers, *Avraham* excused himself from *Hashem's* Presence and ran to greet them and to offer his hospitality. However, he first made certain they removed all traces of their idolatry before entering his home.

The *Gur Aryeh* explains *Rashi* to mean that *Avraham* addressed his guests with great respect as if to intimate that they had the purity of angels who have no desire for sin whatsoever.

. . . .

While praying for the salvation of Sodom and its four sister cities *Avraham* said to *Hashem*, "I am dust and ashes" (*Bereishis* 18:27). The *Midrash Rabbah*, 49:11 (quoted by *Rashi*) explains that *Avraham* was referring to two instances in which he was saved by miracles. Had he not defeated the four kings, he would have been dust, and had he not been saved from *Nimrod* (who cast him into a furnace), he would have been reduced to ashes.

Why were these two miracles evoked by *Avraham* as a component of his prayers for Sodom? The *Maharzu* explains that *Avraham* was arguing that just as *Hashem* performed those acts of kindness on behalf of *Avraham*, so too He should save Sodom in an act of kindness.

HOSPITALITY/KINDNESS

Part I

When *Avraham* was recovering from his circumcision, *Hashem* visited him and inquired about his well-being. This illustrates the essential nature of the *mitzvah* of visiting the sick. When one fulfills this *mitzvah*, he is involved in a G-dlike activity.[2]

Part II

Hashem inquired about *Avraham's* well-being despite the fact that He certainly knew the answer. Furthermore, *Avraham* no doubt recognized that *Hashem* knew the answer. Why then did *Hashem* ask the question?

Obviously, the purpose of *Hashem's* inquiry was not to un-cover information, but rather to demonstrate His concern. Evi-dently, sincerely asking one who is ill about his well-being, even when the answer is manifestly obvious, is a display of car-ing. To the sick person being addressed, this display, in and of itself, is a meaningful act of kindness.

One should not underestimate or overlook the beneficial

---

2.   In *Devarim* (13:5) it is written "And to Him [*Hashem*] you shall cleave." The words of the *pasuk* seem to call upon man to become totally bound to *Hashem*, as if (*kavyachol*) one were in a state where he is miming *Hashem's* every movement. How is this accomplished? *Rashi* explains, "Perform kindness, bury the dead, visit the sick, as *Hashem* does." These deeds are a consummately *Hashem*-like activity.

consequences of a kind word and/or show of concern, however unnecessary or redundant it may appear. This form of kindness was worthy of *Hashem* Himself at the moment of His revelation to *Avraham*.

Part III

Avraham was an elderly person in the most painful stages of postsurgical discomfort. To spare him the toil of serving guests, *Hashem* made that day unbearably hot. Seemingly, *Avraham* should have been relieved. He was spared the exertions of hospitality and thereby afforded the opportunity to rest and to recover from his surgery.

Nevertheless, despite the twin afflictions of painful illness and unbearable weather, *Avraham* sat by the entrance to his tent in the hope that a potential visitor might be out and about, despite the heat. "Since He saw him grieved because there were no guests coming, He brought the angels to him in the form of humans" (*Bava Metzia* 86b). *Avraham*'s sudden inability to help others evidently precipitated greater discomfort than the combination of his postsurgical pain and the unbearable heat. By bringing guests (and the burden of serving them), *Hashem* lessened the overall level of *Avraham*'s pain.

This illustrates the extent to which one should be desirous of performing kindness to others. The conventional understanding of a kind person calls to mind the type of individual who is always willing to extend himself for the needy. When his assistance is requested, there is the sense that the favor is readily given. This trait is accepted as a virtue by almost all civilized peoples.

However, there was no one in need that was then beseeching *Avraham*. Rather, it was Avraham who was searching for someone that he could serve. This demonstrates that the ultimate *baal chessed* does not merely respond to the needs of others. Rather, kindness is so deeply ingrained in his soul that he longs for opportunities to extend help and is driven to find them, personal difficulties notwithstanding. Such a person is deeply pained when unable to give expression to this yearning.

People often hope and pray for financial success and seek out opportunities for profit, not merely waiting for these chances to appear on their own. Some individuals also rightly hope and pray for additional opportunities for Torah study and other *mitzvos*. *Avraham's* example demonstrates that one should hope for and actively seek out the opportunity to help others, even when proffering that assistance will be extremely difficult. [3]

Part IV

To greet his guests, *Avraham* had to first take leave of *Hashem*. *The Talmud (quoted in Rashi)* deduces from this example that the *mitzvah* of receiving guests is greater than the act of receiving the Divine Presence.

Many Jews feel that merely being in the presence of a truly righteous person exerts a powerfully positive influence. If so, what can be said of being with the Almighty Himself? Is this not the supremely sacred environment? *Avraham's* behavior teaches that the *mitzvah* of helping three such guests is deemed a higher priority than remaining with the Divine Presence.

---

3.   R. *Yisroel Salanter* once quipped: One often hears the cry of *"Ah tsenter, ah tsenter!"* (Nine men wishing to *daven* are waiting and seeking a tenth in order to further sanctify their davening with a *minyan*.) However, how often does one hear *"Ah seudah, ah seudah!"* (People wishing to begin a sumptous meal are nonetheless waiting and calling out for a guest so they can further sanctify their feast through the *mitzvah* of sharing it with someone needy.)

This idea can be developed further. *Avraham* was a wealthy man with a large household. As such, someone else could have presumably served as the host until *Avraham*'s audience with *Hashem* was concluded. However, because being served by "the boss" himself bestows greater kindness and honor upon the guests, such hospitality is therefore a greater *mitzvah*. Even attaining that additional dimension to the performance of *chessed* took precedence over communing with an open revelation of the Divine Presence.[4]

4.   An elderly and very devout Jewish woman would often say to R. *Dovid Leibowitz*: "*M'darft zein frum un m'darft zein gut* (One must be pious, and one must be good)." He would respond: "*M'darft zein gut un m'darft zein frum* (One must be good, and one must be pious)." Once she was being especially persistent, and he added: "We must learn from *Hashem* Himself; the Torah teaches that He is exceedingly good, but not necessarily that He is exceedingly *frum*." *(See preface, section A, quoted from Or Hatzafun.)*

Two vignettes of the *Alter* of *Slabodka* come to mind that are also evocative of this theme. Both were related by my *Rebbe*. The *Alter* once asked a young married student whether he helps his wife with her preparations for *Shabbos*. The student responded in the affirmative, and proceeded to quote the Talmud (*Kiddushin*, 41a) concerning *Rava* who personally salted the fish being prepared for *Shabbos*. The *Alter* sharply berated the student, in effect saying: "Is that your principal basis for helping her? What type of *frumkeit* is this? Don't you realize that salting the fish for *Shabbos*, as per the Talmud, is infinitely less significant than doing *chessed* to your wife? She is a living and feeling *tzelem Elokim* and one to whom you especially owe so much kindness and gratitude. True *frumkeit* is to imitate *Hashem* who constantly bestows kindness upon people, first and foremost. The Talmud is only saying that in addition to responding to

Part V

The following is based on a text found later in Vayeira. However, because it in part deals with the concept under discussion, it was included with this chapter.

Upon hearing that Sodom and its sister cities were about to be destroyed, *Avraham* offered a series of prayers on their behalf to *Hashem*. Those prayers are described at relatively great length in the *Chumash*. One argument mentioned by *Avraham* was that *Hashem* had saved *Avraham's* life on two previous occasions. He was saved from *Nimrod*, who threw him in a fiery furnace, and he emerged victorious in his war against the overwhelmingly superior armies of the four kings.

Why were these two miracles evoked as a component of *Avraham's* prayers for Sodom? The *Maharzu* explains that *Avraham* was arguing that just as *Hashem* performed those acts of kindness on behalf of *Avraham*, so too should He act out of

---

whatever primary motives for helping that existed (such as *chessed* to a wife), Rava also made a special point of salting the fish."

Another incident involved a student in the yeshiva's main study hall who stooped to pick up a small scrap of paper which he then promptly dropped. The *Alter* noticed and asked for an explanation. The young man explained that he had suspected that the paper was a scrap from a *sefer*, in which case it had to be buried. Upon seeing that such was not the case, he simply let go of it. The *Alter* rebuked the student in a similar vein. "What type of *frumkeit* is this? You should have thought of what will transpire if you drop the paper. Another person will then have to trouble himself (and possibly interrupt his Torah study for a moment) to retrieve the same paper, thinking it to be from a *sefer*. You are so fretful over the possible dishonor to a tiny scrap from a *sefer*. One should be far more focused on the honor of a *tzelem Elokim*, a fellow Jew, and probably a *talmid chacham*."

kindness and save Sodom.

How can the logic of *Avraham's* prayer be understood? *Avraham* was one of the greatest and most virtuous individuals in the annals of mankind; the Sodomites, on the other hand, were among history's most amoral and depraved. Does it follow that if *Hashem* saved that one incredible *tzaddik*, He should likewise save five cities whose inhabitants were supremely evil?

This reveals a basic definition of *Hashem's* trait of kindness which man is called upon to emulate. For the most part, the extent and enthusiasm of one's kindness should not depend upon who will be the recipient of that goodness. If one performs *chessed* for the *Avraham* of his generation, it should follow that he will retain the urge to practice similar kindness to the Sodomites of his time. If one only has the urge to perform kindness to the "deserving," he is likely not in the main motivated by *Hashem's* sacred attribute of *chessed*, but rather by some other, possibly unholy, trait.

A personification of a truly remarkable *baal chessed* of recent times was R. *Aryeh Levine, z"l*, of Jerusalem. He was known throughout Israel for his incredible and almost indiscriminate kindness to all: to his family, his neighbors, secular Jews, prisoners, lepers, and so on.

. . . .

Parts III and IV help illustrate the extent of *Avraham's* hospitality and *chessed* to others. It should also be noted that *Avraham* presumed his guests to be of less-than-exemplary character; he thought they were idolaters. Nevertheless, *Avraham* ignored his pain and the weather, and he left *Hashem's* Presence and rushed to serve them. This demonstrates that in a general sense, the Torah's lofty dictates that govern interpersonal conduct were intended not only for organizations that offer *chessed*, for family, friends, those who share similar beliefs or those who are clearly righteous, but for almost any Jew.[5]

The obligation of kindness is certainly greater if:

5. There was a secular Israeli Jew who, for many years, oversaw distributions of major governmental financial assistance to *yeshivos*. At one point he was asked how, as an irreligious person, he felt about being the conduit for significant help to Torah education.

This man replied that his background was most unique. Prior to World War II, he was a university student leader in Vilna and a committed nonbeliever. Furthermore, he and many of his friends had been exposed to various degrees of *yeshivah* education. As such, they rebelled against traditional Judaism despite a reasonably thorough knowledge of Torah.

At one time it became necessary to meet privately with the great R. *Chaim Ozer Grodzensky* regarding a community issue. R. *Chaim Ozer* was then the unofficial head of the Vilna Jewish community as well as the final Torah authority for many, if not most, communities and rabbis throughout the world. He was looking forward to the meeting with a sense of dread, anticipating that R. *Chaim Ozer* would berate him for his ways.

Instead, R. *Chaim Ozer*, who was then elderly and ill, greeted him with an overwhelming attitude of warmth, of love and respect. He provided tea and refreshments, and insisted on personally serving him (as *Avraham* did). He then made inquiries as to whether he or any of the other Jewish students on campus required assistance of any sort — i.e., food, lodging or money, and he offered his personal help.

The man continued to explain that helping *yeshivos* and their students was not difficult for him, for he was idealistic and always interested in helping others. Although he never became a *baal teshuvah*, the memory of his encounter with R. *Chaim Ozer* always stayed with him. Accordingly, he would never allow a difference in theology to in any way interfere with what he would otherwise do for a fellow Jew.

1) one is not in great pain and weather conditions are not unbearable,

2) the recipient is not an idol worshiper,

3) the recipient is righteous,

4) the one performing the *chessed* is not occupied so justifiably as *Avraham* was at that moment (interacting directly with *Hashem*).

5) All other factors being equal, there is yet a far greater obligation to perform *chessed* in cases where additional gratitude or honor is due the recipient (e.g., to a parent, spouse or *rebbe*).

Part V illustrates further that if one bestowed a true kindness upon the most righteous of individuals, it should automatically follow that he would have the urge to do almost the same for the most unsavory of people.

Part VI

Heavenly angels are entirely spiritual and do not harbor a desire to sin; they possess a common unity of exalted purpose and a single-minded pursuit of *Hashem's* will. However, the focus of each human life is unique and diverse. That is because people, unlike angels, harbor the *yetzer hara*, which drives them to many different forms of sinful behavior.

The *Nachalas Yaakov* explains *Rashi* to mean that *Avraham* addressed his guests using the words, "your heart," as if saying to them, "your single heart." This figure of speech was meant to imply that the visitors were endowed with a singular purity of intent that is particular to angels only. In truth, they actually were angels, and *Avraham's* words were thus appropriate.

The *Gur Aryeh* asks, but *Avraham* did not yet realize that they were angels, so why was the singular used when referring to their hearts? The *Gur Aryeh* answers that although assuming them to be idol-worshiping humans, he used that terminology out of honor for them. Because these people were his guests, *Avraham* addressed them with a special measure of deference. He said, in effect, that he held them in such high regard that, to him, they were people who had achieved the sublime unity of purpose particular to angels only.

This teaches (1) that extending honor to one's guests is a component of hospitality, (2) the incredible extent to which this veneration should be carried, and (3) that one is obliged to sincerely extend this level of deference to almost any guest, even an idolater. (See section V, numbers 1-5 regarding the obligation to actively perform acts of kindness to a typical present-day guest. Evidently, the same holds true for the obligation to honor one's guest as a component of one's hospitality.)

Part VII

Avraham addressed his guests as if they were as sanctified as G-d's angels. In fact, *Avraham* presumed them to be idolaters for he commanded them to wash their feet to remove idolatry before entering his home (*Rashi*, 4). If the honor was sincere (as it no doubt was) how could *Avraham* simultaneously deal with them both as angels and as people who would profane his home with idolatry?

Evidently, the two relationships can coexist. A person can extend the very highest level of deference to others while at the same time recognizing and acting upon their every shortcoming. The savvy and insight that sees human failings and depravity is compatible with the innocence and purity that can honor every person as a veritable angel of G-d.[6]

6.   A similar idea can be found in Tractate *Derech Eretz Rabbah*, chapter 5. There it is written that one should consider all people as if they were, or might be, robbers, yet he should honor them as if they were R. *Gamliel* (the prince of the Jewish people). The example given is that of R. *Yehoshua* who treated a guest with enormous respect. Yet, at the same time he also took precautions to protect himself from being treacherously robbed by that same person.

In fact, the two cases are different. R. *Yehoshua* wasn't certain of the true character of his guest. As such, it could be argued that he honored him while at the same time taking precautions just in case the guest was a thief. However, *Avraham*'s view of his visitors went beyond suspicion. "He [*Avraham*] assumed them to be Arabs who bow down to the dust of their feet, and he was scrupulous about not bringing idol worship into his house." Nevertheless, he simultaneously accorded them the deference appropriate to *tzaddikim* who had purified themselves to the extent of Heavenly angels.

CHAPTER 9

בראשית, וירא כא: ט-יב,יד

ט. ותרא שרה את-בן-הגר המצרית אשר-ילדה לאברהם מצחק:
י. ותאמר לאברהם גרש האמה הזאת ואת-בנה כי לא יירש בן-
האמה הזאת עם-בני עם-יצחק:
יא. וירע הדבר מאד בעיני אברהם על אודות בנו:
יב. ויאמר אלהים אל-אברהם אל-ירע בעיניך על-הנער ועל-אמתך כל
אשר תאמר אליך שרה שמע בקלה כי ביצחק יקרא לך זרע:
יד. וישכם אברהם בבקר ויקח-לחם וחמת מים ויתן אל-הגר שם על-
שכמה ואת-הילד וישלחה ותלך ותחע במדבר באר שבע:

ספורנו

ט. את בן הגר המצרית: חשבה שהתעורר לזה הלעג מפני ששמע
כך מאמו, כאמרם ז"ל "שותא דינוקא בשוקא או דאבוהי או
דאמיה".
מצחק: מלעיג על המשתה שנעשה בבית אברהם, באמרו שנתעברה
מאבימלך.
י. גרש את האמה הזאת ואת בנה: כי בעצתה עשה הבן שהוציא
דיבה למען יירש בנה הכל, לפיכך גרש מפני שאינו דין שיירש
אפילו בקצת.
יב. אל ירע בעיניך על הנער ועל אמתך: כל אשר תאמר אליך
שרה - אל ירע בעיניך מה שתאמר בדבר הנער והאמה לגרשם עם

שמע בקולה: כי　　(שם על שכמה (פס' יד)״　סימני עבדות, כאמרו
וישמעאל　כי ביצחק יקרא לך זרע:　.בדין אמרה לעשות כך
ובניו יהיו עבדים לו,

יד. שם על שכמה: את החמת לאות שפחות, על דרך ״והתעני
תחת ידיה (טז, ט), אבל לא חדל הצדיק מתת להם די מחסורם,
כמו שאמרו ז״ל ״ויהי אלהים את הנער (פס' כ) - לרבות חמריו
גמליו ופועליו״, ולכן לא חסרו דבר זולתי המים בתעותם במדבר,
וישלחה: ליוה אותה ברוב חסדו, כמו ואברהם הולך עמם
לשלחם (יח טז).

BEREISHIS, VAYERA 21:9-12,14

9. *And Sarah saw the son of Hagar the Egyptian, whom she bore to Avraham, mocking.*

10. *And she said to Avraham: Drive out this slave woman and her son, for the son of this slave woman will not inherit with my son, Yitzchak.*

11. *And the matter regarding his son was very bad [distressing] in the eyes of Avraham.*

12. *And Hashem said to Avraham: It should not be bad in your eyes over [the matter of] the lad and your maidservant; heed whatever Sarah says to you, for through Yitzchak you will be considered as having offspring.*

14. *And Avraham arose in the morning, and he took bread and a jug of water, and he gave it to Hagar; he placed [it] on her shoulder, together with the boy, and he sent her off, and she went, and she strayed in the desert of Beersheva.*

SFORNO

9. **The son of Hagar the Egyptian:** She [Sarah] thought that he [Yishmael] was inspired to this slander for he heard such from his mother, as they [the Rabbis, Talmud Sukkah 56b] of blessed memory said, "The words of a child in the street emanate either from his

father or his mother."
Mocking: *Scoffing at the feast that was made in the house of Avraham [over the birth of Yitzchak; Yishmael was] saying that she [Sarah] had conceived from Avimelech....*
10. Drive out this slave woman and her son: *For it was because of her advice that the son slanders; this was so that her son would inherit everything.*
12. It should not be bad in your eyes over [the matter of] the lad and your maidservant: *What she tells you regarding banishing the lad and the maidservant with manifestations of enslavement, as it is written, "He placed on her shoulder" (verse 14).*
Heed whatever Sarah says to you: *For what she instructs you to do is proper.*
For through Yitzchak you will be considered as having offspring: *And Yishmael and his descendants will be slaves to him.*
14. He placed [it] on her shoulder: *The pitcher [was placed on her shoulder] as a sign of her servitude, as it is written (Bereishis 16:9), "You should be dominated by her." But the tzaddik [Avraham] did not refrain from giving them their adequate needs, as they [the Rabbis] of blessed memory said [referring to the sentence], "'And Hashem was with the lad': This is to include his donkeys, his camels and his workers" [which were provided by Avraham]. And therefore, they did not lack anything except for water [and that was because] of their straying in the desert....*
And he sent her off: *He accompanied her with his abundant kindness, as [it says] "And Avraham went with them to send them off"(Bereishis 18:16).*

OVERVIEW OF TEXT

As *Yishmael* grew older, he became increasingly out of step with the spiritual purity of *Avraham*'s household. In Sarah's opinion, *Hagar*, *Yishmael*'s mother, shared the responsibility for this improper behavior. Sarah therefore insisted that both *Hagar* and *Yishmael* be banished from *Avraham's* home and relegated thereafter to eternal subservience to *Yitzchak* and his descendants. *Avraham* was initially distressed by Sarah's counsel, but was advised by *Hashem* to accede to her judgment.

Avraham provided adequate sustenance for *Hagar* and *Yishmael's* journey, and he then placed a pitcher of water upon *Hagar's* shoulders. This (in keeping with Sarah's dictate) was to ordain that *Yishmael's* descendants would be forever subservient to the descendants of Sarah. *Hagar* and *Yishmael* were then sent off to the desert, a trek fraught with peril. (They later lost their way and exhausted their water supply, and it was only *Hashem's* miracle that prevented their deaths from thirst.)

As *Hagar* was leaving, *Avraham* acted toward her with a traditional component of his legendary hospitality and kindness (see chapter 8). He accompanied her from his house as he did when the three visiting angels departed from his home (*Vayeira* 18:16).

THE TONE OF RELATIONSHIPS

The saga of *Hagar* is certainly most heartrending. She voluntarily gave up her position as a princess of Egypt to become a servant in *Avraham*'s home (see chapter 7, note 2). Subsequently she became *Avraham*'s wife. Now, however, she and her son were being

- relegated to eternal servitude,

- forever banished from *Avraham*'s home and

- sent off to the dangerous uncertainties of the desert.

At the traumatic moment of her departure, *Avraham* could have been ill at ease and/or disappointed with *Hagar* for causing his family to be forever split. *Avraham*, the paradigm of kindness, was also put into the position of having to inflict these three great blows upon *Hagar* and *Yishmael*. (And *Avraham* truly loved *Yishmael*; see *Rashi, Bereishis* 22:2).

Nevertheless, according to the *Sforno*, *Avraham*, in his abundant kindness, accompanied *Hagar* from his home. His conduct toward *Hagar* was likened to the kindness he extended to the three visiting angels when they departed from his home. Seemingly, *Avraham*'s gesture of kindness toward *Hagar* was extremely discordant with the suffering that he was in the midst of inflicting upon them.

In truth, *Hagar*'s being banished from *Avraham*'s house did not require a diminution of the protocols of kindness routinely practiced by *Avraham* (such as escorting those who were leaving his home). Thus, even while in the act of justifiably

expelling *Hagar* from his home, *Avraham's* customary consideration and graciousness remained unchanged. He comported
himself in a manner that was characteristic of his "abundant
kindness."[1]

    Avraham's conduct teaches that if difficulties, tensions or
disagreements crop up between people, care should be taken
that they are circumscribed. The specific problem should not
be allowed to impact upon their other interactions. Rather,
courtesy and kindness should continue to characterize the
overall tone of their relationship.

POSSIBLE APPLICATIONS

    People may disagree with each other — at times, in a
fairly intense fashion. (As a rule, quarreling itself is almost always antithetical to Torah.) Very often, the most severe damage does not emanate from the disagreement itself, but from
the breakdown in civility, consideration and respect that can
accompany strife. Two people arguing over a specific matter

---

1.   One might ask, perhaps this tenderness of *Avraham* to *Hagar*
was based on the fact that she had been his wife. As such,
Avraham bestowed upon her a special measure of warmth,
even at that unpleasant moment. If so, one could not prove
that this lofty ethic is germane to dealings with the public at
large.

    The *Sforno*, however, indicates otherwise. The *Sforno* explains
that *Avraham's* conduct toward *Hagar* was a component of his
general kindness toward all others, previously demonstrated
when he accompanied the three visitors (who were strangers)
when leaving his home. The indication is that he would have
acted similarly toward individuals with whom he had no prior
relationship. Evidently, this type of kindliness should be practiced universally.

may soon find themselves embroiled in a broad-based multi-level conflict that includes a total personal negation of each other.

The concept of the *Sforno* can prevent this breakdown. Even while in the midst of the dispute, the prior attitude of kindness and love on all other matters that characterized the relationship should continue unabated. This would enormously halt the escalation and limit the harm that can ensue from an initially circumscribed dispute.[2]

. . . .

The rebuking or disciplining of children poses a similar

---

2.   R. *Avraham Trop* developed a somewhat similar point from *Rashi* in *Bereishis, Vayeira* 21:25. That *pasuk* describes *Avraham's* rebuke of *Avimelech* over a well that was stolen. *Rashi* adds that he called him to task over "this matter" (of the well). What was *Rashi* adding? The text clearly states that it was over "this matter" of the well that *Avraham* rebuked *Avimelech*.

R. *Trop* answered that *Rashi* was pointing out that *Avraham's* rebuke concerned the well, and the well only. Openly criticizing someone face-to-face can beget a dredging up of past grievances totally unconnected to the subject at hand. *Avraham* was above this practice, and thus, his reproof of *Avimelech* was limited to the matter of the well alone.

Rashi in *Vayeira,* according to R. *Trop,* teaches that rebuke should be issue-specific, and it should not evolve into "warfare" and denunciations on many different fronts. The *Sforno* adds that at difficult moments, it is not sufficient to merely avoid broad-based conflict. Rather, all of the Torah's most lofty requirements concerning human interaction should remain in place. The ongoing attitude and practice of "abundant kindness," as practiced by *Avraham* (see chapter 8) in all other matters, should never cease.

challenge. Chastisement over a finite issue should not evolve
into a total condemnation of the child as a person. The habit
of sending a unilaterally negative message to children in such
moments can cause lasting harm. The ethic of the *Sforno* calls
upon the parent or teacher in the midst of rebuke or discipline
to maintain and express his previously warm attitude toward
the child in every other respect.

CHAPTER 10

בראשית, וירא כב:ב

ויאמר קח־נא את בנך את־יחידך אשר־אהבת את־יצחק ולך־לך אל־
ארץ המריה והעלהו שם לעלה על אחד ההרים אשר אמר אליך:

רש"י

את בנך: אמר לו שני בנים יש לי אמר לו את יחידך אמר לו זה
יחיד לאמו וזה יחיד לאמו אמר לו אשר אהבת אמר לו שניהם אני
אהב אמר לו יצחק. ולמה לא גילה לו מתחילה שלא לערבבו פתאום
ותזוח דעתו עליו ותטרף...

שפתי חכמים על רש"י

כדי שלא יאמרו הקב"ה הטריף דעתו ולכך עשה אבל אי לא היה
מטורף מדעתו לא היה עושה:

BEREISHIS, VAYERA 22:2

*And He said, "Please take your son, your only son, that you love,
Yitzchak, and go to the land of Moriah and bring him up there for
an offering upon one of the mountains that I shall relate to you."*

RASHI

Your Son: He [Avraham] said to Him [Hashem], "I have two sons." He said to him, "Your only son." He said to Him, "This one is only for his mother and this one is only to his mother." He said to him, "That you love." He said to Him, "I love both of them." He said to him, "Yitzchak."

Then why didn't He reveal [that it was Yitzchak] to him from the beginning? So as not to confuse him suddenly, and his mind would be disoriented and torn...

SIFSEI CHACHAMIM on Rashi

So that they shouldn't say that the Almighty confused his mind and therefore he did it [that is, went to sacrifice Yitzchak] but had he not been confused, he would not have done it.

OVERVIEW OF TEXT

Hashem commanded *Avraham* to sacrifice his son *Yitzchak* upon an altar. The actual directive contained seemingly unnecessary detail. *Avraham* was ordered to take

- your son,
- your only son,
- that you love,
- (and finally) *Yitzchak*.

Why was the command articulated with a progressive unfolding of descriptive detail? *Rashi/Sifsei Chachamim* explain that *Hashem's* intention was to uphold *Avraham's* reputation of righteousness. Had the order been stated directly, people might incorrectly say: "*Avraham* heeded *Hashem* only because he was suddenly disoriented and overwhelmed, and he agreed due to haste. However, had *Hashem's* words been spoken slowly, thereby allowing time for contemplation, *Avraham* might have disobeyed."

Avraham's compliance after being gradually apprised of *Hashem's* command confirmed his piety beyond any doubt.

INTRODUCTION TO THE IDEAS

Hashem addressed *Avraham* in stages when issuing the command to sacrifice *Yitzchak*. However, *Rashi* explains that if the order had come suddenly, many would have disparaged *Avraham's* piety and attributed the great deed to a decision made in a moment of confusion. This chapter discusses the hypothetical scenario (which never actually occurred) of *Hashem* speaking suddenly to *Avraham* and what people would have subsequently said — namely, that *Avraham* decided to sacrifice *Yitzchak* only due to confusion and haste.

That possible derision of *Avraham's* devotion is, in fact, a two-part argument claiming:

A) *Avraham's* original decision to obey *Hashem* was due to haste and confusion and,

B) even if *Avraham* had actually sacrificed *Yitzchak*, people would denigrate the great deed, saying that it was a consequence of the original decision that was made in haste. They would say that *Avraham* acted out of character and his deeds were thus not reflective of outstanding piety.

The Torah does not discuss or refute utterly absurd arguments; stupidity need not be disproved (see preface, section H). Yet, Hashem made certain to disprove these naysayers. Evidently, both accusations A and B were theoretically feasible.

Following is a closer analysis of that theoretically feasible two-part minimizing of *Avraham's* deed that would have been leveled against him had the command been issued suddenly.

A) HASTY DECISIONS

According to this false accusation, *Avraham's* agreeing to sacrifice *Yitzchak* was motivated by the haste of *Hashem's* command and *Avraham's* subsequent disorientation. An opportunity to first reflect on the matter would have prompted a different response.

It is hard to imagine something more momentous and irreversible than taking the life of one's own child. (*Yitzchak* was thirty-seven at the time.) Additionally, *Yitzchak* was the future of the Jewish people, making his death additionally catastrophic. Could the decision of a *tzaddik* like *Avraham* on an issue of this gravity be altered by haste? How could he allow such a thing to happen?

Evidently haste and confusion can alter almost any determination — even when

- the dilemma at hand involves whether to kill another human being, a most irrevocable act,

- the person being killed is also one's own son,

- the issue being weighed has global and historic significance (i.e., the destruction of the Jewish nation), and

- the individual making the decision is one of the kindest and wisest people to have ever walked the face of the earth (in this instance, *Avraham*).

It was at least theoretically possible that *Avraham's* judgment in this case could be altered by haste. Certainly then, haste and confusion can easily influence a decision by people of lesser stature in more mundane matters.[2]

Whenever possible, one must take pains to decide upon important matters only after serious deliberation in an environment of calm. One cannot assume that somehow, the combination of sincerity and an important issue at hand will automatically produce a correct determination. Virtually any decision can be altered and corrupted by haste.

---

2.   The claim of the nay-sayers would have been that *Avraham* performed the *mitzvah* of sacrificing *Yitzchak* only because of haste. This teaches that haste can cause one to perform a *mitzvah* that he might not otherwise do. It is also true that a hasty decision can be the factor that causes wrongdoing. The following is a sobering example:

The *Ralbag* at the end of *Vayechi* (*Toeles* 2 and 3) discusses the sin of *Reuvain* who defiled *Yaakov's* bed after *Rachel* died. As *Yaakov's* eldest son, *Reuvain* was entitled to the status of both the firstborn and royalty. However, due to this one sin, *Reuvain* lost both of these crowns. The rights of the firstborn were given to the tribe of *Yosef*, while *Yehudah* ascended to the throne. (The *Targum Onkeles* in *Bereishis*, *Vayechi* 49:3 adds that *Reuvain* would have also been heir to the priesthood, and that too was lost because of this sin.) The *Ralbag* writes that *Reuvain's* misfortune teaches that one should not decide matters in haste, for it was *Reuvain's* haste that caused him to err.

Apparently, in every other respect, *Reuvain's* motives and thinking were impeccable and suffused with holiness; he was sincere, and he was acting out of pure idealism and fear of *Hashem*. His only error was that he made this one decision in haste, and in turn, that haste caused his error in judgment. That single hurried moment, in and of itself, caused *Reuvain* to lose so much, and to lose it for eternity.

B) THE INFLUENCE OF DECISIONS

Avraham and *Yitzchak* journeyed for three days to the site of the sacrifice. If, as argued, *Avraham*'s original acceptance of *Hashem*'s command was due only to haste and confusion, why didn't he change his mind when haste was no longer a factor? He had the three days of travel to come to his senses. Wouldn't making that journey without a change of heart retroactively prove that *Avraham* did not act out of character and due to haste? Why then would the accusation of haste have any conceivable validity?

Apparently, a decision might first be made solely as a result of disorientation or haste. However, that point of view soon assumes a life of its own; a secondary process then takes hold. One becomes partial to that decision already made (albeit in haste); having committed himself to the decision, the human mind then loses a measure of objectivity and critical thinking in this matter.

Consequently, if it were true that *Avraham* acted out of character (albeit because of hasty thinking) when agreeing to the sacrifice, that decision would then tend to stick. *Avraham* would be subconsciously predisposed to abide by what he had already deemed correct. Even three days of calm to contemplate the matter would not necessarily lead to a change of heart. Such would be *Avraham*'s bond and commitment to his prior decision.[3] Nonetheless, it could have remained true, that in an environment of calm, *Avraham* would have never agreed in the first place to carry out *Hashem*'s command.

One must be constantly vigilant in reviewing motives, thought processes and past decisions. This search for true objectivity may necessitate consultation with a friend, a mentor or a *rebbe* (see chapter 32, note 4).

POSSIBLE APPLICATIONS

A particular scenario comes to mind. The choice to adopt a certain belief system, to live a certain way or to associate with certain types of people is a decision of enormous significance. It forms a frame of reference for much of what one thinks and does. The group one associates with can largely influence one's self-image; furthermore, one often subscribes to the prevailing views of the group members (see chapter 22, section B). For an entire lifetime, people may be acting upon and influenced by their past judgments and decisions of this type.

Those decisions may not have all been necessarily correct; they need objective reexamination. However, having once opined in favor of a certain stance, one is then subconsciously drawn to live by and defend his original position,

---

3.   It would appear that the source text does not define how exactly this process operates. It could be that the psychological mechanism is a function of human ego. There is a subconscious mental/emotional bias to defend one's previous thinking so that it will endure as the correct decision.

Alternatively, this dynamic might result from habit of thought. If a late riser takes a job that requires him to be at work early, very often, the force of habit will transform him into an early riser. Similarly, thinking along given lines for a period of time becomes an acquired habit that endures – it has a life of its own. One will always tend to think in a similar fashion and see the same issue in that same light. R. *Isaac Sher*, in his preface to *Sefer Cheshbon Hanefesh*, makes mention of the idea of the force of habit in thinking, and he writes that this is a most powerful type of habituation.

even though he might now decide otherwise, were he facing this issue for the first time.

Rashi is revealing that even decisions regarding mankind's most important matters can be unknowingly distorted by this tendency. Theoretically, *Avraham*'s closeness to *Hashem* could have been such that he would never sacrifice his son. Nevertheless he might have actually gone through with the deed, but only because of the tendency to adhere to a hurried past decision that was out of character. Such can be the power of this form of partiality. Certainly then, one's thinking on everyday matters is potentially vulnerable to the ravages of this type of bias.[4]

---

4.   The ideas and especially the texts of this chapter and Chapter 2 were among the most difficult in this entire book to explicate, especially to those with little or no yeshivah background. That is because both deal in the area of "What if." What if the serpent had argued on its own behalf (Chapter 2) – what if *Avraham* was commanded suddenly (this chapter). Although much effort was expended in search of the greatest possible comprehensibility, that goal may not have been adequately realized. The author apologizes for whatever confusion or lack of clarity that these chapters may contain.

CHAPTER 11

בראשית, חיי שרה כד:ג

ואשביעך ביהוה אלהי השמים ואלהי הארץ אשר לא־תקח אשה
לבני מבנות הכנעני אשר אנכי יושב בקרבו:

רלב"ג

התועלת השני הוא במדות: והוא שראוי לאדם להתרחק מהתחבר
עם הפחותים לפי היכולת. ולזה הרחיק אברהם שיקח יצחק אשה
מבנות כנען להיות מנהגיהם פחותים מאד כמו שהתפרסם מדברי
התורה, אמר "וכמעשה ארץ כנען וגו' לא תעשו" (ויקרא יח, ג).

BEREISHIS, CHAYA SARAH 24:3

*And I [Avraham] will make you swear by Hashem, the G-d of
Heaven and G-d of the earth, that you will not take a wife for my
son from the daughters of the Canaanites among whom I dwell.*

RALBAG

*The second benefit [or lesson that can be derived from this in-
cident] is in character traits. That is, that it is proper for man to
distance himself from fraternizing with lower [less noble] people as*

much as possible. As such, Avraham distanced himself from Yitzchak taking a wife from the daughters of Canaan because of their base customs, as is explained from the words of the Torah, which says, "And like the actions of the land of Canaan...you shall not do" (Vayikra 18:3).

OVERVIEW OF TEXT

Avraham charged his servant *Eliezer* to seek a wife for *Yitzchak*. One requirement *Avraham* insisted on was that a woman from *Canaan* should not be chosen. This was because the *Canaanites* were an immoral people.

The *Ralbag* deduces from *Avraham's* instructions that one should similarly avoid friendships with individuals whose conduct is ignoble.

THE INFLUENCE OF FRIENDS

Avraham did whatever possible to insure that *Yitzchak* would marry the proper wife. According to the *Ralbag*, this teaches that one should be similarly discriminating when choosing a friend with whom to associate.

In the marital relationship, the wife's influence is immeasurable. The *Midrash Rabbah* (*Bereishis* 17:7) describes a husband and wife who were both exceedingly pious. They eventually divorced because, together, they could not produce children. Both married again — but to spouses who were evil. In each of the new marriages, it was the woman's spiritual influence that predominated. The righteous woman made a *tzaddik* of her evil husband, while the formerly devout male became an evildoer. The *Midrash* concludes with the words, "All comes from the woman," meaning that it is typically the wife who sets the moral tone in a marriage. This effect endures for the duration of the marriage, which can be for the greater part of one's lifetime.

This being the case, one could question the *Ralbag*'s analogy. Where is the proof that comparable prudence must be exercised before selecting a friend? Because a wife's influence is inordinately powerful and normally long-lasting, profound forethought must precede the choosing of a wife. Seemingly, one's friend exerts far less influence than his wife. How then can the *Ralbag* deduce from *Avraham*'s vigilance in seeking a proper spouse that similar caution is necessary when choosing a friend?

Apparently, the *Ralbag* is saying a great deal about the underlying dynamics of close camaraderie. Friendships may not normally endure as long as marriages, and they are more easily broken. However, during the period of the companionship, one friend's sway over the other may be as strong as that of a wife over her husband; the friend's influence can permeate the innermost depths of one's soul, creating a lasting impression. (Presumably, the *Ralbag* is discussing a close friend.) It is for that reason that the *Ralbag* was able to make this analogy. The extreme caution required when choosing a wife is thus equally imperative in the selection of a friend. This can apply to the choosing of friends, both for oneself and (to the extent that it can be controlled) for one's children.[1]

---

1.   An often discussed question concerns whether a young rabbi should move with his family to a mostly irreligious environment in order to spread and teach Torah. Many have argued that this *mitzvah*, in most cases, should not be undertaken — there is a significant potential for spiritual hazard. However great the *mitzvah*, the rabbi, and especially his children, could be negatively influenced by associating with the very society they seek to reform. The idea of the *Ralbag* on the enormity of a friend's influence would seem to bolster this view.

The following is a different response:

In a private discussion I had with R. *Yaakov Kamenetsky*, he endorsed the idea that one may move with his young children to a spiritually alien environment to teach Torah. He mentioned that he himself moved his young family from Eastern Europe to Toronto, Canada. He added that to whatever extent possible, a rabbi in this situation should see that the Torah education of his children is supplemented. He mentioned that accordingly, while in Toronto, he hired a private tutor to teach his son *Gemara*.

· · · · ·

The following was related by an eyewitness:

In the early 1950s there was a convention held by the *Torah Umesorah* organization. R. *Aharon Kotler* addressed the gathering and urged *yeshivah* students to make a career of teaching Torah in *yeshivah* elementary schools in the far-flung communities of America. A questioner rose to challenge this view, citing the spiritual peril to one's family.

R. *Kotler* responded immediately to the questioner, quoting the *Rambam* (*Hilchos Malachim* 7:15): "Anyone who goes to war without fear with the intention to sanctify the Name of Heaven, he is guaranteed that damage will not find him and evil will not reach him. And he will build for himself a proper house in Israel, and he will provide merit to himself and his descendants for eternity, and he will merit the World to Come." R. *Kotler* then continued that there is no greater war for the sake of Heaven than the struggle to save Jews from assimilation.

Someone related to me that R. *Mordechai Gifter* expressed a similar view to that of R. *Kotler*. But R. *Gifter* also added another thought. He said that the dedication and sacrifice of the parents to spread Torah where it would not otherwise be taught is itself a positive influence over the children; and the impact of their commitment far exceeds what they could imbibe from the circumstance of living among more Torah-minded Jews.

. . . .

Following are two thoughts I have heard from my *rebbe* on this subject:
1) The *Sforno*, at the beginning of *parashas Chukkas* in his discussion of the *parah adumah*, states clearly that people are always affected by those with whom they come in contact. However, there is one exception to that rule: People who teach Torah are protected from moral and spiritual contamination. There is a special Divine assurance that their interactions with those they teach will not be harmful.

The question was raised, While the rabbi himself may be impervious to this contact, what of his children? Wouldn't their spirituality suffer? My rebbe answered that there can be no greater damage to an individual than having his children drawn away from the service of *Hashem*. If so, when the *Sforno* writes that there will be no harm to the teacher of Torah, the guarantee applies to his children as well.

The *Sforno* does not mean that the child of a teacher of Torah will automatically grow up to be the individual that his parents yearn for. Children often do not live up to the expectations of their parents, even when raised in a totally "protected" environment. The *Sforno* only states that harm will not befall them as a consequence of spreading Torah.

2) My *rebbe* also related that he was brought to America in the 1920s, prior to his *bar mitzvah*. His father was then a student in the famous *Slobodka Kollel* and was asked to head a New York *yeshivah* that was then being founded. The contrast between New York City and the *yeshivah* world of Eastern Europe was indescribable. The *yeshivah* of *Slobodka* was at its glorious peak, and people had no inkling of the Holocaust that would soon come. In America, meanwhile, several million eastern European Jews had recently arrived, and almost all of them had quickly abandoned their observant ways.

R. *Dovid Leibowitz's* question concerned whether or not he should leave Europe with his wife and son to move to America where he was needed to teach Torah. R. *Leibowitz* wrote the *Chofetz Chaim*. The *Chofetz Chaim* wrote back advising him to leave *Slobodka* for New York.

CHAPTER 12

בראשית, חיי שרה כד:לט

ויאמר אל־אדני אלי לא־תלך האשה אחרי:

רש"י

אלי לא תלך האשה: אלי כתיב, בת היתה לו לאליעזר, והיה
מחזר למצוא עלה, שיאמר לו אברהם לפנות אליו להשיאו בתו, אמר
לו אברהם: - בני ברוך ואתה ארור, ואין ארור מדבק בברוך:

משכיל לדוד על רש"י

והטעם שבחר טפי אברהם בבנות ענר אשכול וממרא אם לא תאבה
וכו' יותר מבת אליעזר אעפ"י שגם הם היו כנענים כמותו והיו גם
הם בכלל ארור כנען עם היות שאליעזר היה ת"ח וצדיק גדול
המושל בתורת רבו דאפשר עוד שאילו לא היה שואל אליעזר על
בתו אולי אם לא היה מוצא ממשפחתו היה פונה אליו להשיאו בתו
טפי מבנות ענר וכו' אבל הואיל והעיז פניו לשאול בפיו כאלו היה
הגון וכאו' לזה אמר לו אין ארור מדבק בברוך וה"ט דלא קא"ל אין
ברוך מדבק בארור אלא איפכא כלומר אין מן הראוי שהארור ישאל
ויבקש לדבק בברוך מבלי הכיר את מקומו:

BEREISHIS, CHAYA SARAH 24:39

And I said to my master [Avraham]: Perhaps the woman will not follow me.

RASHI

Perhaps the woman will not follow: Eliezer had a daughter, and he went about [searching] to find an excuse, so that Avraham would say to him [Eliezer] that he should turn to him [Avraham] to give his daughter [to Yitzchak] as a wife. [But] Avraham said to him: "My son is blessed and you are cursed [i.e., of Canaanite stock], and the cursed are not joined to the blessed."

MASKIL L'DOVID on Rashi

And [what is] the reason that Avraham preferred the daughters of Aner, Eshkol and Mamreh to the daughter of Eliezer even though they were also Canaanites like him and were also in the category of the "cursed of Canaan" — despite the fact that Eliezer was a talmid chacham and a great tzaddik who supervised the Torah [study] of his master...?

It is possible [to answer] that if Eliezer had not asked about his daughter, [and] perhaps had he [Avraham] not found [a suitable match for his son Yitzchak] from his own family, he would have turned to him [Eliezer] for the marriage of his daughter ahead of the daughters of Aner, Eshkol and Mamreh. But since he [Eliezer] was brazen and asked openly [for the match], as if [to say that he thought himself to be] suitable for and worthy of it, he [Avraham] said to him, "One who is cursed does not join with one who is blessed."

And this is the reason why he [Avraham] did not say to him, "One who is blessed does not join with one who is cursed," but rather he said the opposite — meaning that it is not proper for one who is cursed to ask...to join with one who is blessed without recognizing his place.

OVERVIEW OF TEXT

Avraham set out to choose a wife for his son *Yitzchak*, and he charged his servant *Eliezer* with the responsibility of finding the right person. *Avraham's* instructions were to begin the search in the household of *Bisuel*. If someone appropriate from *Bisuel's* family could not be identified, a second choice would be a woman from the households of *Aner*, *Eshkol* or *Mamreh*. They were three upstanding individuals, referred to in the Torah (*Bereishis* 14:13) as people who were associated by treaty with *Avraham*.

Rashi, quoting the Talmud, relates that *Eliezer* sought to have his own daughter become *Yitzchak's* wife. *Avraham* responded to *Eliezer's* suggestion by saying that one who is accursed (*Eliezer*) could not join in marriage with one who is blessed (*Avraham*). Although in his own right a great *tzaddik*, *Eliezer* was a descendant of *Canaan* whose family was cursed by *Noach*.

The *Maskil L'Dovid* raises a question: The curse upon *Canaan* was indeed a justifiable reason for choosing *Bisuel's* family ahead of that of *EliezeR*. But *Aner*, *Eshkol* and *Mamreh* were themselves *Canaanites*. If so, why wasn't *Eliezer*, who was an outstanding *talmid chacham* and *tzaddik*, preferred ahead of *Aner*, *Eshkol* and *Mamreh*? Whereas they may have been people of relative distinction, they were in no way *Eliezer's* equals in matters of stature and piety.

The *Maskil L'Dovid* answers that while *Eliezer* had great overall merit, his request demonstrated a critical personal deficiency. He did not recognize the limitations of his own stature and his true place in the world. This led to the inappropriate suggestion that it was his own daughter that deserved to be chosen as *Yitzchak's* wife. Were it not for this request, *Eliezer* might have been chosen second after *Bisuel*. However, due to this failing, *Aner*, *Eshkol* or *Mamreh* were deemed more desirable than *Eliezer*.

KNOWING ONE'S PLACE

Rashi writes (*Bereishis* 24:42) that even *Eliezer's* everyday conversation was dearer to *Hashem* than the words of Torah that *Moshe* would speak in later years. While that *Rashi* may be somewhat difficult to understand, it certainly says a great deal about the towering stature of *Eliezer*.

But *Eliezer* had a devastating personal shortcoming. He had an inflated view of his status which in turn led to the mistaken suggestion that his daughter was the appropriate match for *Yitzchak*. That failing alone made *Aner*, *Eshkol* and *Mamreh* the second choice, despite the factor of *Eliezer's* far greater piety. One might think that *Eliezer's* G-dly stature and knowledge of Torah should outweigh this one particular flaw.

Evidently, there are grave implications to overestimating one's own status and doing so to the point where important decisions are influenced. This deficiency alone can undermine and negate much of an entire lifetime of exalted holiness.

An intermittent unrealistic fantasy about one's own stature is not necessarily catastrophic. To one extent or other, people may occasionally imagine themselves to be what they are not. However, *Eliezer's* mistake led him to act inappropriately in a matter of great significance. It is a self-delusion which influences major decisions that is so devastating.

This understanding is apparent in the words of the *Maskil L'Dovid*: "It is not proper for one who is cursed to ask...to join with one who is blessed without recognizing his place."[1]

---

1.   The Torah contains numerous references to the idea that man

Eliezer not only failed to recognize his place, but he actually acted upon his self-delusion.[2]

---

should strive to attain the very heights of spirituality. Presumably, a component of that pursuit would be the desire to secure the best *shidduch* possible, both for oneself and for his child. Why then was *Eliezer's* request on behalf of his daughter viewed so negatively?

In fact, this is not a question at all. The Torah calls upon every Jew, even one on the lowliest of levels, to climb the spiritual ladder and to eventually attain an exalted state of G-dliness. *Eliezer* would not have been criticized for striving to ascend to greater heights in all matters, including the proposed *shidduch*. *Eliezer's* error was that he acted as if he already occupied a certain lofty position that in truth he did not. Put more simply: one who is on level one should recognize his level and aspire to level ten. But *Eliezer* acted as if he already was at level ten when in fact he was not.

2.   It is somewhat difficult to understand why this shortcoming is so damaging. The *Maskil L'Dovid* says only that such is the case, but he does not appear to be saying why it is so. As such, any explanation cannot be proven from the words of the *Maskil L'Dovid*.

Perhaps it can be compared to one's approach to spending money. "A man does not leave the world with half of his desires in his hand. If he has in his hands one hundred, he desires two hundred; if his hands acquire two hundred, he desires to make it four hundred" (*Midrash Rabbah, Koheles* 1:13). Human desire is boundless. It is normally financial constraints that prevent unlimited spending to satisfy one's limitless desires. Accordingly, it is all but guaranteed that one who refuses to live within his means will eventually dig his own financial grave. He will likely continue to respond to his desires and to spend ever more until his resources are expended and he is hopelessly in debt.

Similarly, an overinflated self-assessment that influences one's decisions is a sure recipe for ruination. Freed from the constraints

POSSIBLE APPLICATIONS

A large contributor to a *shul* or *yeshivah* is normally treated with considerable deference. He also may exert inordinate influence over that entity (see chapter 16, section A). In some cases, the benefactor's power and honor goes to his head. He may soon wrongly fancy himself an expert on how the rabbis should run the institution and subsequently expect his recommendations to be heeded. This encroachment upon the domain of the rabbis can engender enormous misfortune and damage, both to the institution, and perhaps even more so, to the one offering the advice.

. . . .

This type of self-delusion can also be personally devastating in many different ways. People who overestimate their status may strive to attain the honor that they assume to be theirs and make fools of themselves in the process. At the very least, they may live with constant bitterness over their lack of recognition. Similarly, this same feeling has no doubt prevented or delayed many marriages. The mistaken exaggeration of one's own stature (or that of an offspring) can cause one to unrealistically insist on a type of match that may not be available.

---

of reality, one's personal expectations and/or demands will tend to continually mount and be increasingly unrealistic. What is anticipated will never materialize, and the consequences may be disastrous.

CHAPTER 13

בראשית, חיי שרה כד:סא

ותקם רבקה ונערתיה ותרכבנה על־הגמלים ותלכנה אחרי האיש
ויקח העבד את־רבקה וילך:

רלב״ג

התועלת השתים עשרה הוא במדות: והוא שראוי לאדם בלכתו
עם אשה שילך ראשון והיא אחריו. ואף על פי שתהיה באופן שיהיה
ראוי לו לתת לה כבוד. וזה שאם היתה האשה הולכת תחלה יהיו
עיני האדם בה ויביאהו זה לחשוק בה ואולי יבא לידי עבירה. ולזה
תמצא שהלכה רבקה ונערותיה אחרי האיש, עד הגיעם למקום אשר
היה שם יצחק.

BEREISHIS, CHAYA SARAH 24:61
*And Rivkah and her servants arose and rode on the camels and
went after the man; and the servant took Rivkah and he went.*

RALBAG
*The twelfth benefit [or lesson that can be derived from this
incident] is in character traits. That is, that it is fitting for a
man, when he goes with a woman, that he should go first and she
after him — even though it may be in a case where it is proper for*

him to give her honor. This is because, if the woman walked first, the eyes of the man would be upon her, and this will bring him to lust after her and perhaps come to sin. For this reason, you will find that Rivkah and her servants went after the man [Eliezer] until they came to the place where Yitzchak was.

OVERVIEW OF TEXT

Eliezer was dispatched by *Avraham* to seek out a suitable wife for *Yitzchak*. He found *Rivkah*, and the match was arranged. While returning together to *Avraham*, *Eliezer* traveled at the head of the procession. The women, including *Rivkah*, followed behind him.

Proper form would have been for *Rivkah* to precede *Eliezer*, for he was the servant of her father-in-law-to-be. Nevertheless, the order was reversed. The *Ralbag* explains that this was done because a man should not walk behind a woman, for it may cause him to lust after her and possibly sin.[1] Therefore, *Eliezer* went before *Rivkah* for the duration of the journey, despite the violation of the master-servant protocol.

---

1.   The *halachah* does not prevent women from walking or journeying behind men. Such was permissible to *Rivkah*, despite being improper for *Eliezer*. This indicates that men are at a greater risk than women of being led to sin by sight stimuli.

MALE/FEMALE PROPRIETY

The *halachah* spells out restrictions regarding the social contact between men and women. These parameters help prevent the development of improper relationships and subsequent sin. The *Shulchan Aruch* (*Even Ezra*, 21) says: "One should distance himself from women very much ...for the soul of man lusts after them [women]...[2] The *Shulchan Aruch* there additionally states "Man should not follow behind a woman in the street." On this the *Be'er Hetev* comments "Even if she is fully clothed."

There are individuals who somehow feel comfortable with a wholesale disregard of *Even Ezra* 21. They claim that the laws are not essential for them because:

- they are overly restrictive and unnecessary, especially for this day and age, or

- while these laws may be needed by others, they are completely unaffected by this contact, or

- the intention of the Torah is that man should control himself — and this is something that they can always do.

Eliezer was a *tzaddik* of the very highest caliber (see *Rashi*, *Bereishis* 24:42 on the stature and piety of *Eliezer*). Can one

2.   It should be noted that *Even Ezra* does not seek to eliminate all contact between men and women. Many in our generation observed the conduct of the great rabbis of the recent past such as R. *Moshe Feinstein*. As needed, he interacted with women and courteously and attentively responded to their questions. In a general sense, it is social contact between men and women for its own sake that *Even Ezra* 21 proscribes.

even imagine such a great *tzaddik* succumbing to sin just because of his travel position during one journey? *Rivkah* was traveling to join *Yitzchak* in marriage, and *Eliezer* was charged with bringing her there by his revered master and *rebbe*, *Avraham*. Nonetheless, the *Ralbag* indicates that *Eliezer* might have actually sinned had he ignored the *halachah's* guidelines of decorum.[3]

Evidently, there are certain universal human traits and weaknesses. One universal circumstance of humanity is that man is always potentially vulnerable to sins of passion, no matter how G-d fearing and holy he may be. The Torah therefore contains certain strictures that are binding upon all Jews which, if observed, help prevent this type of sin.

When these laws are ignored, the human mechanism of self-control, however strong, may fail — even in a *tzaddik* of biblical stature. Choosing to ignore *Even Ezra* 21 for even a short period of time (such as during the course of *Rivkah's* journey), would have placed *Eliezer* in peril of iniquity. Certainly, those who are less than *tzaddikim* of historic dimensions must scrupulously observe these Torah principles. The failure to do so could evolve into catastrophic sin.[4]

---

3.   The *halachah* was known to the great people of that age even though it was many years before Sinai. In fact, *Eliezer* is described as the one who taught the Torah of *Avraham* to others (Talmud *Yoma* 25b).

4.   *Even Ezra* 21 spells out many of the strictures that should govern interactions between men and women. From the *Ralbag* one can infer that tragedy can ensue when these laws are ignored, even amongst the most righteous.

Following is another aspect of this issue:The Talmud (*Bava Basra* 57b) heaps great praise upon one who avoids looking at women who are improperly clothed. The reference is to a man who passes an area where women are doing wash and, as a

POSSIBLE APPLICATIONS

In theory, the modern secular world partially subscribes to many of the Torah's ethical precepts and moral standards. For example: the Western world pays at least lip service to such virtues as honesty, charity, and devotion to family and community.[5]

However, regarding this idea of the *Ralbag*, modern thinking diametrically opposes Torah thought. According to

---

result, are immodestly clothed.

Very interestingly, the Talmud concludes that the man's restraint is praiseworthy only if there was no other route to his destination. But if another path was available that did not overlook the sight of women doing their wash, the man is considered a *rasha* for placing himself in jeopardy. This, despite his subsequent exercise of the same heroic and pious self-restraint for which the one with no choice of paths was so lavishly praised. (The term *rasha* is a severe condemnation. It is rarely used in the Talmud or *Midrash* when referring to otherwise observant Jews.)

Evidently, it is a profound depravity, in and of itself, to expose oneself, even once, to a situation where temptation, even simply to look, will have to then be resisted. Although that very temptation was later heroically avoided, the Torah nevertheless considers that man to be a *rasha* for exposing himself to the danger.

An interesting possible modern application of the idea described in *Bava Basra* is the Internet, with its vast potential for exposure to lust and temptations that will later have to be withstood. If unnecessarily passing an area where laundering is occurring deems one a *rasha*, although the temptation was withstood, could not the same be true of recreationally surfing the net?

the *Ralbag*, even a temporary lack of absolutely proper decorum could have caused a consummately righteous individual
to sin. Late twentieth-century secular Western society seems
utterly oblivious to the presence of this type of cause and effect.

In present secular society,

- almost all schools and college dorms (and even the U.S. mil-
  itary) are now fully integrated;

- the media, movies and the Internet now provide a deluge of
  lewdness available to all;

- the general notion of *tznius* in dress is an almost entirely
  alien concept.

And it is also true that society is plagued by an epidemic
of adultery and divorce, resulting in a devastating breakdown
of the traditional family structure.

From the perspective of the Torah it is easy to see the correlation between these developments. If traveling behind
Rivkah for one journey could have possibly caused a moral
breakdown in a *tzaddik* of *Eliezer*'s caliber, certainly then, years
of ongoing impropriety will certainly beget this result among
the general society.

Until society returns to a standard of propriety more akin
to that of the Torah, it will continue to suffer disastrous consequences.

---

5.   Throughout its history, the United States has been a nation that
      has paid much more than lip service to the virtue of *chessed* — it
      has exhibited a national characteristic of kindness. The *Chofetz
      Chaim* reputedly said that, in the merit of her kindness, America
      will be spared the devastation of the wars of *Gog* and *Magog*.

CHAPTER 14

בראשית, חיי שרה כה:ח

ויגוע וימת אברהם בשיבה טובה זקן ושבע ויאסף אל־עמיו:

רמב"ן

זקן ושבע: שראה כל משאלות לבו ושבע כל טובה, וכן ושבע ימים
(להלן לה כט), ששבעה נפשו בימים, ולא יתאוה שיחדשו בו הימים
דבר, וכענין שנאמר בדוד וימת בשיבה טובה שבע ימים ועושר
וכבוד (דהי"א כט כח). והוא ספור חסדי השם בצדיקים, ומדה
טובה בהם שלא יתאוו במותרות, כענין שנאמר בהם תאות לבו נתת
לו (תהלים כא ג), ולא כמו שנאמר בשאר האנשים אוהב כסף לא
ישבע כסף (קהלת ה ט), ואמרו בו (קהלת רבה א יג) אין אדם יוצא
מן העולם וחצי תאוותיו בידו, יש בידו מנה מתאוה מאתים, השיגה
ידו למאתים מתאוה לעשות ארבע מאות, שנאמר אוהב כסף לא
ישבע כסף:

BEREISHIS, CHAYA SARAH 25:8

*And Avraham expired and died at a good old age, old and satisfied;
and he was gathered to his people.*

RAMBAN

Old and Satisfied: *That he saw [attained] the desires of his heart* *and was satisfied of all good. Similarly [it says of Yitzchak] "And sated in days" (Bereishis 35:29). He did not desire that the days should bring something new. As it is written of [King] David: "And he died in good old age, satisfied of days and wealth and honor" (I Divrei Hayamim 29:28). And this is a recounting of the kindness of Hashem to the tzaddikim.*

And it is a good trait of theirs that they do not desire extra things, as it is written of them "The desires of his heart you gave him" (Tehillim 21:3), not as it is written about other people, "He who loves money will not be satisfied with money" (Koheles 5:9). And they [the rabbis in Midrash Rabbah, Koheles 1:13] said of him, "A man does not leave the world with half of his desires in his hand. If he has in his hands one hundred, he desires two hundred. If his hands acquire two hundred, he desires to make it four hundred." As it is written, "He who loves money will not be satisfied with money."

OVERVIEW OF TEXT

Avraham was described at the time of his death as being "old and satisfied." The *Ramban* explains that this was indicative of a most unique status. *Avraham* was able to enjoy his great wealth while remaining unaffected by the craving for more than what he possessed. Normally, human greed prevents one from enjoying whatever he may have. For however great one's fortune may be, he desires that much more. *Avraham* was unique. He had great affluence; he utilized it; he enjoyed it. But he did not desire anything beyond that which he already possessed.

CONTENTMENT WITH POSSESSIONS [1]

Avraham was the great father of the Jewish people. By age three, he fathomed the oneness of *Hashem.* His monotheism and his exalted moral status placed him in sharp contrast to the rest of the world. As such, he was described as an *Ivri,* signifying that he stood at "one side" while the rest of the entire world was at the "other side" (*Midrash Rabbah, Bereishis* 42:8). He withstood ten great tests, including being told to sacrifice his beloved son, *Yitzchak.*

Nevertheless, *Avraham's* sublime lifetime of virtue and holiness did not guarantee that he would be content with this

---

1.   Most of what is contained in this chapter has been already elucidated by my *rebbe.* It appears in both *Chiddushei Halev* and *Majesty of Man,* written by his students in Hebrew and English, respectively. These are books that convey ideas from some of his *mussar shmuessen.* Nevertheless, it is being included in this book as my own idea. Two explanations are possible (other than outright plagiarism):

• I may have once heard the idea from my *rebbe,* forgot it mostly, and later arrived at roughly the same concept after studying the *Ramban,* thinking it to be my original insight. If so, this is an admission.

• I may have independently discerned the same concept in the *Ramban* without ever having heard such from my *rebbe.* (That, if true, is certainly a great personal honor.) In the introduction to his work, *Even Haezel,* R. *Isser Zalman Meltzer* wrote that in such situations, one can declare the idea his own. If so, I claim the same privilege.

immense fortune. It could have very well been that notwithstanding his exalted stature, *Avraham* would have been dissat-
isfied with his great wealth and would have desired to double
his possessions. All of *Avraham*'s piety did not guarantee that
he would be capable of rising above this human tendency.

The *Ramban*'s point is that there was an additional and
heretofore unknown aspect of *Avraham*'s greatness. *Avraham*
was able to enjoy his belongings without being caught up in
the never-ending cycle of disquiet characterized by a yearning
to double what he already possessed. He attained complete
satisfaction with his possessions. That he conquered this tendency was an additional testament to his piety.

Such is the difficulty of being satisfied with what one already possesses. Even if one were to attain the holiness and
the immense wealth of *Avraham*, there is no guarantee that his
serenity wouldn't be constantly jarred by "If he has in his
hands one hundred, he desires two hundred."

POSSIBLE APPLICATIONS

A common self-delusion is that personal dissatisfaction
can be traced to a dearth of riches — happiness will accompany the acquisition of greater wealth. This mistaken notion
consumes and drives many people of all socioeconomic levels
for much of their lives.[2]

One must realize that the notion that greater wealth will
beget greater contentment is nothing but fantasy. However
great a person's fortune may be, he will likely remain unsatis-
fied with what he owns. He will be plagued by "If he has in his

---

2.   Some human desires are needs rather than wants. The pur-
      suit of a true need is generally justifiable, and it does not beget
      the insatiable craving for yet more (see chapter 15, section A).

hands one hundred, he desires two hundred." Despite his G-dliness, *Avraham* had to attain yet an additionally exalted level — simply to be satisfied with what he already possessed.[3]

This knowledge — that increased wealth will not bring increased happiness — if fully assimilated, may inspire one to dedicate more time to lofty objectives and less time to the pursuit of affluence. For even if a fortune is acquired, it will not necessarily promote satisfaction and peace of mind. Rather, it will likely initiate a fresh and insatiable longing for ever more wealth.[4]

---

3.   How one can strive to attain contentment with one's possessions is not spelled out by the *Ramban*. An obvious approach is a strengthening of one's *bitachon* — the inner conviction of the mind and the heart that the amount of money a person will acquire in a given year is preordained on *Rosh Hashanah*. There is a direct correlation between the level of one's *bitachon* and the absence of lusting for additional riches.

4.   A prominent Jewish businessman recently observed that he had met several multibillionaires in the course of his work. It was his observation that they all possessed one common characteristic. They shared an all-consuming, almost maniacal drive to earn yet more money. In truth, every self-made billionaire was once a self-made half-billionaire that felt he needed much more money.

CHAPTER 15

בראשית, תולדות כה:כב,כג

כב. ויתרצצו הבנים בקרבה ותאמר אם־כן למה זה אנכי ותלך לדרש
את־יהוה:
כג. ויאמר יהוה לה שני גיים בבטנך ושני לאמים ממעיך יפרדו
ולאם מלאם יאמץ ורב יעבד צעיר:

רש"י

כג. שני גוים בבטנך: גיים כתיב, אלו אנטונינוס ורבי, שלא פסקו
מעל שולחנם לא צנון ולא חזרת, לא בימות החמה ולא בימות
הגשמים (ברכות נו:):

ט"ז על רש"י

ויש מקשים הא אמרינן בגמרא דרבי אמר בשעת פטירתו ולא
נהניתי מעוה"ז אפי' באצבע קטנה. ולק"מ דכיון דרבי היה עשיר
גדול ומזונות שלו כדרך העשירים, היה זה להכרח המאכל שלא היה
יכול לאכול בלא זה ולא קרוי תענוג אלא מה שיכול לאכול בלא זה,
והוא מתאוה למותרות:

גור אריה על רש"י

ומרמז על כלל ישראל שיש להם ענין מיוחד שהם גאים ורוצה לומר
כי נפש חשוב יש להם, ונוהגים במאכל שלהם בחשיבות, וזהו
שאמרו כי 'לא פסקו מעל שלחנם לא צנון ולא חזרת'. ורוצה בזה
כי יש אוכל אכילתו כבהמה ואינו מחשיב עצמו, אבל ישראל ועשו
אין נוהגין כך, רק מתקנין תקון הראוי לאדם להחשיב עצמו...
והשתא נראה מה שאמר רבי בשעת פטירתו שלא נהנה מן העולם
הזה אפילו באצבע קטנה, זה אין דומה לזה, דצנון וחזרת אין זה
הנאה כלל, אלא שהיה בוחר בזה להחשיב את עצמו, והוא דרך
החשובים כאשר ראוי לפי חשיבות הנפש שלהם, אבל שיהיה נוטה
אחר הנאתו ותאותו - לא נטה.

שפתי חכמים על רש"י

וי"ל דבני ביתו היו אוכלין ולא פסקו משולחנו וזה היא גאות אבל
רבי בעצמו לא היה אוכל.

BEREISHIS, TOLDOS 25:22,23

22. And the children struggled within her, and she said, If so, why is it that I am? And she went to inquire of Hashem.

23. And Hashem said to her: Two nations are in your womb and two peoples will be separated from your insides, and one people will be stronger than the other people, and the elder will serve the younger.

RASHI

*23. **Two nations are in your womb:** The word which we pronounce נוים is written ניים [here] as if to connote proud ones. Those [referred to] were Antoninus and Rebbe, from whose tables there never ceased neither radishes nor lettuce, both in summer or in the rainy season [winter]. They were so exceedingly wealthy that they could afford out-of-season produce throughout the year.*

TAZ on *Rashi*

There are those that ask: The Talmud (Kesubos 104a) writes that Rebbe, at the time of his passing, said "I have not had benefit from this world even like a small finger [to the extent of livelihood that one could earn with the labor of one small finger]." [If so, how could he indulge himself in out-of-season produce throughout the year?]

And it is not a question at all. Since Rebbe was a very wealthy man and the manner of his eating was like that of the wealthy, this [extravagance] was a necessity for his eating; he was not able to eat without this [extravagance]. And [unnecessary] pleasure [in matters of eating] is only in cases where one could eat without [the additional pleasures], and he nevertheless desires the extras.

GUR ARYEH on *Rashi*

And it [the word "nations"] alludes to Klal Yisrael and Edom, who are special, in that they are haughty. And it is as if to say that they have very exalted souls and they conduct themselves importantly with their eating. And that is what they [the Rabbis] said [regarding Antoninus and Rebbe] "from their tables there never ceased neither radish nor lettuce,..." And it means [to say] with this that there is [such a person who] eats his food like an animal and does not consider himself important. But Yisrael and Eisav do not conduct themselves this way, but make appropriate preparations to enhance their importance....

And now it would appear that what Rebbe said at the time of his death, that he did not have benefit from this world even like a small finger, can be understood. For the radish and lettuce are not indulgences at all, but show his [level of lifestyle in order] to render himself distinguished. And this is the way of those who are exalted, as is appropriate according to the exalted nature of their soul. But [the intention is not to say] that he was drawn after his pleasure and his lust — [for certainly] he was not [thus] drawn.

SIFSEI CHACHAMIM on Rashi

[He begins with the question of the Taz and Gur Aryeh. He answers that nevertheless,] the members of his household ate [radishes and lettuce] and there never ceased from his table [radishes and lettuce]. And this was his status as a "proud one." But Rebbe himself never ate them.

OVERVIEW OF TEXT

Rivkah was seeking out the reason for her unusually difficult pregnancy. She was informed, prophetically, that she was carrying *Yaakov* and *Eisav*, from whom would issue two great nations; their struggle for control of the world had already begun in utero.

The prophecy also identified two of *Rivkah's* prominent descendants who would live at the same time: R. *Yehudah Hanasi*, and *Antoninus*. R. *Yehudah Hanasi*, usually referred to as *Rebbe*, a descendant of *Yaakov*, was the compiler of the *Mishnah; Antoninus*, a descendant of *Eisav*, was a Roman ruler. Both individuals were extraordinarily wealthy as evidenced by their tables that were always graced by out-of-season produce (a luxury then available to only the most affluent).

The Talmud writes of *Rebbe* that he did not partake of his wealth more than was absolutely necessary. When dying, he raised his fingers, stating that he did not have (any unnecessary) benefit from this world — even to the extent of the profit earned through working with one finger only. Several commentaries therefore ask, How can *Rashi* describe *Rebbe* as one who lived in great opulence? Did not the Talmud write that he partook of only the bare necessities? (This question is also cryptically asked by *Tosafos* in tractate *Avodah Zarah* 11a.)

The *Taz* answers that both statements are true. *Rebbe* never indulged himself with even one extra penny's worth of luxury. However, due to his great affluence, his opulent lifestyle was a necessity without which *Rebbe* could not function. It was only relative to others that *Rebbe* lived immoderately. However, with regard to his own requirements, he partook of only the bare necessities.

. . . .

The *Gur Aryeh* answers the same question differently. *Rebbe* was not in any way drawn after lust or the desire for excesses. However, his elaborate lifestyle was called for by his most lofty soul. Living in this grand fashion was appropriate to the level of his *neshamah*.[1]

. . . .

The *Mizrachi*, quoting *Tosafos* in *Avodah Zarah*, offers yet another answer. *Rebbe* did not personally partake of even the slightest unnecessary pleasure. However, his table was laden with such excessive luxury for the many other people who ate there. That was the evidence of *Rebbe's* status as a "proud one." (According to the *Taz* and *Gur Aryeh*, *Rebbe* himself actually ate in this extravagant manner; according to the *Mizrachi*, *Rebbe* himself ate modestly – it was those who ate at *Rebbe's* table who partook of the sumptuous meals.)

---

1.   The *Gur Aryeh* explains that *Eisav* as well as *Yaakov* possessed a somewhat similar loftiness of the soul. *Eisav's* exalted *neshamah* is still evident among his present-day descendants in the grandeur of their clothing and architecture. This is in contrast to the offspring of *Yishmael* who are endowed with less lofty souls. As such, until this day, the Ishmaelites are relatively unconcerned with the dignity of their eating and living conditions. (The *Vilna Gaon* and R. *Yaakov Emden* taught that the modern-day German people are the descendants of *Eisav* [see ArtScroll Press, *Guardian of Jerusalem*, pages 202, 203; also see notes of R. *Yaakov Emden* on Talmud *Megillah* 6b].)

A) NEEDS

Many are aware of the Talmudic dictum "He who has one hundred desires two hundred" (*Midrash Rabbah, Koheles* 1:13). Man can never achieve satisfaction from material possessions; whatever one obtains fosters the desire for twice that amount. As such, yielding to one's desires in search of contentment is pointless, for self-indulgence will only create the desire for yet greater indulgences (see chapter 14). Yet the *Taz's* explanation apparently sanctions maintaining a most opulent lifestyle such as *Rebbe's*; *Rebbe's* "indulgences" were not criticized. How can this be understood?

In truth, it is the lust for ever more possessions which cannot be satisfied. However, each person has a threshold of personal need. *Rebbe* required this grade of lifestyle; due to his circumstances, he could not eat from a less lavish table. Thus, although *Rebbe's* expenditures were exorbitant relative to others, it was personal necessity and not, *chalilah*, self-indulgence that inspired his consumption.[2] As such, it would have been wrong for *Rebbe* not to satisfy his needs.[3]

---

2.   The concept of human "need" that is nonetheless lavish is also found in the laws of *tzedakah* (*Yoreh Deah* 250:1). The *halachah* there stipulates that a wealthy man who was reduced to penury should ideally be supported in the luxurious manner to which he was previously accustomed. Such is his need.

3.   It can, at times, be difficult to differentiate between one's true needs and his longing for excesses. A telling sign of an unwholesome want is when satisfying that desire is soon followed by a strong urge to acquire yet more of the same. The

Presumably, if possible, one should satisfy his needs as *Rebbe* himself did.

The words of the *Taz* also illustrate the enormous variance of human material needs. *Rebbe's* lifestyle was indeed out of reach to all but the world's most affluent. However, that was what he personally required, due to his station and wealth. If his table were more modest, he would have been uncomfortable eating altogether. *Rebbe* partook of only what was necessary for *him* and not one iota more.[4]

A given indulgence cannot be unilaterally deemed as ei-

---

appearance of the secondary lust would seem to indicate that the original indulgence was "greed rather than need." Satisfying a true need does not beget a secondary hunger for yet more.

The following might be a scenario of justifiable need: A middle-aged adult who lived in a well-maintained private home was traveling and had to sleep for several days in an inexpensive motel together with others from the lower rungs of society. The environment and squalid living conditions caused him real suffering and a need for better lodgings. Satisfying that need will bring about peace of mind, without the never-ending desire for ever more luxurious accommodations.

4.   R. *Yoel Adelman* pointed out that this is a striking example of the *Mesillas Yesharim's* words "True and desirable *chassidus* is far from being conceptualized by us [True piety is very different from what people would imagine it to be]"(introduction to *Mesillas Yesharim*).

As he was leaving this world, the one self-praise *Rebbe* chose to mention was his abstinence. According to the *Taz*, that abstinence referred to *Rebbe's* huge expenditures on himself that were nonetheless tightly controlled. That was indicative of the great piety *Rebbe* had attained during his lifetime. *Rebbe* did not even mention the fact that he had compiled the *Mishnah*, the basis of the Oral Torah until this very day.

ther a necessity or a luxury; what constitutes need is a highly subjective consideration. What is an outrageous extravagance to most of the world may in fact be a justifiable imperative to some. [5] Rebbe's example demonstrates that one can be living

---

5.   The *Taz* discusses the differences in need that are a consequence of one's socioeconomic level. Another determining variable is one's spiritual level. Heightened spirituality can diminish one's physical requirements. All other factors being equal, a Torah scholar's improper overindulgence may be another person's absolute requirement.

On this topic, my *rebbe* quoted the *Midrash* (*Yalkut Shimoni, Mishpatim*, 363). That *Midrash* describes R. *Yochanan* who was walking with R. *Chia bar Abba* past a group of properties. At each spot R. *Yochanan* proclaimed, "This was mine, but I sold it in order to study Torah." Finally, R. *Chia bar Abba* began to weep, saying, "What have you left for your old age?" R. *Yochanan* answered that he exchanged something that took six days to give over to man (i.e., the material world) for something that took forty days to transmit (to *Moshe* — i.e., the Torah).

R. *Chia bar Abba* was himself a great Torah scholar. Certainly he recognized R. *Yochanan's* theoretically advantageous "good deal." Why then did he weep?

My *rebbe* explained that R. *Yochanan* was at a higher spiritual level than R. *Chia bar Abba*. The same sacrifice for Torah that was appropriate and uplifting to R. *Yochanan* was a painful and inordinate deprivation to one of somewhat lesser spirituality. Despite understanding intellectually what R. *Yochanan* had accomplished with his tradeoff, R. *Chia bar Abba* nonetheless wept over that same monetary loss which was, to R. *Yochanan*, a source of joy.

People must be wary of challenges and undertakings that are too far removed from their level of spirituality. Had R. *Chia bar Abba* attempted R. *Yochanan's* sacrifice for Torah, his overall devotion to *Hashem* could have been set back by weeping for

in the world's most sumptuous manner while at the same time being the Torah's eternal paradigm of one who subsists on bare necessities alone.

POSSIBLE APPLICATIONS

This concept gives additional impetus to observe the Talmudic dictum (*Avos* 1:10) "Judge all people meritoriously [always give others the benefit of the doubt]." A typical instance of being judgmental is when one points a finger at another and accuses him of extravagance. The *Taz* is teaching that there can be an enormous disparity between the needs of different individuals. And it can often be most difficult for others to comprehend the differences.

Rebbe (like *Antoninus*) expended as much on his own material consumption as perhaps anyone else alive at that time. To those who observed from afar, *Rebbe* may have appeared to have been, *chalilah*, the archetype of wasteful consumption. Nevertheless, *Rebbe* became the Torah's model for all ages of one who subsisted for an entire lifetime on bare necessities.

. . . .

Wealthy individuals can glean from the *Taz* that their legitimate needs may indeed exceed those of others. However, it is also true that *Rebbe* never lost sight of the absolute definition of what his needs were and what they were not. Despite the outlay of tremendous sums to satisfy his needs, *Rebbe* scrupulously avoided even the slightest unwarranted pleasure. If, in modern denominations, three hundred dollars was needed

---

himself (as he did for R. *Yochanan*) and a spirit of depression. Obviously, as a general rule, one should seek out new challenges and opportunities for growth. However, they must be within realistic reach.

for his every breakfast, he made certain that $301 was not spent. That extra dollar would have been the "small finger" of indulgence that *Rebbe* always shunned.

Large sums of money are oftentimes spent on weddings, bar mitzvahs, and so forth. These expenditures are, upon occasion, appropriate and contributory to the *mitzvah*. However, at other times, the relationship between the *mitzvah* and the money spent is harder to discern — the expense is inappropriate. It is not only unwarranted major expenditures that should be avoided; even the smallest unnecessary expense should be shunned — as per *Rebbe's* example. Notwithstanding his enormous affluence, *Rebbe* did not spend even a "small finger's worth" more than necessary.

B) MAN'S G-DLY IMAGE

The famous work *Tomer Dvorah* begins with the idea that man was created *b'tzelem Elokim*...in G-d's image. The author writes that primarily, the pragmatic outgrowth of *tzelem Elokim* is in the realm of human behavior. Mankind has an innate predisposition to always act in a G-dlike manner that is merciful and sanctified.[6]

---

6. My *rebbe* once spoke of the centrality of the concept of *tzelem Elokim* and cited a proof from the *Yerushalmi* (*Nedarim* 30b) where the following quote appears: "Love thy neighbor as thyself.' R. *Akiva* said, This is a great [central] rule of the Torah. *Ben Azai* said, 'This is the book of man's generations' [*Bereishis* 5:1, which articulates that man was created in God's image]; this is an even greater [more central] rule of the Torah." All are aware that "Love thy neighbor as thyself" is crucial to the smooth functioning of society. If people extended the same consideration to others as they do to themselves, almost all societal strife would end. The world would be free of discord and war; instead there would be universal fellowship, brotherhood and love.

How can it be said that the concept of man being created in God's image is yet more central? Seemingly, that concept is abstruse, esoteric and hence, far less relevant to everyday behavior. My *rebbe* explained that the *Yerushalmi* is teaching that the idea of *tzelem Elokim* is within the pragmatic reach of all people; furthermore, understanding this concept will do more to upgrade human behavior than R. *Akiva*'s idea. Once a person begins to see himself in terms of his own G-dliness, his conduct will become uplifted in a very profound manner.

The *Gur Aryeh* reveals some additional aspects to the concept of *tzelem Elokim*. One's attitude to his eating[7] and cloth-

---

The idea was once explained in the following manner: How
would one act if he lived in centuries gone by and was of royal
lineage and the real-life sovereign of a country that wielded absolute power over the lives of his subjects? Not only would he
dress and speak in a regal manner; his every action would be
suffused with modesty, distinction and majesty.

Humans, who are created with *tzelem Elokim* (and especially
Jews, who have yet an additional *neshamah*), are endowed
with infinitely greater majesty than the royal personage of the
previous paragraph. *HaShem* Himself — the King of kings —
the Creator of Heaven and Earth — resides permanently
within us! We are thus called upon to always see ourselves in
this light and to act accordingly at all times.

7.   A similar concept can be found in *Or Hatzafun*. The Talmud
(*Bava Metzia* 83a) describes laborers who were hired with the
provision that they would be fed. When the owner of the field
realized what agreement had been struck, he hurried to rene-
gotiate. He made sure that there would be an agreed upon
maximum as to what these people would be fed.

The Talmud explains that if no specifics were articulated,
even lowly workers would be entitled to the world's most opulent feast. This is because of their *tzelem Elokim*. The *Alter* of
Slobodka explained that on a conscious level the workers certainly did not expect to be fed in such a grand manner. However, their *tzelem Elokim* created a different subconscious expectation. As the descendants of *Avraham*, *Yitzchak* and
Yaakov, their majestic *neshamos* called out for the most exalted
of eating conditions.

The *Gur Aryeh* and the *Alter* are each focusing on somewhat different aspects of *tzelem Elokim*. The *Alter* discussed providing for
others on a level appropriate to their *tzelem Elokim* (despite the fact
that those others never consciously even imagined that such royal
treatment was their due). The *Gur Aryeh*'s idea is that *tzelem Elokim*

ing is also impacted upon by the notion of *tzelem Elokim*. Were man just another part of an evolutionary cycle, then theoreti- cally, his food and clothing could be similar to that of an animal. However, *tzelem Elokim* dictates that his every moment and movement should be suffused with G-dlike majesty.[8]

Rebbe was cognizant of the inner grandeur of his own *tzelem Elokim*. As such, he understood that the manner of his eating should be accordingly exalted and regal. It was not *Rebbe's* personal desires and animalistic lusts that were being indulged; it was his *tzelem Elokim*. As a function of his *tzelem Elokim*, *Rebbe* lived in a most opulent manner. Yet at the same time, he himself was considered the model of one who lived with an attitude of excessive modesty and existed on bare necessities alone.

---

dictates that man should provide for *himself* on that level.

8.   The great *yeshivah* in *Slobodka* was known for its stress on the doctrine of seeing man as a *tzelem Elokim*. People were charged, to whatever extent possible, to comport themselves in a most G-d like fashion — including in their manner of dress. A former student once remarked that in *Slobodka*, one's *frumkeit* was considered lacking if even his necktie was askew.

C) ROLE PLAYING

The *Sifsei Chachamim* explains that *Rebbe* himself ate with extreme restraint. The extravagant meals were for the benefit of those who ate at *Rebbe*'s table.

If *Rebbe* himself ate with such frugality and modesty, why was his table laden with such excessive opulence? It must be that the elaborate circumstances of *Rebbe*'s table were dictated by his position. He was the prince of the Jewish people as well as one of the world's wealthiest individuals. Thus, although he himself did not in any way partake in the extravagance, *Rebbe* (as one of the "proud ones") was obliged to prepare his table with superabundance. (It does not appear that *Rebbe*'s extravagance was done primarily out of kindness to his guests. *Rebbe*'s practice is described by the *Sifsei Chachamim* as a function of his being a proud one.)

This teaches that there are times when a person must play a role expected of him; and often, that role will run diametrically contrary to his basic inclination of character. *Rebbe*'s personal piety led him to partake of only life's bare necessities. Nevertheless, because of the role he had to play, the lavishness of his table was on a par with the world's most excessive levels of consumption.

POSSIBLE APPLICATIONS

Some people are often faced with a dilemma. Though possessed with an innately modest disposition, they find themselves called upon to act as authority figures. They must suddenly function as a parent to children, a boss to employees, a teacher before a class, and the like. Generally speaking, for the job to be conducted properly, a certain amount of role playing is called for.

Some react by following the inclination of their basically humble or reticent nature, and they eschew the expected play-acting needed for the exercise of their authority. The result is almost always unsatisfying. Very sadly, others grow into the role by simply becoming more immodest. One must realize that personal leanings of character should rarely be blindly adhered to. In a given situation, the Torah could theoretically call upon the world's most unassuming individual to act in an excessively regal and/or authoritarian manner while at the same time retaining his own most praiseworthy humility.[9] In the case of *Rebbe*, history's paradigmatic example of one who avoids self-indulgence felt obligated to host the world's most extravagant table.

---

9.   There were recent American presidents who would attempt to demonstrate their basically humble and populist nature by being seen in the most informal of positions, e.g., jogging in shorts on the White House lawn. Even if one grants that they were motivated by sincerity (and not merely by political considerations) they were probably acting improperly.

The presidency of the United States is one of the primary leadership positions in the world. Any man elected to that office should act accordingly. One's having a truly modest personality is not necessarily justification to abrogate the formality and dignity expected from the representative of that august office.

CHAPTER 16

בראשית, תולדות כו:טז

ויאמר אבימלך אל־יצחק לך מעמנו כי־עצמת ממנו מאד:

ספורנו

כי עצמת ממנו: ותוכל בעשרך להתקומם עלינו:

BEREISHIS 26:16

And Avimelech said to Yitzchak: "Go from among us, for you have become much stronger than us."

SFORNO

For you have become much stronger than us: And with your wealth you are able to rise up over us.

OVERVIEW OF TEXT

Yitzchak became enormously wealthy while living in the land of the Philistines. The Torah relates that Avimelech (the Philistine king) then asked Yitzchak to leave the country, for he had become "much stronger than us." What exactly was the nature of this strength that was cause for Yitzchak being asked to leave?

The *Sforno* explains that the riches gave rise to the fear that *Yitzchak* would assume power over the country. According to the *Sforno*, that is why *Yitzchak* was asked to leave.

THE INFLUENCE OF MONEY   197

THE INFLUENCE OF MONEY

According to the *Sforno*, *Yitzchak's* immense fortune made him a threat to the sovereignty of the Philistines and their ruler *Avimelech*. His riches could empower him to rise up and become the sovereign of the country.

Yitzchak was an outsider, a visiting foreigner. As a monotheist, he propounded a belief system radically different from local practice. *Yitzchak* was thus hardly the ideal choice to become leader of the Philistines. He certainly did not pose a physical menace, for he had no army. How then was *Yitzchak* threatening *Avimelech's* supremacy?

The *Sforno* is shedding light on the power that can go hand in hand with extreme wealth. When an immensely affluent individual moves to an area, he brings employment to the region, and his spending thus enriches the populace; he may even soon become the lifeblood of the local economy. He can not only immediately rise to a position of prominence; he can quickly become the single most influential and powerful person in his area.[1] This remains true even in the case of a completely apolitical rich man with a different belief system (as *Yitzchak* was). Realizing this very real threat, *Avimelech* asked *Yitzchak* to depart.

One should be mindful and wary of the enormous influence that exceedingly wealthy individuals will almost automatically exert over society (as well as over a *shul, yeshivah,*

---

1.   In terms of realpolitik, it many very well be that, as a group, the heads of big business wield more political power than the politicians themselves.

and the like).[2]

---

2.   A prominent fund-raiser for one of the large American
      yeshivos was recently asked the following: Does a *yeshivah* for-
      feit its independence by accepting a large amount of money
      from a single wealthy individual? If so, should it be avoided?
          His off-the-cuff answer was that a one-time contribution
      without conditions attached would certainly be fine. Every in-
      stitution hopes for the one huge gift that will alleviate its fi-
      nancial uncertainties.
          However, he continued, an ongoing pattern of large dona-
      tions is different. Such gifts create a reliance on the donor.
      Ideally, such amounts should be accepted only by an organiza-
      tion that could survive a sudden termination of the gifts. Oth-
      erwise, the establishment becomes entirely dependent on the
      ongoing goodwill of the donor. His every wish will likely be
      heeded, for without him, the institution will be forced to close.
      The contributor thus becomes the de facto supreme authority
      within the *yeshivah* — a position for which he is likely unquali-
      fied, his beneficence and philanthropy notwithstanding.
          This need not be a disincentive to contributing large sums to
      institutions of Torah. In fact, a person capable of making large
      contributions to Torah causes is likely obligated to do so.
      Rather, the *Sforno*'s idea underscores the potential for harm
      that can evolve from the relationship of a major donor with an
      institution. Those capable of such gift giving should exercise
      special caution and restraint so that their *tzedakah* does not ul-
      timately harm the very entity that it was intended to support.
          R. *Dovid Leibowitz* believed that ideally, a *yeshivah*'s finances
      should be controlled by its rabbis. He once quipped, "The *baalei
      battim* say that they should be in charge of a *yeshivah*'s finances,
      while the rabbis should reign supreme over the spiritual aspects
      of the *yeshivah* — I say that the *baalei battim* should be in charge
      of the spirituality, leaving the checkbook in the hands of the rab-
      bis." (In other words, he who controls the *yeshivah*'s money also
      controls its *ruchnius*.)

CHAPTER 17

בראשית, תולדות כז:יב

אולי ימשני אבי והייתי בעיניו כמתעתע והבאתי עלי קללה ולא
ברכה:

דברי שאול

אולי ימשני אבי והייתי בעיניו כמתעתע והבאתי עלי קללה
ולא ברכה: לדעתי הכונה כי יעקב היה מדתו אמת ולא לבו הלך
לבדות שקרים ולאמר לאביו שהוא עשו אמנם היה נבוך מאוד כי
כבוד אמו לוחצתו שיקיים מאמר אמו אך מרוב תשוקתו אל האמת
היה אומר הן עשו אחי איש שעיר ואנכי איש חלק אולי ימשני אבי
והייתי בעיניו כמתעתע כאדם האומר הלואי שימושני אבי והייתי
בעיניו כמתעתע וירגיש בזה שרציתי לרמות אותו והבאתי עלי קללה
בזה אני רוצה האף שיהיה לי רעה למען האמת שלא יברך אבי כ"א
עשו אחי שרוצה לברך כ"כ היה דבוק באמת ומה נכבד בזה דרשת
חז"ל במכות כ"ד לא רגל על לשונו זה יעקב שאמר אולי ימשני אבי
ועיין בזה באפיקי יהודה דרוש עין רוגל לפמ"ש הרב מה' עמנואל
בספר לוית חן שההבדל בין אולי לפן שאולי הוא הדבר הנוטע יותר
שחפץ שיהיה כן ופן הוא דבר שאין אדם רוצה וא"כ כאן הרי יעקב
לא חפץ שימושהו ולמה אמר אולי ולפמ"ש א"ש אדרבא מזה
הוציאו חז"ל שכ"כ היה יעקב דבוק באמת ולא רגל על לשונו דבר
שקר עד שחפץ יותר שימושהו אביו ויהי' בעיניו כמתעתע ויביא
עליו קללה ולא ברכה משילך להטעות אביו וזה"ש לא רגל על לשונו
זה יעקב שאמר אולי ימושני אבי.

BEREISHIS, TOLDOS 27:12

Perhaps my father will touch me and I will be in his eyes as one who mocks; and I will bring upon myself a curse and not a blessing.

DIVREI SHAUL

Perhaps my father will touch me and I will be in his eyes as one who mocks; and I will bring upon myself a curse and not a blessing: *I believe the meaning is that Yaakov's trait is truth, and his heart [his being] could not be brought to utter falsehoods and to say to his father that he was Eisav. However, he was very torn, for the honor of his mother pressured him to fulfill the word of his mother. But, because of his great desire for truth, he said, "Behold, my brother Eisav is a man of hair and I am smooth-skinned. Perhaps my father will touch me, and I will be in his eyes as one who mocks."*

[It is like] a man who says, "I wish that my father would touch me, and I would be in his eyes as a mocker, and he will realize that it was my intention to fool him, and I will bring upon myself a curse. [Yet] this is what I desire, even though evil will befall me, because of this truth, that my father will not bless me but Eisav my brother whom he wished to bless." So extremely was he [Yaakov] attached to truth.

How exalted in this matter is the drashah of the Rabbis, of blessed memory, in tractate Makkos 24, "It was not common on his tongue." This is Yaakov, who said, Perhaps (אולי) my father will touch me." And see in Afikei Yehudah, Drush Ein Rogel, according to Rav Emanuel in the Sefer Leveyas Chen, that the difference between the Hebrew words אולי and פן is this: אולי refers to something that one wishes to be so, and פן is something that a person does not desire.

And if so, here Yaakov [seemingly] did not wish that his father should touch him. Why then did he say אולי? According to what I said [about Yaakov's overriding desire for truth], it is good [under-

standable]. From this the Rabbis deduced that Yaakov was so attached to truth, and there was no falsehood upon his tongue, to the point that he would have desired that his father touch him and he should be in [his father's] eyes like a scoffer, and he would bring upon himself a curse and not a blessing [rather than] that he fool his father.

And this is what is meant [in the Talmud in Makkos], "It was not common on his tongue." That was Yaakov who said, "Perhaps my father will touch me."

(In the Vilna Gaon's Kol Eliyahu, parashas Chayei Sarah 24:22, virtually the same interpretation as that of the Divrei Shaul is brought in the name of R. Yitzchak Hamburg.)

OVERVIEW OF TEXT

Having reached old age, Yitzchak expressed his intention to bless Eisav, his firstborn son. Rivkah, however, realized that Yaakov, rather than Eisav, should receive the blessing. Seeking to thwart Yitzchak's plan, Rivkah instructed Yaakov to appear before Yitzchak disguised as Eisav. (It should be noted that Rivkah's stratagem did not require Yaakov to actually utter an outright lie, but to create a false perception [Sifsei Chachamim 27:19].)

The Torah relates that Yaakov expressed the reservation, "Perhaps my father will touch me [and realize that I am not Eisav]... and I will bring upon myself a curse and not a blessing." The conventional understanding of these words is that Yaakov feared that if Yitzchak discovered the duplicity, he might curse rather than bless Yaakov. Rivkah therefore assured Yaakov that he would emerge unharmed. (Rivkah's assurance was based on a prophetic vision communicated to her; see Targum Onkeles 27:13.)

The Divrei Shaul, interpreting the Talmud in Makkos, explains the issue differently. Yaakov's attachment to truth was absolutely compelling, and he was therefore conflicted. On one hand, he was obligated to heed his mother's command; on the other hand, his extreme honesty was preventing him from presenting himself as *Eisav*. He acquiesced to *Rivkah's* dictate, for that was his obligation, but he was actually hoping to be discovered by *Yitzchak*. Rather than successfully perpetuate a deceit, *Yaakov* preferred being apprehended, despite the fact that it could precipitate a curse from *Yitzchak* rather than a blessing.

A) TRUTH

Rivkah had prophetically guaranteed that no harm would befall *Yaakov* while he was attempting to pose as *Eisav* in order to receive the blessings. Nevertheless, *Yaakov's* response was one of extreme reluctance. Though doing *Rivkah's* bidding, he actually hoped that the ruse would be uncovered by *Yitzchak* and the truth established.

What were the parameters of *Rivkah* and *Yaakov's* discussion? Had *Rivkah* been advocating sinful behavior, *Yaakov* would have been forbidden to listen to her. The *halachah* (*Yoreh Deah* 240:15) clearly states that parental commands to violate the Torah must not be heeded. Evidently, *Rivkah's* advice to *Yaakov* to behave in this seemingly deceptive manner was in accordance with *halachah*. That is why *Yaakov* was obligated to comply with the parental command. But if *Rivkah's* plan was within the context of *halachah*, why then did *Yaakov* hope that he would be discovered?

Yaakov's actions demonstrate that even when deception is required by the Torah, one's personal reaction should be one of extreme distress. It should always be deeply discomforting to depart even slightly from absolute truth. Furthermore, one should earnestly wish that the false impression created should not be allowed to stand. It does not appear that *Yaakov's* response was one of *lifnim mishuras hadin* and hence not necessarily relevant to others of lesser stature; no mention is made of such. Rather, *Yaakov's* actions represent ideal conduct for all righteous people.

There is a further insight into *Yaakov's* actions. *Yaakov* realized that were he detected (which was his wish), *Yitzchak* would have likely given the blessings for future generations to *Eisav*, and

Yaakov's descendants might have been cursed instead. This would have resulted in a long-term catastrophe for *Yaakov,* his family and the future generations of the Jewish nation. Nonetheless, *Yaakov* was hoping to be discovered. He preferred truth despite the risk of terrible long-term consequences for getting away with a one-time deception and being blessed as a result.

Such is the extent to which one should refrain from anything less than absolute truth. It was proper to risk so much to avoid participating in a deception that was (1) permissible, (2) dictated by parental command, (3) supported by prophecy, (4) vital for the future of the entire Jewish people and (5) never actually an outright lie. Certainly then, far greater efforts and sacrifices are required to avoid outright and unjustified misrepresentations and falsehoods that have no such noble and sacred justification.

"Torah observance" connotes the extreme avoidance of anything but absolute truth. Any departure from that ethic is an enormous wrongdoing, in and of itself. Small, everyday falsehoods of convenience are generally a violation of Torah.[1] Major deceptions and deliberate fraud are yet a far greater transgression.

There is yet another aspect to this idea that emerges from the text. Creating a false impression is not only improper while it is being committed. Even after a lie was communicated, one should harbor the burning desire for the falsehood to be uncovered and the truth known. Thus, even after consenting to and executing the deceit, *Yaakov* was hoping to be discovered by *Yitzchak,* notwithstanding the possible consequences.

---

1.   R. *Simcha Zisel* of *Kelm* once said that one should constantly train himself to never deviate from absolute truth. An example given concerned the scenario of a person being asked for the time. R. *Simcha Zisel* taught that if, for example, the actual time is 9:12, the answer should be that the time is 9:12. Rounding the time off and responding that it is 9:10 is a departure from truth.

B) THE MEANS TO THE END

When viewed more globally, the words of the *Divrei Shaul* also highlight the proper response to one of life's classical dilemmas. At times, the pursuit of a worthy objective may necessitate trampling upon a seemingly "minor" *halachic* or ethical precept. To cite an example, it is generally improper to publicly flatter an individual who willfully and knowingly defies the Torah. Can this behavior be permitted if it would cause significant monies to be donated to the cause of Torah? What option should be chosen? Is it the overall and larger good or the avoidance of the "small" violation needed to achieve the "greater" goal? Do righteous ends justify unbefitting or unallowable means?

In truth, although each individual case may be different, there are general principles that govern this issue.

The *Divrei Shaul* is teaching that necessity does not justify lying, deception or, presumably, anything else that is otherwise improper. *Yaakov needed* to delude *Yitzchak* so that thirty-four centuries of Jews would be blessed rather than cursed. Can there be a more urgent exigency? Seemingly, a one-time departure from absolute truth was well worth it if it would help the hundreds of millions of Jews that have walked the earth since *Yaakov's* lifetime. Seemingly, *Yaakov* should have thus enthusiastically embraced his mother's (prophetically inspired) dictate without reservation.

Nevertheless, *Yaakov* acquiesced to his mother's wishes only because *halachah* required him to do so. Otherwise, *Yaakov* would have refused to participate in the ruse. Further-

more, *Yaakov* was actually hoping that *Yitzchak* would discern
the truth, despite the possibly dire consequences for the future. Such was the extent of *Yaakov's* eagerness to avoid even
the very slightest impropriety.[2]

    Yaakov's preference, at that moment, for honesty can be
explained. Man as an individual is required to adhere to the
Torah. The big picture (i.e., matters such as the future of the
Jewish people) is largely in *Hashem's* hands. While one should
certainly be concerned with the world's future, those problems do not normally engender specific *halachic* mandates.
Thus, except when clearly sanctioned by *halachah*, an attempt
to help rectify the "big picture" cannot justify the violating of
one's primary responsibility — heeding every nuance of the
Torah. [3]

    Yaakov was, no doubt, most concerned about the future

---

2.   There are individuals who support sacred causes such as a
yeshivah through dishonorable fiscal practices. The rationale
of dire necessity is often invoked. My *rebbe* (who has always de-
cried these practices) has often said that, irrespective of all
other arguments that attempt to either forbid or condone this
behavior, absolute honesty in these matters should be pursued
for yet another reason — avoiding *chillul Hashem*. Dishonest or
illegal practices on behalf of a *yeshiva* are often (if not usually)
eventually discovered, creating an enormous desecration of
Hashem's Name, one of the greatest of sins (*Rambam, Hilchos
Teshuvah* 1:4). *Chillul Hashem* is forbidden, even if it is to avert
an institution's collapse; see chapter 5, note 7.

3.   This concept deals with a different aspect of the idea discussed in chapter 5, section B. There it is pointed out that a desire for holiness, when uncontrolled, can itself become the
driving force behind wrongdoing. This chapter makes the
point that even a small violation of Torah must be avoided. In
a situation of "either or," that avoidance is often of greater significance than grandiose overall goals.

of his people. However, *Yaakov* understood that his primary
duty was his customary level of Torah observance. Therefore,
Yaakov's preference would have been to maintain his prior
level of honesty and to leave the future of the Jewish people in
Hashem's capable hands. **⁴**

POSSIBLE APPLICATIONS

4. The following is a classical illustration of this concept:
    During the last twenty-five years of R. *Yisrael Salanter's* life,
    the *haskalah* was ravaging eastern Europe. Yet, R. *Yisrael* dedi-
    cated most of his efforts during that period to helping the Jews
    of Germany and France. In those areas, the *haskalah* had al-
    ready been almost totally "victorious."
    (He is reputed to have said that the Jewish people could be
    compared to an unmanned train that was rolling . While hur-
    tling down a hill, it is most difficult to seize control of the
    train. However, once it levels off at the bottom, the train's mo-
    tion could possibly be halted. He continued that the east Euro-
    pean Jews were then in the midst of a free fall, while the west
    European Jews had already hit their spiritual bottom and were
    thus more approachable.)
    R. *Yisrael* came upon a plan that he felt would significantly
    impact upon all of west European Jewry. He would build a ma-
    jor *yeshivah* in Paris. However, at the time, there was a Parisian
    rabbi who would have been disaffected by the existence of the
    yeshivah. He would have been completely overshadowed by
    the presence of the world-renowned R. *Yisrael,* and he could
    not truly bring himself to be totally oblivious to that fact.
    R. *Yisrael* abandoned his plan. He declared that the future of
    west European Jewry was ultimately in the hands of *Hashem,*
    Who has many other agents of *kiruv* at hand. R. *Yisrael's* first
    responsibility was to follow every subtlety of right and wrong.
    That responsibility included refusing to aggrieve the local
    rabbi.

This basic idea sharply differentiates Torah from secular idealism, *lehavdil*. The supreme ideal of Torah is observing the 613 *mitzvos* — there is no higher ethic. Accordingly, any cause, whether it be helping the world, building a *yeshivah* or earning a livelihood must be pursued only within the context of what is allowed by Torah.

An impassioned secular idealist, however, will tend to begin making judgments — what is most important, the end or the means? Oftentimes it is the all-important and glorious end that is deemed supreme. Violations in the name of that higher goal soon follow, and when the goal is not realized, the violations increasingly worsen (see "possible applications" to chapter 5) .

CHAPTER 18

בראשית, ויצא כח:י

י   ויצא יעקב מבאר שבע וילך חרנה:

רש"י

ויצא: לא היה צריך לכתוב אלא וילך יעקב חרנה ולמה הזכיר
יציאתו אלא מגיד שיציאת צדיק מן המקום עושה רושם שבזמן
שהצדיק בעיר הוא הודה הוא זיוה הוא הדרה יצא משם פנה הודה
פנה זיוה פנה הדרה וכן (רות א) ותצא מן המקום האמור בנעמי
ורות:

שפתי חכמים על רש"י

הוא זיוה: ר"ל בעוד שהצדיק בעיר האנשים והעם ג"כ צדיקים לפי
שמתביישין מן הצדיק וגם הוא מוכיחן. **פנה זיוה**: ר"ל העם שבעיר
עושין עבירות.

אמרי שפר על רש"י

והר"ר אברהם בר אשר ז"ל כתב שם בפירושו לבראשית רבה
שהכוונה בזה... ובהיותו אצלם הם מתהדרים בו כאדם המתהדר
במלבושים נאים או בחפץ יקר אשר לו והכל מהללים אותם
בשבילו.

רלב"ג

התועלת הראשון הוא במדות: והוא שראוי לאדם לשמוע בקול
הוריו. ולזה העיד הכתוב שיציאת יעקב מבאר שבע היתה ללכת
לחרן כאשר צוו אותו הוריו.

BEREISHIS, VAYATZE 28:10

And Yaakov went out from Beersheva and he went toward Charan.

RASHI

And he went:...It was only necessary [for the pasuk] to [say], "And
Yaakov went to Charan." Why then does [the pasuk] mention his departure? It is only to tell [us] that the departure of a righteous man
from any place makes an impression. For during the time that the
righteous man is in a city, he constitutes its glory; he is its splendor,
he is its crown. [But when] he departs from there, there departs its
glory, there departs its splendor, there departs its crown. Similarly [it
says,] (Ruth 1:7), "And she went out of the place," which is stated regarding Naomi and Ruth [i.e., righteous women who departed from
an area].

SIFSEI CHACHAMIM on Rashi

Splendor: Meaning: while the tzaddik is in the city the people are
also tzaddikim — for they are embarrassed before him, and he also
rebukes them.

There departs: Meaning: people in the city commit sins [after the
tzaddik's departure].

IMREI SHEFER on Rashi

Crown: R. Avraham ben Asher wrote in his commentary to the *Midrash Rabbah on Bereishis* that the intention *[interpretation]* is: *...while he [the tzaddik] is with them, they are honored by him as a man is honored by fine garments or an expensive possession that he has. And all praise them because of him [the tzaddik]...*

RALBAG

The first benefit is in character traits. That is, that it is proper for one to listen to the voice of his parents. Therefore the pasuk testified that Yaakov departed from Beersheva in order to go Charan as his parents commanded him.

OVERVIEW OF TEXT

The sidra of *Vayetzei* opens by recounting *Yaakov's* taking leave from the city of *Beersheva* and his journey to *Charan.* Seemingly, it was the destination that was of significance, but where *Yaakov* departed from was already known. *Rashi* explains that this geographical citation teaches the consequences of a *tzaddik's* move from an area. When a *tzaddik* departs, the glory of that city takes leave with him.

Why does a *tzaddik* endow the city of his residence with such distinction?

The *Sifsei Chachamim* explains that the distinction a *tzaddik* brings to a city is the uplifted conduct of the townspeople. That is because the *tzaddik* promotes exemplary behavior on the part of the citizenry, thereby ultimately causing them to become *tzaddikim* themselves. His influence is twofold, both passive and overt. People are embarrassed to sin in the presence of the *tzaddik*. Furthermore, a *tzaddik* actively criticizes misconduct. Therefore, those around him act as *tzaddikim*, and thus they are *tzaddikim*. When the *tzaddik* departs, his influence takes leave as well, and the people resume their sinning.

. . . .

The *Imrei Shefer* explains the benefit of the *tzaddik*'s residence differently. The inhabitants of the town enjoy a sense of self-importance when living in close proximity to the *tzaddik*. The comparison drawn is to the self-aggrandizement engendered by one's possessions or fine clothing. Similarly, the townspeople pride themselves in the *tzaddik* residing in their midst. When the *tzaddik* departs, the honor of his presence amongst them takes leave with him.

. . . .

The *Ralbag* offers an entirely different interpretation from *Rashi* as to why *Yaakov*'s departure was described. *Rivkah* was aware that *Eisav* planned to kill *Yaakov*. She therefore commanded *Yaakov* to flee *Beersheva* to save his life. Consequently, when *Yaakov* left *Beersheva*, he had a specific purpose in mind; it was to fulfill the *mitzvah* of parental honor by heeding *Rivkah*'s command to *Beersheva*. The *Ralbag* thus concludes that *Yaakov*'s actions illustrate the supreme importance of heeding parental edicts.

A) ACTING PROPERLY

Understanding human behavior often requires an analysis of underlying motives. In fact, it is often assumed that one's inner character is the true measure of his being. An example of such is found in the *Chovos Halevavos* (*Shaar Yichud Hamaaseh* 6) which says: "You should not refrain from guarding your superficial and inner thoughts and the depths of your heart, for the majority of loss or benefit to one's actions will occur only because of them, corresponding to their repair or loss. [One should guard his thoughts, for one's inner being will strongly color his actions.]"

Yet, the measure of man is not always one and the same as his inner being. The *Sifsei Chachamim* writes that because the townspeople act like *tzaddikim* they are *tzaddikim*. Did the people of the town attain inner piety? Their praiseworthy deeds were seemingly temporary and superficial, for they were entirely dependent upon the ongoing presence of the *tzaddik* — it was indisputable that they would resume their sinning immediately upon the *tzaddik's* departure. How can it be said of them "They are also *tzaddikim*"? The words suggest that they had attained a level of sanctity somewhat akin to that of the *tzaddik* himself (whose piety is certainly not dependent upon the continued presence of another *tzaddik*).

Certainly, underlying human character is an enormously significant barometer of the human personality. However, the *Sifsei Chachamim* is teaching that the true measure of man is also largely calibrated by what one actually does — human actions, in and of themselves, are of great consequence. *Mitzvos* and good deeds performed are building blocks of holiness; a *tzaddik* is one who consistently acts as a *tzaddik* without ever wavering from this course of activity. Thus, if the townspeople act with righteousness, they are considered *tzaddikim* on that basis alone. This remains true despite the fact that

- their behavior is not really self-motivated, but externally provoked (by the *tzaddik*), and

- their exemplary behavior is not self-sustaining; it will take leave together with the *tzaddik*.

This is not to say that a *mitzvah's* purity of heart is not vital. When all other factors are equal, a *mitzvah* performed with deeper sincerity is deemed greater. However, the appellation *tzaddik* is appropriate even to one whose piety is akin to that of the townspeople described by *Rashi*.

This underscores the importance of performing *mitzvos*, even those that may not feel just right. In a very profound manner, they can change and uplift one's entire being.[2]

POSSIBLE APPLICATIONS

In a general sense, the explicit commands of the Torah such as observing *Shabbos* and holidays apply to all Jews equally. However, the appropriate fulfillment of other *mitzvos* may change for different people or even for the same person at different times. For example, the obligation to dedicate a set period daily to Torah study is incumbent upon all Jews. However, exactly how much time one must devote to this *mitzvah* can vary, depending upon personal circumstances.

The decision on how much time should be devoted to Torah study may be determined by what feels natural and spontaneous to the individual involved. In this spirit, one might conclude that if an hour of daily Torah study appears to be comfortable, then this would fulfill that individual's requirement. The determination may be based on the rationale that if one does not feel an instinctual urge for additional study time, it probably would not be constructive.

This text might elicit a different conclusion. Even a *mitzvah* deficient in internal enthusiasm is of enormous consequence; deeds of this ilk can totally transform a person into a *tzaddik*. Thus, the feeling that it's absolutely right is not necessarily a requisite for the activity in question to be pursued.

---

2.   It should be noted that it is not always true that all mitzvos performed are praiseworthy. The Torah decries a *mitzvah* done for ulterior motives only, such as public acclaim. The Talmud (*Berachos* 17a) goes so far as to write: "One who studies Torah without doing so for the sake of Heaven...it would be better that he wasn't created." *Tosafos* (*Pesachim* 50b) explains that this refers to one who studies to further his arrogance or to belittle another person.

The case of *Tosafos* in *Pesachim* is a *mitzvah* motivated by a hidden or dishonorable agenda. The scenario of *Rashi* is different, for the praiseworthy conduct of the people was not prompted by anything improper. Rather, their righteousness was the result of the *tzaddik*'s ongoing influence and prodding, and it was not internally motivated or self-sustaining. The *Sifsei Chachamim* is teaching that even such behavior can make of one a *tzaddik*.

B) TRUE HONOR

It is obvious, even without textual source, that what may appear to be an outpouring of sincere honor may, in fact, be something else entirely; it may be an endeavor to achieve personal gain. For example, when the president of the United States visits an area, he is typically mobbed by crowds of people. On the surface, this would appear to be an outpouring of adoration and respect. In reality, people are likely hoping for the personal thrill of being close to a powerful person (and/or boasting about it afterward). Thus, what is being bestowed on the president is primarily selfish self-aggrandizement rather than honor.

What is being discussed in *VayEtzei* is not the departure of a president from *Beersheva* but, *lehavdil*, that of *Yaakov*. *Yaakov* was the ultimate *tzaddik* and *talmid chacham*. It is written, "There is no honor but Torah" (*Pirkei Avos* 6:3) — the only authentic reverence in this world is that which comes to a person because of his involvement with Torah. Seemingly then, the honor accorded *Yaakov* was a very real acknowledgment of his greatness.

Yet, although the people of *Beersheva* grieved over *Yaakov*'s departure, their sadness was not a function of their veneration for either *Yaakov* or for the Torah. Rather, their attitude to having *Yaakov* in their midst was akin to their feelings toward their costly garments and possessions; he was a resource for the enhancement of their self-regard. When *Yaakov* departed, the residents of *Beersheva* experienced the consequent loss of self-gratification.

This is an example of how what appears to be a gesture of

honor may in truth be an expression of something completely different. This phenomenon could even apply to the most richly deserved deference accorded a true *gadol hador*. The ostensibly sincere tribute may in reality be a case of others utilizing the *talmid chacham* for their own purposes.

POSSIBLE APPLICATIONS

The pursuit of honor is one of the three powerful lusts which the *Mishnah* (*Avos* 4:21) teaches can "drive a person from the world." The idea of the *Imrei Shefer* provides a potent antidote to this potentially deadly pitfall.

One should bear in mind that the scenario of a person being honored is very possibly nothing but an apparition. What may in fact be occurring is that others are using the honoree for their own personal gain. This may be true even when the world's greatest *talmid chacham* is receiving his richly deserved acclaim. It is certainly a possibility when people of lesser stature are being honored for reasons other than Torah scholarship.

C) PARENTAL COMMANDS

The *Ralbag* explains that *Yaakov's* departure from *Beersheva* was primarily a fulfillment of a parental dictate — his mother had commanded him to flee in order to protect himself from *Eisav's* murderous designs. As such, Yaakov was also fleeing in order to avoid being killed.

Certainly the drive to save one's life at a moment of imminent threat is a most powerful and universal human impulse. As such, most people faced with a similar situation would flee, first and foremost, to save themselves. Appended to the instinctive drive of self-preservation might be the awareness that such was also a technical fulfillment of the *mitzvah* of parental honor. Exceedingly righteous individuals in this situation might act with a duality of purpose, reflexive self-preservation and, to a lesser extent, the *mitzvah* of parental honor.

Evidently, there was a different hierarchy of motives that drove *Yaakov*. Though fully mindful of the need to save himself, that was not *Yaakov's* primary focus as he left *Beersheva*. First and foremost, *Yaakov* was setting out to fulfill a parental command.

One might argue that the drive for self-preservation is a far more fundamental human instinct than the urge to observe a parental dictate. Evidently, the truth is different. The impulse to fulfill a command of the Torah's can become the most central, uppermost and all-powerful of human motives; *Yaakov's* drive to uphold the honor of his mother was a deeper and more innate part of his personality than even the frenzied effort to save his own life.

Such is the appropriate preeminence and fulfillment of the *mitzvah* of heeding parental dictates.

CHAPTER 19

בראשית, ויצא לא:ד,ה

ד. וישלח יעקב ויקרא לרחל וללאה השדה אל־צאנו.
ה. ויאמר להן ראה אנכי את־פני אביכן כי־איננו אלי כתמל שלשם
ואלהי אבי היה עמדי.

רלב"ג

התועלת הל"ב הוא במדות: והוא שאין ראוי לאדם כשירצה דבר
מה מאנשי ביתו, שיכריחם על זה על צד האונס והנצוח. אבל
ישתדל לפתות אותם ולהכניעם אל מה שירצהו בתכלית מה שאפשר
כדי שיתעוררו לזה מעצמם, כי זה יותר טוב משיעשו זה על צד
האונס וההכרח. ולזה תמצא שאמר יעקב לנשיו דברים נכוחים,
יביאום להשמע אליו להפרד מאביהן. והודיע להן בסוף דבריו כי
השם ית' צוהו ללכת ולשוב אל בית אביו. כדי שיתרצו בזה מזה
הצד גם כן שלא ימרו פי השם ית' כי הן היו מאמינות בו. כמו
שהתבאר במה שקדם.

BEREISHIS, VAYATZE 31:4,5

4. And Yaakov sent, and he called to Rachel and to Leah to the field
to his flock.

5. And he said to them: I see the face of your father, that it is not toward me like yesterday and the day before; and the G-d of my father was with me.

RALBAG

The thirty-second benefit is in character traits. That is, when a man wants something from the members of his household, it is not proper that he coerce them, but he should rather endeavor to ultimately sway them toward what he wants, so they will be inspired [to that same decision] on their own. For this is better than if they would [be brought to] do it through force. Therefore you will find that Yaakov spoke appropriately to bring them [to the point of wanting] to listen to him and to depart from their father. And he informed them when concluding his words that Hashem commanded him to go and to return to his father's house, so that they [his wives] would additionally agree to this [decision to leave] so as not to defy the word of Hashem, for they believed in Him, as we have explained previously.

OVERVIEW OF TEXT

Yaakov fled from his home because of his brother *Eisav* and eventually took up residence in the house of *Lavan*. There he married his wives, and became the father of a large family. After twenty years had passed, *Lavan*'s sons suddenly became overtly hostile to *Yaakov*. *Hashem* then appeared to *Yaakov*, instructing him to return to his homeland.

Yaakov then called his wives together and privately discussed with them why he thought that it was an appropriate time for them all to leave. He subsequently mentioned that *Hashem* had also commanded him to return home.

The *Ralbag* writes that if one seeks to influence his family members to embrace a particular ideology or behavior, it is inadvisable to compel them.[1] Rather, one should endeavor to

---

1.   The *Ralbag* is discussing *Yaakov*'s avoidance of "force" as a method of winning over his wives. Presumably, "force" need not connote only that which is purely physical. People can be forced into something just as surely by other coercive methods, i.e., withholding of privileges and/or affection or

bring them to the point of independently arriving at the same goal, decision or activity. That was why *Yaakov* first dialogued with his wives to effect their independent and enthusiastic support of his decision. Only then, to yet further deepen their commitment to his plan, *Yaakov* added that *Hashem* had commanded them to leave.

---

continually browbeating the other party into succumbing. In *Yaakov's* case, one type of force would have consisted of informing them that his request was the will of *Hashem.*

WIELDING INFLUENCE

The *Ralbag* clearly states that coercion is not the most effective method for influencing others — even where force is available. Rather, it is preferable to bring people to the point where they will arrive at a hoped-for decision on their own. When this process occurs, the conclusion and commitment is more profound. This is evident in the words of the *Ralbag* who describes the household members as acting either out of their own will or acting because they were forced and defeated.

In *Yaakov's* scenario, there were three possible factors that could have motivated his wives to wholeheartedly endorse his decision. They were:

- force (of whatever form),

- influencing them to the point of adopting the preferred view on their own, and

- calling to their attention that *Yaakov's* decision was also *Hashem's* explicit command.

Yaakov first opted for the second approach. He spoke to his wives as to why he thought it best to depart, hoping that they themselves would arrive at the same conclusion. It was only afterward, in order to further strengthen their commitment to his plan, that *Yaakov* also disclosed the third argument — that this was also *Hashem's* order.

Why didn't Yaakov simply relate from the onset that *Hashem* had commanded him to depart?

Seemingly, to a truly great *tzaddik* or *tzaddekes*, there is no higher imperative than obeying the specifically stated will of *Hashem*. How, for example, would the *Chofetz Chaim* have acted if *Hashem* revealed Himself and overtly decreed that he should perform a specific deed? His commitment to the task would know no bounds. Every fiber of his being, conscious and subconscious, would be dedicated to the task.

Yaakov's wives were at a biblical level of G-dliness. As such, if *Yaakov* sought their absolute agreement, wasn't it enough to simply relate that *Hashem* had commanded them to leave? Presumably, this would have been the most potent argument or inducement for people of such exalted spirituality.

It was mentioned in chapter 8, part VI, that a circumstance of humanity is that every individual has a distinct disposition and leaning. Furthermore, however spiritual one may be, his inclination will not always necessarily be one and the same as that of *Hashem*. In one who harbors difficulty in performing a given action, a certain internal hesitancy or tension can arise. This remains true even if the given action was the stated dictate of *Hashem*.

Yaakov recognized that his wives might have experienced an infinitesimal trace of inner resistance to leaving their family and homeland. He therefore initially avoided mention of *Hashem's* command. *Yaakov* knew that while they would certainly never overtly disobey *Hashem*, the factor of *Hashem's* dictate alone would not necessarily elicit their utterly wholehearted compliance. Instead, he began discussing the issue in a manner designed to bring his wives to an independent desire to leave. It was only afterwards that he added that such was also the explicit will of *Hashem*.

A state of consent gained through browbeating or coercion may be tentative. However, an independently formed conclusion is much different; it becomes the change of heart to which one is most deeply committed. *Rachel's* and *Leah's* devotion to their own autonomous determination in a sense exceeded even what their commitment would have been to an explicit directive of *Hashem* that ran contrary to their personal inclinations.[2]

Yaakov addressing his wives was:
• one of the greatest people to have ever walked the earth,
• absolutely certain of his rectitude (it was what *Hashem* had commanded), and he was
• addressing individuals of unparalleled piety.

Nevertheless, *Yaakov* took pains to help his wives arrive at the decision on their own. Certainly then, in situations where all three factors are absent, it is usually best to avoid eliciting decisions through pressure.

POSSIBLE APPLICATIONS

Daily living includes continual conflicts of wills. The concept of the *Ralbag* has obvious application to the conduct

---

2.   The *Ralbag* demonstrates how difficult it can at times be for one's thinking to become aligned with that of the Torah. This seems somewhat contrary to the previous chapter (part C), which demonstrated that *Yaakov's* thinking and his drive for the *mitzvah* of parental honor was even more innate than the instinct to save his own life.

The two concepts are not in conflict. When a person's *neshamah* directs him in an unimpeded fashion, his craving for a great *mitzvah* can exceed even the most natural urge, such as the drive for self-preservation. However, in cases where one's inclination may not run parallel to the dictates of the Torah (as with Yaakov's wives who were being asked to leave their family and homeland), then that hesitancy is best overcome by that person's independent conclusion.

of these struggles. One particular scenario comes to mind.

A very critical period in one's development is that of adolescence and early twenties. People then make their seminal decisions on school, career and marriage — choices that will profoundly impact upon the direction of their lives. Close relatives or rabbis often become heavy-handed "advice givers" who overwhelm these young people with what they assume to be the correct choices. This well-intended desire to be of help might also find expression in a variety of quasi-forceful methods. (A prevalent and often partially truthful rationalization for this intrusion is that the young people are unprepared to decide on these weighty matters.)

The *Ralbag* indicates that hesitancy over a given resolution will likely not be resolved and eradicated by external pressure or by truth. The young person will be truly committed only to the decisions that he arrived at on his own. The most powerful influence one can yield is to somehow bring that other person to correctly decide the issue — independently.

An interesting corollary to this application is that pressuring the young individual toward a given decision might not only fail to accomplish its goal, but it can be a recipe for future failure. That is because real success in marriage or career, even under ideal circumstances, is never automatic. Herculean exertions are often necessary to triumph over life's challenges in these areas. And it will likely be incomparably more daunting for one who had never fully embraced the choice of what those challenges would be.

CHAPTER 20

בראשית, וישלח לב:כה

ויותר יעקב לבדו ויאבק איש עמו עד עלות השחר:

חולין צא:ב

ויותר יעקב לבדו א"ר אלעזר שנשתייר על פכין קטנים מכאן לצדיקים שחביב עליהם ממונם יותר מגופן וכל כך למה לפי שאין פושטין ידיהם בגזל.

אורחות צדיקים פרק י"ח

וילמד מיעקב אבינו, שהיה ציקן שאין דגמתו שנאמר: "ויותר יעקב לבדו" (בראשית לב, כה), ואמרו רבותינו, זכרונם לברכה, ששכח פכים קטנים וחזר עליהם... ראה הציקנות הגדולה, שאדם עשיר כמו יעקב, עליו השלום, היה לו לחזור עבור פכים קטנים.

מתנות כהונה על מדרש רבה שמות א כ"ה

שאין פושטין כו' - ולפיכך צריכים לקמץ שלא יצטרכו לפשוט ידיהם בגזל.

בן יהוידע על חולין

וכל כך למה לפי שאין פשוטין ידיהם בגזל. נ"ל בס"ד הכונה שהם
מחמירין על עצמן שלא לגזול אפילו דבר מועט דלא קפידי אינשי
עליה, כגון ליקח קיסם מן אגודה של עצים וכיוצא בזה כי נחשב
עצלם דבר זה לגזל, ולכן הם מייקרים ממונם בביתם שלא לאבד
אפילו דבר מועט כהא דחזר על פכים קטנים שאין נחשבים לכלום
לפי עושרו כדי ללמד את בניו ובני ביתו שלא יזלזלו בגזל שהוא
דבר מועט דלא קפדי אינשי עליה בראותם שהממון חשוב אצל
בעליו דאפילו שהוא עשיר גדול סיכן עצמו לחזור לבדו להביא פכין
קטנים דאין חשובין כלום לפי עשרו, ולכן גם הם יהיו נזהרים בגזל
אפילו בדבר מועט ליקח קסם מאגודה של עצים ולא יהיו מורין
היתר לומר אין זה חשוב אצל בעליו כלום:

BEREISHIS, VAYISHLACH 32:25

*And Yaakov was left alone; and [there] a man wrestled with him,
until the break of dawn.*

TALMUD CHULLIN 91b

*R. Elazar said: He [Yaakov] remained behind for some small jars
[which had been left at the old camp]. From here [we learn] that to
tzaddikim, their money is more dear to them than their bodies. And
why [is their money dear to them] to such an extent? Because they
do not lay their hands on anything stolen.*

ORCHOS TZADDIKIM 18

*...One should learn from our forefather Yaakov who was incompa-
rably frugal, as it is written (Bereishis 32:25): "And Yaakov was left
alone." And our Rabbis of blessed memory said (Talmud Chullin
91b) that he forgot some small jars, and he returned to fetch
them...See the great frugality! That a wealthy man like Yaakov of
blessed memory [felt he] had to return [to the old camp] for some
small jars.*

MATNAS KEHUNAH on Midrash Rabbah Shemos 1:25

Because they do not lay [see Talmud Chullin quoted above]: And therefore they must be frugal so that they will not need to [one day] lay their hands on anything stolen.

BEN YEHOYADA on Talmud Chullin

With the help of Heaven [I say that] the intent [of the Talmud] appears to be that they [tzaddikim] are extra stringent not to steal even small amounts that people do not care about, for example, removing a wood splinter from a stack of logs and [other forms of taking from others] similar to this. For they consider even this to be stealing.

Therefore, they make dear their own money in their households [being careful] not to lose even a small amount [of that which is theirs], like that which he [Yaakov] returned for relatively insignificant objects in relation to his wealth, to teach his sons and the members of his household not to make light of stealing small amounts, with which people are not generally concerned. [And this lesson will be driven home] when they see that the money is dear to its owner, in that even though he [Yaakov] was very wealthy, he endangered himself to return alone to bring these small objects which were not worth anything relative to his wealth.

Therefore, they [the members of his household] will be [trained to be] careful about stealing, even small amounts, [such as] to take a splinter from a bundle of wood, and they will not rationalize, saying the owner does not consider this to be anything.

OVERVIEW OF TEXT

Yaakov and his family were returning to *Eretz Yisrael* after a long absence. He was informed that his brother *Eisav* was approaching with four hundred armed men. It was evident that *Eisav* might attempt to murder them all. *Yaakov* countered with a three-pronged strategy of 1) presents (bribery) for *Eisav*,

2) prayer, and if all else failed, 3) war. *Yaakov* also divided the camp into two sections so that if one group was massacred, the other might escape.

On the eve of his encounter with *Eisav*, *Yaakov* relocated his entire party. He then returned to the old camp to retrieve several small items.[1] The Talmud explains that *Yaakov's* return was in keeping with the practice of *tzaddikim* who guard their money most dearly. According to the *Orchos Tzaddikim*, *Yaakov's* behavior was rooted in the principle that all people, including the wealthy, should take care to avoid the loss of even small amounts.

Why are *tzaddikim* so careful about avoiding small losses? The Talmud clarifies that it is because *tzaddikim* do not partake of that which is stolen. The Talmud's logic appears difficult to comprehend. What is the connection between the two? Seemingly, avoiding theft and frugality are two unrelated characteristics.

The *Matnas Kehunah* explains this to mean that *tzaddikim*, even when wealthy, fear that they may one day be reduced to penury and will therefore have the pressing temptation to engage in theft. Therefore, they are frugal to the extreme; today's unneeded penny saved could be what allows the *tzaddik* to resist the need to steal tomorrow.

---

1.   The *Gur Aryeh* on *Bereishis* adds that the items *Yaakov* returned for were very small and insignificant and that there were very few of them.

The commentary of the *Maharal* on *Chullin* 91a, the *Midrash Pesikta Zuta* (quoted in *Yalkut Yehudah*) and the *Midrash Lekach Tov* all learn the story slightly differently. They explain that there wasn't anything specific that *Yaakov* knew was missing. Rather, *Yaakov's* only concern was that perhaps something small and insignificant was possibly left behind at the old camp.

The *Ben Yehoyada* (differing with the *Orchos Tzaddikim* and the *Matnas Kehunah*) explains that *Yaakov*'s concern over the small items was not a function of his frugality per se. Rather, *Yaakov*, who was quite wealthy, was taking advantage of an opportunity to teach the members of his household a critical lesson. By taking the trouble to retrieve these items, *Yaakov* drove home the idea that even a wealthy individual such as himself might be resolute about holding on to every penny. Therefore the lesson taught was that stealing anything from anyone should always be avoided — even taking the very smallest of amounts from the very wealthiest of individuals.

A) AVOIDING WASTE

Yaakov had just divided his camp so that if one group was slaughtered, the other might be saved. He was clearly in the midst of a true life-and-death struggle for himself, his family, and by extension, the entire Jewish nation of the future. *Avraham* and *Yitzchak*'s sacred heritage of monotheism was thus also at stake, and the climax of this encounter would occur on the following day.

Yaakov's focus upon his salvation was thus no doubt most intense and single-minded. Could any other "unimportant" activity (such as recovering small items) even remotely compare to the importance of the imminent struggle with *Eisav*? It must be that *Yaakov* calculated that this detour would not minimize his chances of saving himself (see section C). However, even if he theoretically had the time to retrieve the items, he could have used the time for other matters or to pray at greater length to *Hashem*. Instead, he chose to return for the forgotten but insignificant objects left behind.

According to the *Orchos Tzaddikim*'s explanation of the Talmud, *Yaakov* returned to the old camp because *tzaddikim* avoid the squander of even small amounts. This demonstrates the enormous significance that the Torah attaches to avoiding even negligible waste. This precept applies irrespective of whether one is idle or busy, wealthy or indigent. It is always true that insignificant waste should be avoided — even in the midst of the life-and-death struggle of a nation.

According to the *Pesikta Zuta* and others (see note 1), *Yaakov* was not only willing to pause to retrieve a small item that was definitely lost; *Yaakov* took steps to check for the possibility that *perhaps* something small was lost, while in the midst of a life-and-death situation. Such is the extent of the Torah's ethic of avoiding waste.

It should be noted that *Yaakov* was not, *chalilah*, categorically tightfisted with his money. To the contrary, he spent extravagantly when such was appropriate (see chapter 5, note 2). It is also true that everyday human needs are often costly and nevertheless called for (see chapter 15, section A). It is *waste* that *tzaddikim* so scrupulously avoid.

B) AVOIDING THEFT

Part I

Section A illustrates the lengths to which a *tzaddik* will go to avoid waste. Why is avoiding pennies of waste of such enormous significance? The Talmud's reason is "Because they [*tzaddikim*] do not lay their hands on anything stolen."

The *Matnas Kehunah* interprets this to mean that *tzaddikim* fear that they may one day be irresistibly tempted to steal a penny; they fear being eventually reduced to penury, when the temptation to steal even a single penny may be uncontrollable. Therefore, even if they are exceedingly wealthy (*Yaakov* is described by the *Orchos Tzaddikim* as being wealthy), *tzaddikim* preserve every penny; that one extra penny may be what will ultimately save them from the terrible sin of stealing.

Seemingly, this is a most unusual fear. Wealthy people may fret over the eventuality of losing their wealth; but if all is well financially, do they make practical plans for the period after they have already joined the ranks of the poor? Do they see that as a real possibility? Furthermore, in this particular instance, *Yaakov* had other pressing worries on his mind — he was fighting for both his own life and that of his family. And needless to say, he was the greatest of *tzaddikim* who would mightily resist every temptation to steal. If so, why did he pause at that moment to guard against such a highly unlikely eventuality?

This demonstrates the terrible fear one must have of the

sin of stealing. Psychologists might deem this measure of fear in almost all other matters as being inadvisably neurotic. But the fear of one's own potential for thievery of even one penny is different. There is almost no limit to the safeguards that one must institute against ever being reduced to such behavior.

Part II

The *Ben Yehoyada* interprets the words of the Talmud entirely differently from the *Orchos Tzaddikim* and *Matnas Kehunah*. He explains that *Yaakov*'s retrieval of the objects was not a function of frugality. Rather, *Yaakov* was attempting to teach his family a lesson. By returning for his own lost objects, *Yaakov* demonstrated that even a wealthy individual such as himself zealously preserves his most insignificant possessions. As such, all stealing should be avoided — even taking the smallest of items or amounts from the very affluent. There is no guarantee that even the loss of one half-penny's worth will be forgiven by its wealthy owner.

Were the members of *Yaakov*'s household thieves? *Chalilah!* They were great *tzaddikim* (see chapter 22, note 1) who no doubt avoided all manner of theft. Why then was there a need for this particular lesson at such a critical moment? It must be that *Yaakov* was taking pains to further deepen their already existing avoidance and abhorrence of stealing. Perhaps his admonition would affect what a descendant would do in a later generation. He sought to insure that a family member would never help himself to even a fraction of a penny that wasn't his, rationalizing that the owner doesn't care.

As mentioned previously, the background of what was transpiring highlights the extreme significance of this idea. This was a moment when the future of all of Jewry was at stake. Didn't *Yaakov* have other more important things to concern himself with? Nevertheless, *Yaakov* paused to impart this ethic. *Yaakov* saw an opportunity to further guard against the possibility that one day a member of his household would do something immoral such as taking a splinter from a wealthy person's woodpile without first asking permission.

How much more vigilant then would *Yaakov* have been if there was a certainty that a household member would take the splinter. What if the household member would actually steal more than a toothpick? *Yaakov* would have been even more dedicated to preventing that from ever happening. All of *Yaakov's* exertion grew out of his determination to prevent someone else from his household from stealing. His concern with making sure that he himself would not steal was no doubt even greater.

POSSIBLE APPLICATIONS

The everyday conduct of business and professions involves numerous challenges to the ethic of absolute financial integrity. Lies and misrepresentations that cause money to change hands may be outright stealing. This text highlights the enormous imperative to scrupulously avoid even the most "meaningless" stealing and to certainly avoid more substantive theft.[2]

---

2.   Stories abound about the care that R. *Yisrael Salanter* took to avoid the slightest possibility of stealing. Following are two examples:

At one point R. *Salanter* resigned from the rabbinate and chose instead to support himself by running a business. He soon left the business only to rejoin the rabbinate. He later explained that as a *rav*, he felt unequal to the grave responsibility of answering questions of *halachah*. However, he quickly realized that the possible misrepresentations and stealing endemic to business raised even greater dilemmas of *halachah*.

C) MULTIPLE FOCUS

The Torah attaches supreme importance to the value of human life. If one must choose between saving a life and observing a *mitzvah*, it is forbidden to perform the *mitzvah*.[3] The Torah must be violated so that the life will be saved. Certainly then, one should not distract himself from rescuing people in order to retrieve pennies.

How then can *Yaakov's* actions be explained? He had two choices before him. One option was to continue his efforts to protect himself and his family; the alternative was to sidetrack over a few small items. He elected to recover the objects, either to save an insignificant amount (*Orchos Tzaddikim* and *Matnas Kehunah*) or to teach his family a lesson (*Ben Yehoyada*). Was this choice correct if it in any way lessened his concentration on the salvation of human life?

It must be that *Yaakov's* focus on saving lives was in no way diminished. All possible preparations had already been

---

It was wintertime, and R. *Yisrael* was walking several paces behind another individual. Both were headed to the same home. When they arrived, the first man deferentially held the door open for several moments until R. *Yisrael* arrived. R. *Yisrael* rebuked the man for his "robbery." In keeping the door open to give honor to Torah he was allowing heat to escape from the home, thereby stealing from the householder.

3.   There are three exceptions to this rule. They are the sins of adultery, murder and idolatry. If one must choose between either violating one of these commandments or losing his own life, he is required to forfeit his life.

completed, and *Yaakov* was certain that retrieving the items
would not divert his attention from the main task before him.
Otherwise, the Torah would have forbidden his actions.

Evidently, man has the ability to rivet his attention on a
complex, all-important undertaking while remaining fully at-
tentive to even the smallest minutia of other far less critical
matters. Furthermore, pausing to attend to the minor issue
need not compromise one's focus on the more important situation. Both undertakings can be pursued with vigor without
imperiling each other.[4] Therefore, recovering the lost items

---

4.   One of the most remarkable personalities of world history
was Napoleon I, emperor of France. He was the undisputed political ruler of his country and a master of palace intrigue. He
was also one of the greatest battlefield generals of all time. He
was also a great thinker. His Napoleonic Code was a visionary
masterpiece; it reorganized the government of France into a
structure that is, to this day, largely intact. The code's ideas of
equality before the law and freedom of religion were revolu-
tionary for those times. The code was largely responsible for
dramatically transforming a thousand years of the political
thinking of European civilization.

Individuals may attain greatness in one field. But how often
do even the most brilliant and successful people change professions, and attain comparable distinction in a second and
completely different career? Napoleon was not only incredibly
preeminent in several disparate endeavors, but he was able to
pursue them simultaneously. How did he do it?

R. *Dovid Leibowitz* once commented that Napoleon possessed a
trait that all people should attempt to emulate. When, for example, he dealt with warfare, the entire universe of his intellect
was focused on that subject alone, and his many different careers did not in any way interfere with his concentration. However, despite riveting his mind on combat, he simultaneously
kept all of the details of all his other responsibilities on the

was not a conflict to the major challenge that faced *Yaakov*.

POSSIBLE APPLICATIONS

There are people who become totally engrossed in their careers. Most often, the greater a person's success, the more all-encompassing the involvement with his work. *Lehavdil*, this is true of Torah scholarship as well. It is normally the most outstanding of Torah scholars who possess the most intense drive to pursue their Torah study.

What of a person's other obligations? At times, that intense pursuit of career (or Torah, *lehavdil*) may engender a disregard of those obligations. The duties neglected may include anything from the attention to one's family or his personal health.

It is apparent from the response of *Yaakov* that a deep commitment to career or to a cause need not interfere with other "less critical" responsibilities. One can be totally absorbed in the world's most important emergency while remaining in touch with the smallest nuances of his other responsibilities. If one's vocation becomes the reason for neglect of spouse, family or other of life's details, it is likely an unacceptable excuse. People are capable of maintaining focus upon even the smallest details of life while pursuing greater causes without compromising either.

"back burner" of his mind. This was necessary in order to avoid having his activities conflict with each other and to be aware of when his attentions had to be diverted to another area.

Similarly, *Yaakov*, *lehavdil*, was focused on both the mortal threat facing him and on other issues as well. Furthermore, *Yaakov* didn't simply keep two or more highly important endeavors in mind. Though involved with a most crucial matter of life and death, *Yaakov* still did not lose sight of even the smallest details of another almost insignificant issue.

CHAPTER 21

בראשית, וישלח לד:כה

ויהי ביום השלישי בהיותם כאבים ויקחו שני־בני־יעקב שמעון ולוי
אחי דינה איש חרבו ויבאו על־העיר בטח ויהרגו כל־זכר:

רש"י

שני בני יעקב: בניו היו, ואף על פי כן נהגו עצמן שמעון ולוי
כשאר אנשים שאינם בניו שלא נטלו עצה הימנו, (ב"ר פ י):

מזרחי על רש"י

שלא נטלו עצה מאביהם כמנהג הבנים אלא עשו עצמן כנכריים.

נחלת יעקב על רש"י

שלא נטלו עצה הימנו: וקשה דהא בעצת כולם השיבו במרמה
בחכמה המול לכם כל זכר כדי שיהרגום בהיותם כואבים וי"ל
שביום השלישי עשו שלא בעצת אביהם שהלכו שניהם לבד ואפשר
שאילו נתיעצו היו הולכים כולם להורג' או אפשר שיעקב היה מציע
דבריו לפני שכיניו יושב הארץ שיסכימו עמו שחייבים מיתה.

BEREISHIS, VAYISHLACH 34:25

It was on the third day, when they were in pain, two of Yaakov's sons, Shimon and Levi, Dinah's brothers, each took his sword, and they came upon the city confidently and killed every male.

RASHI

Two of Yaakov's sons: They were his sons, and even so, they conducted themselves [like] Shimon and Levi, like other people that were not his sons. [This was evidenced by the fact that] they did not seek counsel from him [Yaakov].

MIZRACHI on Rashi

They did not take counsel from their father as is the custom among sons, but they made themselves as if they were strangers [in that they did not seek parental counsel].

NACHALAS YAAKOV on Rashi

That they did not seek counsel: It is difficult [to understand Rashi's commentary on this verse] for it was upon the advice of them all that they [Yaakov's entire family] answered [the people of Shechem] with trickery and wisdom that they should circumcise all males so that they could kill them when they were in pain. [If so, why were Shimon and Levi singled out and criticized for not taking counsel with Yaakov? The entire family had already agreed to this plan of action.]

One can answer that on the third day they acted without the advice of their father, for the two of them went alone. And it is possible that, had they consulted [with Yaakov], they [all the brothers] would have all gone [having been advised to all go together] to kill them. Or it is possible that Yaakov would have presented his words [plans] before his neighbors [those nations] who lived in the land so that they would first agree with him that they [the people of Shechem] deserved to be killed.

OVERVIEW OF TEXT

Shimon and *Levi*, acting alone, killed the males of the city of *Shechem*. This was in retribution for a crime committed against their sister *Dinah* by the son of that city's leader. *Rashi*, quoting the *Midrash*, states that *Shimon* and *Levi* were criticized for acting without first seeking counsel from their father. The *Mizrachi* adds that the practice of seeking parental counsel in this type of situation is customary among sons.

The *Nachalas Yaakov* explains that the basic plan to kill the males of *Shechem* was proper, and in fact, the entire family had already agreed upon it. However, before actually acting, certain details should have first been discussed with *Yaakov*. He might have advised them that all of the brothers should have assaulted *Shechem* together, rather than risk having *Shimon* and *Levi* go it alone. *Yaakov* also feared the reprisals of the neighboring nations. He thus may have also preferred to first present his intentions before his neighbors regarding *Shechem*. Presumably, discussing and explaining the justification for the attack before it actually occurred might have mitigated some of their antagonism.

PARENT/CHILD RELATIONSHIPS

Shimon and *Levi* were criticized for failing to first discuss their intentions with *Yaakov*. The topics discussed might have included (1) how and with whom to conduct the actual attack, and (2) how to create political damage control vis-à-vis the other locals. The *Mizrachi* adds that it is normal for children to bring home questions of this type for parental counsel.

Based on *Rashi* alone, this text would not prove that, as a general rule, parental advice should always be sought out before acting. *Yaakov* was the greatest scholar and the wisest man of that age (or of almost any other age). As such, *Shimon* and *Levi* should have first consulted with *their* father.

But the *Mizrachi* adds that such is the "the custom among sons" — all sons — regardless of who their parents may be.

How can the *Mizrachi* be understood? The issue at hand was not of a familial nature, such as a dispute between parents and children. Rather, their quandary concerned how exactly to wage war. Is it the widespread custom to seek parental counsel when facing a comparable situation? Most parents are expert neither at politics nor warfare; there are others who are normally far more capable and knowledgeable advice givers.

Apparently, the *Mizrachi's* words ("as is the custom among sons") are describing the normative and ideal parent/child relationship. When family dynamics are wholesome and as they should be, children will interact with parents much as the *Mizrachi* depicts.

More often than not, the parents are not the most competent resources on the subject at hand. However, their overwhelming love and concern can be of great significance. Despite lacking the technical expertise to advise personally, there are other "services" that loving parents are uniquely qualified to provide. They can bolster the children with emotional support, they can be a sympathetic sounding board for ideas, or they can help direct the children to a more knowledgeable consultant. [1]

It could perhaps be compared to two twins that were in-

---

1. The *Mizrachi* describes the bottom line of how the child should relate to parents. However, he does not discuss exactly how children can be reared to effect this ideal.

Presumably, the family environment should feature open communication, trust, emotional support and unconditional love as well as parental guidance and discipline. Furthermore, to whatever extent possible, the family should also be suffused with a spirit of learning and theoretical, intellectual dialogue. Family milieus of this ilk will likely help produce children that would interact with parents in the manner described by the *Mizrachi*.

. . . .

Some parents seem to feel that they help their children most by constantly criticizing their deficient conduct. Common sense dictates that there is an appropriate time and place for the reproof and discipline of children. In fact, in I *Malachim* 1:6, the *Radak* explains that *Dovid*'s son *Adoniyahu* rebelled against *Dovid* because when, as a child, he would misbehave, he was not reproved by his father. *Adoniyahu* therefore wrongly deduced that his improper conduct was acceptable.

However, continual faultfinding should not be the basic communication of parent to child. A child subjected to constant reproof will likely be disinclined to discuss real issues with his parents; raising serious topics with parents of that ilk would likely be an invitation for further censure. Such home dynamics are the antithesis of the *Mizrachi*'s model.

credibly close to each other. Each would automatically first discuss all personal dilemmas with the other, notwithstanding the factor of others being more qualified to give advice on the issue. Similarly, the Torah's ideal is a family environment where children will automatically first come home for advice on virtually anything. Raising children in the manner prescribed by the Torah entails establishing parent/child relationships of this type.

Chapter 22

בראשית, וישב לח:א

ויהי בעת ההוא וירד יהודה מאת אחיו ויט עד-איש עדלמי ושמו
חירה:

מדרש רבה שמות מב:ד

בשעה שאחיו של יוסף מכרוהו והלכו לנחם אביהם ולא נתנחם.
אמרו כל הדברים הללו עשה לנו יהודה שאלולי בקש לא מכרנו
אותו כשם שאמר לנו אל תהרגוהו ושמענו לו. אלו אמר לנו אל
תמכרוהו נשמע לו אלא אמר לנו לכו ונמכרנו לישמעאלים ועמדו
ונדוהו שנאמר (שם לח) ויהי בעת ההיא וירד יהודה מאת אחיו ולא
היה לו לומר אלא וילך יהודה שהיה לו ירידה מצד אחיו.

יפה תואר הארוך על המדרש

עשה לנו יהודה: שאף על פי שהיו שם יותר מרשיעים שבקשו
להרגו האשימו יותר את יהודה כי הוא הגדול שבהם ועליו מוטל
לעיין יותר בדברים אי נמי איפשר שכל אחד כבר שככה חמתו אחר
שהשליכו הבור אלא שהיו יראי' איש מאחיו לאמר שחמל עליו אבל
יהודה כי לא יפחד מאחד מהם להוציא כל רוחו עליו אשמה כי
כשם שנשמעו לו למכירה היה בטוח שישמעו לו להצלה ולכן לא

האשימו את ראובן שכמו שאמר השליכו אותו הבורה ושמעו לו אלו
אמר נעזבנו היו שומעים לו כי כי ידעו שראובן כוונתו רצויה ולא בקש
הצלתו בידעו כי לא יהיו דבריו נשמעים אצלם מה שאין כן יהודה
שהיה מלך.

BEREISHIS, VAYESHEV 38:1

And it was at that time, and Yehudah went down from his brothers
and turned toward an Adullamite man, whose name was Chira.

MIDRASH RABBAH SHEMOS 42:4

At the time that Yosef's brothers sold him, they went to comfort
their father [Yaakov], and he was not comforted.

[And among themselves] they said, all of these things [misfor-
tunes] were done to us by Yehudah. For had he requested [that we
not sell Yosef], we would not have sold him [and we would have returned him to his father]. Just as when he said to us, "Do not
abandon him," we listened to him, when he said to us, "Go and let
us sell him to the Ishmaelites" [we listened to him].

And they [the brothers] rose, and they excommunicated him
[Yehudah]. As it says, "And it was at that time, and Yehudah went
down from his brothers." But it should have said, "And Yehudah went
[rather than saying that he went down]." This [addition of the word
"down"] indicates that he had a "going down" from his brothers.

YEFE TOAR HAARUCH on the Midrash

Were done to us by Yehudah: For even though they were more involved in the wrongdoing, since they sought to kill him [Yosef], they
faulted Yehudah more, because he was the gadol [leader] among them,
and it was his responsibility to think more deeply into the matter.

Or else, it is possible [to answer] that the anger of each one of
them [the brothers] had already abated after they threw him
[Yosef] into the pit. But each [brother] feared his brothers [and thus
was afraid] to say [before them all] that he was compassionate to
him [Yosef]. However, the sin was upon Yehudah, because he feared

not one of them [and therefore was able] to express himself completely. For just as they listened to him regarding the sale, he [Yehudah] was certain that they would listen to him to save him [to bring Yosef back to Yaakov, rather than selling him].

And therefore, they did not fault Reuvain [who had convinced them to throw Yosef into a pit rather than to kill him. Regarding Reuvain, the brothers did not reason as follows:] "Just as he [Reuvain] said, throw him into the pit, and [we] listened to him, had he said, let us leave him, [we] would have listened to him" [and therefore Reuvain is the cause of these misfortunes. The brothers did not reason thus], for they knew that Reuvain's intentions were pure but he did not request his [Yosef's] outright salvation because he knew that his words would not be heeded by them. Not so Yehudah, who was a king.

OVERVIEW OF TEXT

The brothers of *Yosef*, who were *tzaddikim* of the highest caliber, sincerely believed that *Yosef* was guilty of a capital offense, and it was their duty to put him to death.[1] Initially, they

---

1.   It may be true that something about what the brothers did to *Yosef* was in error. However, in an overall sense, *Yosef's* brothers cannot, *chalilah*, be viewed as sinners. To the contrary, they were the greatest of *tzaddikim*. The following provides an inkling of their greatness: After selling *Yosef*, the brothers convened a *beis din* to excommunicate anyone who would reveal what they had done. A *beis din* for this purpose requires a quorum of ten. *Binyamin* and *Reuvain* were then with *Yaakov*, leaving only nine brothers. They summoned *Hashem*, Who joined them to complete the *minyan*, and He then participated in the *cherem* (*Rashi* on *Bereishis* 37:33). Clearly, they were the most sanctified and G-d-fearing individuals, and their decisions regarding *Yosef* were suffused with holiness. Otherwise, *Hashem* Himself would not appear after being summoned to join in their *cherem*.

This still appears difficult to understand. If *Hashem* joined the brothers in the *cherem*, why was their sale of *Yosef* deemed

unanimously resolved to kill *Yosef* outright. *Reuvain* then convinced them to instead leave *Yosef* in a pit to die. *Yehudah* subsequently proposed selling *Yosef* as a slave to a caravan of Ishmaelites that was headed to Egypt. *Yehudah's* suggestion was accepted, and *Yosef* was sold.

After being led to believe that *Yosef* was killed by a wild animal, *Yaakov* began a period of intense and inconsolable mourning. Seeing *Yaakov's* unremitting suffering, the brothers regretted their abduction of *Yosef*. However, they laid the blame for the mistake upon *Yehudah*, arguing that had *Yehudah* advocated returning *Yosef* to *Yaakov* rather than selling him, they would have heeded his words. The *Midrash* continues that the brothers therefore excommunicated *Yehudah*.

The *Yefe Toar* asks the following: It was true that *Yehudah* suggested selling *Yosef*. However, the alternative favored by the brothers was far more extreme. They were seemingly content with the original decision to execute *Yosef*. They had to be convinced to accept the ideas of both *Reuvain* and *Yehudah*. Why did they fault *Yehudah* and not themselves?

The *Yefe Toar* offers two answers: A) As the *gadol* (leader)[2]

improper at all? In truth, this is a valid question irrespective of the issues raised in this chapter (see foreword, part IV). However, some clarification of the matter can be found in the *Sforno* (*Bereishis* 42:21). The *Sforno* indicates that the only error in the sale was that since *Yosef* was their brother and was pleading for clemency, they should have released him out of mercy, even though he deserved to die according to *halachah*.

2.   The Hebrew word *gadol*, as applied by the Yefe Toar to *Yehudah*, presumably means to denote that he was their leader. There are various references in the Torah to the fact that *Yehudah* was their leader or king, but it does not appear that in this text, he was singled out for greater responsibility because he was clearly more righteous than his brothers.

among them, *Yehudah* should have examined the matter more deeply. Had *Yehudah* pondered the matter more deeply, he would have realized that *Yosef* should have been returned to *Yaakov* rather than sold.[3]

B) The brothers' anger had subsided, and they therefore were willing to recant and to return *Yosef* to *Yaakov* unharmed. However, each brother feared revealing his change of heart to the others. *Yehudah*, however, had no such fear, for he was their leader whose opinions were heeded. Thus, they faulted *Yehudah* for not pushing for complete clemency toward *Yosef* — advice that would have been accepted.

The *Yefe Toar* also explains why the brothers did not also fault *Reuvain*. *Reuvain* had recommended leaving *Yosef* in a pit to die, but he did not press for complete salvation. *Reuvain* understood that his advice would have been disregarded altogether if he asked for too much (unlike *Yehudah*, who would have been heeded since he was their leader).

In fact, when comparing the advice offered by *Reuvain* and *Yehudah*, the *Yefe Toar* clearly states that *Yehudah's* counsel was heeded because he was a king (and not because he was either more righteous or more learned).

3.   At first glance, this would appear to be in conflict with the idea of chapter 2, section A. There the point was made that one cannot hold others responsible for his own wrongdoing — Adam and *Chavah* could not exonerate themselves and blame the serpent, for one is ultimately responsible for his own deeds. Yet here the brothers apparently blamed *Yehudah* more than themselves; they did not excommunicate themselves as they did *Yehudah*.

This is not a question. Chapter 2, section A makes the point that if one person successfully entices another to sin, the latter cannot absolve himself by blaming the forme. This *Yefe Toar Haaruch* is saying that a leader who has a heightened capacity to see the truth of an issue may be more blameworthy in the event of a sin than those he leads.

A) GROWING FROM LEADERSHIP

The brothers all agreed to sell *Yosef*, but *Yaakov's* terrible suffering caused them to later regret the decision. Yet it was *Yehudah* who was excommunicated as the responsible party. Why did *Yehudah's* guilt exceed that of the brothers? The *Yefe Toar's* first answer is that, as their leader, *Yehudah* should have put more thought into the matter; had he done so, he would have realized that *Yosef* should have been released unharmed.

The resolution to kill another human being is certainly one of the most weighty and irreversible decisions that man can make; it cannot be recalled after the execution. Furthermore, in this case, the person whose fate they were ruling upon was their own brother, who was himself a great *tzaddik* (and is referred to in Torah literature as *Yosef Hatzaddik*). Additionally, the brothers undoubtedly realized that killing *Yosef* would cause terrible anguish to their revered and beloved father, *Yaakov*.

Any responsible and upstanding human being would exert every ounce of his intellectual capacity before ruling that another human should be put to death. Certainly this was true of the brothers, who were great *tzaddikim* sitting in judgment of their righteous brother. Without doubt, they decided to execute *Yosef* only after first considering the decision to the absolute limit of their capacity.

Yet the brothers were so critical of *Yehudah* that they placed him in *cherem*. They contended that *since he was their leader*, his additional contemplation would have shed new light upon the matter. Of what significance was the factor of his leadership? Each one of the brothers including *Yehudah*, had already expended his intellect to its absolute outer limit. Seemingly, *Yehudah*'s further concentration on the issue would have been pointless.

In truth, there are many critical instances when man is able to expand his known capacities and access previously unattainable strengths. At almost any time when life is at risk people can greatly exceed their previous limits of physical strength and endurance; for example, the mother whose child is being threatened can lift a phenomenally heavy object to save him.

In a similar vein, a leader's capacity to comprehend critical issues can also be expanded. This is because when considering a personal matter, it is one's own issues that are at stake. However, a leader must decide on behalf of others, and a conscientious leader will not be oblivious to that added responsibility. The extra gravity attending the decision will elicit newer and greater depths of wisdom that were absolutely unattainable prior to assuming a leadership position.

This differential can be compared to two people of comparable eyesight who are observing a distant view; one has binoculars, while the other has to rely on the naked eye. Very obviously, the binoculars enable the person to more accurately observe the scene. So, too, the circumstance of leadership augments the capacity of the leader. The brothers thus felt that *Yehudah*'s wisdom was more profound, for it was aided by the fact of his being the leader. Only *Yehudah* could have perceived the mistake in selling *Yosef* after further pondering the matter.

Even the wisest of leaders must ponder his leadership decisions more than his determinations of a personal nature. When the effort is expended, new vistas of wisdom will be opened before the leader that would be otherwise unattainable. That remains true even in situations where wisdom was presumably already expended to its absolute maximum outer limits (as with the case of the brothers, who were brilliant *tzaddikim* deciding on a matter of such grave significance).

POSSIBLE APPLICATIONS

Most adults may suddenly find themselves in a position of leadership to one extent or another — a parent to a child or a boss in an employment setting. The newly "ordained" leader must realize that the typical effort, energy and breadth of contemplation over issues prior to his assumption of leadership may not be sufficient. When considering the fate of others, the leader is called upon to additionally consider the rectitude and implications of decisions and judgments. He may then realize a level of understanding that was previously unattainable.

A corollary to this idea is that one should have great regard for the comprehension, responses and judgments of his leaders. It is true that all humans can err, including leaders. However, one must realize that a leader's insight into a given issue may be more profound and all-encompassing. All other factors being equal,[4] the responsibility for others bestows a clarity of vision that is completely inaccessible to anyone not shouldering that responsibility.

---

4.   The phrase, "all other factors being equal" is of critical significance. An unqualified leader will not necessarily grow into the role simply because he assumes responsibility for others. To the contrary, even slight differences in a leader's qualifications are of great significance (see chapter 26). However, an otherwise acceptable leader can attain yet greater wisdom as a result of his position – wisdom that was previously beyond his reach.

B) BIAS AND DEFYING A GROUP

The question at hand is why the brothers blamed *Yehudah* for the sale of *Yosef* and not themselves. The second answer of the *Yefe Toar* is that the brothers individually may have reconsidered their decision to harm *Yosef*. However, each one feared revealing his change of heart to the others. *Yehudah* who was their king had no such fear. Thus, he alone was faulted for the failure to openly advocate returning *Yosef* to their father unharmed.

Why did the brothers "fear" revealing their change of heart? They certainly were not afraid that arguing to save *Yosef* would endanger them personally. *Tzaddikim* such as the brothers would never harm one of their own for expressing an opposing *halachic* view. (They considered harming *Yosef* only because they judged him guilty of a capital offense according to *halacha*.) Yet, the *Yefe Toar* clearly indicates that the brothers remained silent because they "feared" verbalizing their change of heart.

Apparently, their fear was social in nature; they feared "bucking the trend." Nevertheless, the *Yefe Toar* requires further explanation. How could social pressure prevent such *tzaddikim* from expressing a view that might forestall this tragedy?

The following basic premise of Torah and *mussar* will help explain the *Yefe Toar*: The *Orchos Tzaddikim* (*Shaar Hasheker*) writes that "Every person is influenced in his logical thoughts by his character traits; the lazy person by his laziness, the man of anger by his anger..." The concept that deficient character traits exert an influence over one's logic is a revealing insight that is typically unrecognized. Yet, once pointed out, it is a readily observable phenomenon.

The following is an illustrative: The emotion of anger is a character traits mentioned by the *Orchos Tzaddikim* that influence one's thought. Among spouses or friends, when one party is feeling anger toward the other, common everyday annoyances are often viewed in a wildly unrealistic light. Everyday annoyances such as a wife's simple tardiness may be "logically" interpreted by an angry husband as proof-positive of a decades-old pattern of arrogance and inconsideration. And the husband is absolutely certain that his thinking is entirely based on rationale rather than upon emotion. But when that same husband is harboring a loving attitude to his wife, he may interpret an identical lateness as being utterly insignificant. The first thought process was subconsciously altered by the emotion of anger, and the person didn't see its influence at the time. After the anger subsided, a true perception of the same event became possible.

The *Orchos Tzaddikim* is teaching that any deficient character trait and its attendant subconscious bias can activate this same syndrome. A person given to jealousy may suddenly feel that he "needs" a new car when his neighbor purchases the same, etc.

The judgment of the brothers was not swayed by a fear that they were aware of. Such *tzaddikim* would never knowingly allow social censure to play a role in the life or death of their brother. Their decision was altered by the subconscious fear of standing alone socially. This unidentified fear created a subconscious bias with the result that in all sincerity, their reasoning dictated that it was righteous and proper to sell *Yosef.*

It is not merely that one may consciously fear opposing improper group standards. Rather, unbeknown to the person himself, subconscious social fear can beget the distorted opinion that those standards are indeed just.[5] This process is so powerful and insidious that it can becloud and alter the determinations of even the greatest of *tzaddikim* on the most critical of life-and-death matters.[6] (See chapter 32, note 4.)

POSSIBLE APPLICATIONS

The circumstance of living in a vibrant Jewish community can confer great benefit. When the standards of the group are exemplary, a strong and wholesome influence to conform is exerted upon the individual members of the community. However, as with *Yosef*'s brothers, group pressure can also act as a negative factor, by being not only a force that is difficult to resist, but a factor that confuses one's judgment.

To cite a contemporary example, when a couple is engaged, many within the Torah observing world fall prey to certain widely observed conventions: "This and that party must

---

5.   The third chapter of the *Mesillas Yesharim* describes something similar. The *Mesillas Yesharim* mentions that the failure to introspect can give rise to two problems. The first is that one will fail to recognize that something before him is bad or sinful. The second more insidious problem is that he may see something evil as being good, and something truly good as evil.

The idea described by the *Mesillas Yesharim* seems similar to that of the *Yefe Toar*. However, the *Mesillas Yesharim* merely indicates the existence of this dynamic. The *Yefe Toar* demonstrates further that this tendency to confuse good and evil can be instigated by social fear and that it can even distort decisions on life and death being made by the greatest of *tzaddikim*.

be made leading up to the wedding by this or that side; each side must buy such-and-such presents at various stages of the engagement; the *ofruf*, wedding and *sheva berachos* all must conform to the *accepted* standard, etc."

At times, these expectations are not only difficult to comply with, but they can bring families to the brink of financial ruination. Yet, based on the *Yefe Toar*, it may require enormous wisdom and purity of heart to even recognize the difference between the truly necessary and the outright folly.

. . . .

The general idea of common bias subverting everyday thinking has almost universal application. To whatever extent one has not perfected his character traits, each and every one of those deficient traits will exert a subconscious influence over one's thought processes. This highlights the need for *tikkun hamiddos*, because one's ability to think accurately correlates directly to the refinement of his character.

---

6.   My *rebbe* has often said in the name of the great *baalei mussar* that it is the mechanism of subconscious bias that explains the wrongdoing of the great people of the *Chumash*. For example, the Talmud (*Shabbos* 10b) relates that a factor that led the brothers to sell *Yosef* was jealousy. Is this possible? Would even a moderately upstanding person of this day and age sell his own brother (if he could) due to jealousy? How then could *tzaddikim* of that caliber be influenced by jealousy and so hurt their father in the process?

It must be that the jealousy referred to was not in their awareness. Rather they harbored a minute trace of unseen subconscious jealousy that interfered with their otherwise most righteous and sophisticated judgment. However, they were faulted for jealousy because such *tzaddikim* should have cleansed themselves of even microscopic traces of subliminal envy.

CHAPTER 23

בראשית, וישב לט:יא,יב

יא. ויהי כהיום הזה ויבא הביתה לעשות מלאכתו ואין איש מאנשי הבית שם בבית:
יב. ותתפשהו בגדו לאמר שכבה עמי ויעזב בגדו בידה וינס ויצא החוצה:

רש"י

לעשות מלאכתו: רב ושמואל, חד אמר מלאכתו ממש וחד אמר לעשות צרכיו עמה, אלא שנראית לו דמות דיוקנו של אביו וכו' כדאיתא במסכת סוטה:

אמרי שפר על רש"י

עוד אני אומר שדרשה בזאת איננה כנגד מעלות הצדיק כיון שהוא דבר במחשבה ולא יצא לפועל אף על פי שתהיה לאיזו סבה שתהיה. ויש לנו דמחשבה רעה אין הקדוש מצרפה למעשה בישראל זולתו בע"ז ולכן אין זה חסרון בצדיק דכל הגדול מחבירו יצרו גדול ממנו אדרב' הוא לו מעלה כיון שבלסוף ניצול מהעבירה ואין כוונת הפסוק להודיענו מחשבת אלו הצדיקים אבל הכוונה להודיענו שניצולו ושהקב"ה הרחיק מהם העבירה ההוא.

מדרש רבה שיר השירים א:א

ור"נ אומר יום טיאטרון שלנילוס היה והלכו כולם לראות והוא נכנס
למלאכתו.

עץ יוסף על המדרש

וכתב היפ"ת ולי נראה שהוא היום שפורצים שפת נילוס כדי שיעלה
על כל ארץ מצרים שעושים בו שמחה וגיל בארץ מצרים. וזהו
שמסיים ר' נחמיה והלכו כולם לראות והוא נכנס למלאכתו. כלומר
דלפי"ז ניחא הא דקמ"ל קרא שבא הביתה לעשות מלאכתו דנ"מ בהא
לאשמועינן חסידותיה דיוסף דאע"פ שכל העבדים והשפחות היו
תחת ידו והם הלכו לטייל על הצחוק מ"מ הוא לא הלך בסוד
משחקים ולא ישב במושב לצים אלא בא הביתה לעשות מלאכת
רבו באמונה.

סוטה לו-ב

ותתפשהו בבגדו לאמר שכבה עמי: (תנא מלמד שעלו למטה שניהם
ערומים) באותה שעה באתה דיקנו של אביו ונראית לו בחלון אמר
ליה יוסף (יוסף) עתידין אחיך שיכתבו על אבני אפוד ואתה ביניהם
רצונך שימחה שמך מביניהם ותקרא רועה זונות.

ילקוט שמעוני בראשית קמה

ולא שמע אליה אמר רבי שמע לה אלא שהביא הקב"ה איקונין של
אב ונתבייש וברח. פעם שניה נכנס נטל הקב"ה אבן שתיה א"ל אם
תגע בה הרינו משליכו ואחריב את העולם.

ילקוט שמעוני על תהילים קיד:ג

הים ראה וינוס: ד"א ראה ארונו של יוסף יורד לים אמר הקב"ה
ינוס מפני הנס שנאמר ויעזוב בגדו בידה וינס ויצא החוצה.

BEREISHIS, VAYESHEV 39:11,12

11. *And it was on that day and he came to the house to do his work;
and there was no person from the people of the household there in
the house.*
12. *And she grabbed him by his garment, saying, "Lie with me!"
And he left his garment in her hand, and he fled, and he went outside.*

RASHI

11. **To do his work:** *Rav and Shmuel: One said, it was his actual
work [he came to perform his regular tasks], and one said to do his
matters with her [to commit adultery], but the image of his father
appeared to him, as it is written in tractate Sotah.*

IMREI SHEFER on Rashi

*...this drashah [the second opinion quoted in the Talmud that
Yosef came with the intention to sin] is not contrary to the greatness of the tzaddik [Yosef]. This is because it was something in his
thoughts and did not evolve into action, despite it [his absention
from sin] being for [other] reasons [the miraculous appearance of
his father's image]. And we have [in the Torah] that Hashem does
not consider evil thoughts in a Jew the same as sin, except for idolatry. And therefore, this is not a failing in the tzaddik [Yosef], for
"Anyone greater than his friend has a greater inclination to sin"
(Talmud Sukkah 52a). To the contrary, it demonstrates [Yosef's]
greatness since in the end, he was saved from sin. And it is not the
intention of the pasuk to inform us of the thoughts [of sin] of these*

righteous people; rather, the intention is to inform us that they were
saved and that Hashem distanced the sin from them...

MIDRASH RABBAH SHIR HASHIRIM 1:1

R. Nechemiah said, It was a day of tiatron of the Nile, and they all
went to see, and he [Yosef] entered to do his work, to calculate the
accounts of his master.

ETZ YOSEF on the Midrash

Tiatron: *[and the Yefe Toar wrote:] And to me it appears that it was*
the day that the Nile burst forth from its banks to rise upon the en-
tire land of Egypt, [and therefore] they made on it [that day] a re-
joicing in the land of Egypt. And that is what R. Nechemiah con-
cludes: "and they all went to see and he [Yosef] entered to do his
work." According to this, it is understandable that the pasuk [took
the trouble and] taught that he came to the house to do his work.
For this is significant in that it demonstrates the chassidus of Yosef.
For even though all the servants and maidservants were subordi-
nate to him, and they all went to be present at the merriment, nev-
ertheless, he did not go with the counsel of the revelers, nor did he
sit with scoffers. But he faithfully came to the house to do the work
of his master.

TALMUD SOTAH 36b (quoted in Rashi)

And she grabbed him by his garment, saying, "Lie with me!":
This teaches that they both entered unclothed into the bed.[1] At that
time, the form of his father came to him and appeared at the win-
dow. He said to him, "Yosef! Your brothers are destined to be writ-

---

1.   Their entry into a bed in an unclothed state is recounted in
      the version of the Talmud found in *Ein Yaakov*, and it is
      parenthesized. However, the commentary of *Rif* (on *Ein*
      Yaakov) and the commentary of *Divrei Shaul* (on the *Chumash*)
      both include this phrase as part of the Talmud's narrative.

ten upon the stones of the breastplate [of the high priest], and you are among them. Is it your desire that your name should be erased from among them and you be called a shepherd of prostitutes?"

MIDRASH YALKUT SHIMONI 145

Rebbe said, He listened to her [and was about to sin], but Hashem brought the form of his father, and he [Yosef] was embarrassed and fled. The second time he entered [to sin], Hashem took the even shisia. He [Hashem] said to him [Yosef], "If you touch her, I will throw it [the stone] down, and I will destroy the world."

MIDRASH YALKUT SHIMONI on Tehillim 114:3

The sea saw and fled: It saw the bier of Yosef entering the sea. Hashem said, Let it [the sea] flee because of the fleeing [of Yosef], as it is written, "And she grabbed him by his garment, saying, Lie with me! And he left his garment in her hand, and he fled, and he went outside."

OVERVIEW OF TEXT

The wife of *Potifar* was ceaselessly attempting to entice *Yosef* to sin. On the day of an Egyptian celebration, *Potifar's* entire household left to join in the rejoicing, save his wife who feigned illness and remained at home. *Yosef* then entered the house. According to one opinion in the Talmud, *Yosef* came to do his regular work, but he then almost succumbed. According to another opinion in the Talmud, *Yosef's* intention in coming was to sin with *Potifar's* wife.

The *Midrash* on *Shir Hashirim* accepts the view that *Yosef* came to do his work. The *Etz Yosef* explains the *Midrash* to be saying that *Yosef's* reporting to work was a testament to his great *chassidus*. Although the other slaves all took off work to attend a celebration, *Yosef* nevertheless remained at home in order to faithfully perform his duties.

Yosef came perilously close to sinning, entering a bed

with *Potifar*'s wife, unclothed. The image of *Yaakov* then miraculously appeared, threatening that *Yosef* would be eternally severed from his heritage if he sinned. *Yosef* then seized control of himself and fled. According to the *Midrash Yalkut Shimoni*, *Yosef* once again returned with the intent to sin. He refrained from adultery the second time as well, but only after *Hashem*'s threat to destroy the entire world.

The *Imrei Shefer* explains that the Torah's description of *Yosef*'s close brush with wrongdoing does not in any way diminish his stature. To the contrary, *Hashem*'s miracles that protected *Yosef* from sin are themselves proof-positive of *Yosef*'s piety. Furthermore, *Yosef*'s act of controlling himself, albeit only after *Hashem*'s miracles, was itself an act of enormous holiness. The *Midrash Yalkut Shimoni* writes that when the Jews left Egypt and were facing the Red Sea, it was the merit of *Yosef*'s fleeing from temptation that caused the sea to flee from the Jews and to split.

(The *Imrei Shefer* also quotes the *Rambam* [introduction to *Avos*, 6], who writes that temptations of the natural and unnatural variety are viewed differently. With natural desires such as stealing and adultery, a person who naturally lusts for sin and yet controls himself is deemed greater than one who never harbored the temptation. With an unnatural urge, such as one who would like to drink blood, which is prohibited, it is greater to have never had the desire. If so, the *Imrei Shefer* concludes, this description of *Yosef*'s taking flight from this transgression testifies to his G-dliness.)

A) SIN — INTENTIONS AND DEEDS

Yosef is referred to in Torah literature as *Yosef Hatzaddik* — *Yosef*, the ultimate righteous man. Yet, *Yosef* came so perilously close to the cardinal sin of adultery. In fact, he escaped abomination only because of the miraculous appearance of his father's image. According to the *Midrash*, even after this miracle occurred, he again returned with the intent to sin. That second attempt was thwarted only by *Hashem's* threat to destroy the world.

Yosef was saved from adultery only by *Hashem's* miracle. How can a person who succumbed to the lust for mortal sin be referred to as a *tzaddik*? Seemingly, whether or not the misdeed actually occurred was almost anticlimactic; *Yosef's* true and inner being was defined by his intention to sin with *Potifar's* wife.

The Torah's understanding is different. Even the greatest *tzaddik* could be momentarily overcome by an urge to sin that is so intense and humanly irresistible that nothing short of an outright miracle would save the *tzaddik*. However, as long as the actual iniquity did not occur, the *tzaddik's* general sanctity and closeness to *Hashem* is not necessarily negated or even diminished. As a rule, as long as the transgression did not actually occur and thoughts of sin are not actively cultivated,[2] one can remain a *tzaddik* of the highest caliber. It is the performance of wrongdoing that is critical.

Unexpected circumstances that somehow prevent transgression from occurring can themselves be proof-positive of the *tzaddik's* greatness. Furthermore, a person who refrains from sin, even if only because of external factors, may in fact be acting with great piety. It was in the merit of *Yosef*'s fleeing from *Potifar*'s wife (albeit only after the miracles) that the Red Sea also "fled" and parted for the Jews.[3]

This text also reveals the monumental significance of a sinful deed. *Yosef* was so close to supreme evil; he was extricated from the situation only by miracles. Yet, he remains *Yosef Hatzaddik*. Had he actually committed the act, he would have plummeted in stature to the point of being severed from his brethren.[4]

POSSIBLE APPLICATIONS

When an individual is seized with a strong desire for wrongdoing, the *yetzer hara* will often inspire a two-part reaction.

• The evil urge is proof-positive of one's lack of religiosity. This demoralizing feeling can foster a negative self-image and discourage one from seeking to draw himself closer to *Hashem*. He assumes that, unlike himself, truly virtuous

---

2.   The *halachah* (*Even Ezra* 21) enumerates activities that must be avoided, for they foster sinful thoughts. *Yosef* did not in any way bring the *yetzer hara* upon himself, for that would have been a transgression, in and of itself (see chapter 13, note 4). Rather, circumstances were such that even without active participation on his part, *Yosef*'s uncontrollable urge brought him to the brink of adultery.

3.   This concept is somewhat similar to that discussed in chapter 18, section A. That idea was that exemplary conduct, though only due to external factors, is enormously significant; it can transform a person into a *tzaddik*. The idea of this section is that refraining from sin, though aided by unforeseen happenstance, may be considered righteousness of the highest order.

people would never harbor these sinful cravings.

* Being overcome by low and evil thoughts means that it makes almost no difference whether or not one actually sins. One might reason that he may as well sin, for the deed itself is all but an anticlimax. His righteousness has already been utterly repudiated by terrible thoughts and/or his uncontrollable desire for abomination.

Both of the above reactions could not be further from the truth. *Yosef*, at one point, was beset by the intense and uncontrollable desire for sin. Nevertheless, he never ceased being

---

4.   A phenomenon of present times is the proliferation of easy-to-read biographies of great *tzaddikim* of yesteryear, written in the vernacular. These stories can certainly be most inspiring.

However, some have found many of these works somewhat demoralizing. That is because the lives depicted often seem impossibly unrealizable. A possible reason for this reaction is the frequent failure to portray the struggles that the protagonists faced. The descriptions in these books are often of otherworldly subjects; the life histories described are often fairytale-like, untouched by the serious challenges and obstacles of everyday living.

Someone recently quipped that dozens of Torah personalities of the last several hundred years are described in modern biographies as being far more more untouched by temptations and frustrations than all seven *ushpizin*.

The reality is different. If the Torah attributes occasional temptations and frustrations (and even rare mistakes) to people of *Yosef*'s caliber, the same is likely true of later *tzaddikim*; their humanity and vulnerability were very real. But their everlasting greatness was manifested in, among other things, their ability to constantly resist the *yetzer hara*, with *Hashem*'s help, and to promptly repent and rebound from any wrongdoing, however slight.

Yosef Hatzaddik. Furthermore, though helped by an outright miracle, *Yosef*'s refusal to sin was the supremely meritorious deed that caused the Red Sea to later split for the Jews.

This text also illustrates the enormous difference between the burning desire for wrongdoing and the actual performance of the sin. Had *Yosef* actually sinned, he would have been severed from the Jewish people. By resisting his urge to sin, to this very day he remains *Yosef Hatzaddik*.

B) EXTREME CHASSIDUS

The following is not meant to in any way allude to or comment upon the popular movement known as Chassidus. Rather, the term "chassidusis" utilized is in its classical context as defined by the Mesillas Yesharim and mentioned throughout the Torah.

According to the *Etz Yosef* on the *Midrash, Shir Hashirim*, *Yosef*'s dedication to his duties on that day was indicative of his great *chassidus*. Much is written throughout the Torah describing *Yosef*'s piety. Yet, according to this *Midrash*, the Torah is here teaching that *Yosef* had also attained this additional and heretofore unknown dimension of *chassidus*.

Following is some of what is known of *Yosef*'s piety:

- *Yosef*'s brothers were all people of enormous holiness (see chapter 22, note 1), and *Yosef* apparently stood out from among them as the one of greatest piety. *Yosef* is referred to in the *Midrash* as *Yosef Hatzaddik*. Although Adam, *Noach* and the patriarchs had already lived, it was the merit of *Yosef* that caused the Red Sea to split.

- *Yosef* was also a great scholar of Torah. By age seventeen, *Yosef* had already mastered all of the Torah acquired by *Yaakov* during fourteen consecutive years of adult Torah study during which time *Yaakov* did not even interrupt his study in order to sleep (*Rashi* on *Bereishis* 13:3).

What could eclipse all else that *Yosef* had accomplished spiritually? What conceivable act of extreme *chassidus* could demonstrate yet greater piety than that which is otherwise known about *Yosef*? This *Midrash* provides the answer. *Yosef* did his work faithfully for his master *Potifar*.

Evidently, extreme integrity in matters of money requires consummate righteousness and sanctity. Thus, *Yosef's* being a faithful employee demonstrated an additional level of *chassidus* that would not have been otherwise evident, notwithstanding all of his other G-dly attributes (see chapter 20, note 2).[5]

POSSIBLE APPLICATIONS

The feeling that their daily work does not provide the opportunity for spiritual growth besets many individuals who are not directly involved in Torah-related fields. This *Etz Yosef* teaches that, in fact, almost any workplace is a milieu in which to acquire exalted holiness of the *neshamah*. That sanctification can be attained when, in addition to observing the other areas of the Torah, one deals with utmost integrity in all matters involving money.

---

5.   Chapter 52 of the *Kav Hayashar* decries those who are excessively devout to the point of inappropriateness. The author goes so far as to say that those who adopt such behavior may in fact be committing major sins such as adultery or murder. The author concludes:

"One should not rely on what he sees with his eyes — that [the person observed] is acting with perfection, for one man does not know what is in the other's heart. And always remember this principle: He who does not wish to have benefit from the money of his friend and certainly does not wish for stolen money, and [one whose] financial dealings are with integrity — he is certainly a man that is a *tzaddik* and is just. But when one sees his friend kissing *tefillin* and *davening* and not dealing with money with integrity, one must distance himself from him with all forms of distancing. For the fundamental fear [of *Hashem*] and piety is [expressed] in matters of money. And every man that maintains his piety in financial matters, he is the consummate *tzaddik*."

CHAPTER 24

בראשית, וישב מא:נ-נב

נ. וליוסף ילד שני בנים בטרם תבוא שנת הרעב אשר ילדה־לו אסנת בת־פוטי פרע כהן און:

נא. ויקרא יוסף את־שם הבכור מנשה כי־נשני אלהים את־כל־עמלי ואת כל־בית אבי:

נב. ואת שם השני קרא אפרים כי־הפרני אלהים בארץ עניי:

רלב"ג

התועלת השלישי הוא בדעות: והוא להודיע שכל הטובות השופעות בזה העולם הם שופעות מהשם יתעלה ולזה יחס יוסף כל הטובות השופעות לו לשם ית'. ומפני זה אמר בקריאת השמות לבניו כי נשני אלהים" כי הפרני אלהים.

התועלת השמיני הוא במדות: והוא שאין ראוי לאדם שישתדל לבטל מה שנגזר מהשם יתעלה בכמו זה העופן אשר השתדלו לבטלו אחי יוסף כשמכרוהו. כי הם חשבו שהוא רחוק שיהיה מושל עליהם אחר שהרחיקוהו מעליהם ועם היותו נמכר לעבד. וזה היה כלי אל שהגיע יוסף לתכלית הממשלה והשררה. וכזה יקרה הרבה במי שישתדל לבטל גזרות השם יתעלה בזה האופן. כמו שסופר לנו מרומוס ורומילוס, שחלם אביהם בליל לידתם ששני אודים יצאו

מנחיריו ושרפו עיר ממשלתו. וכאשר הקיץ הודיעוהו שכבר ילדה
אשתו תאומים. ושפט שהם האודים אשר חלם. וצוה להשליכם
היערה ולהמיתם שם. ונזדמנה להם שם דובה והניקה אותם. כמו
שאמרו במדרש תלים. וכאשר גדלו החריבו עיר אביהם ובנו רומי,
ובהם המשפחות הגדולות מרומי והם הדובּיים.

BEREISHIS, MEKETZ 41:50, 51, 52

50. And to Yosef were born two sons before the onset of the years of famine, whom Asnas, the daughter of Potifera, the priest of On, bore to him.

51. And Yosef called the name of the firstborn Menashe, for Hashem made me forget all of my toils and the house of my father.

52. And the second he called Ephraim, for Hashem made me fruitful in the land of my affliction.

RALBAG

The third benefit [or lesson that can be derived from this incident] is in concepts to inform [us] that all the good things that flow in abundance in this world flow in abundance from Hashem, Who is exalted. And that is why Yosef attributed all of the good things that came to him to Hashem, Who is exalted. And because of this, he stated, in the naming of his sons, "for Hashem made me forget... for Hashem made me fruitful."...

The eighth benefit [or lesson that can be derived from this incident] is in concepts. And that is, that it is not proper for a man to endeavor to nullify that which is decreed from Hashem, as the brothers of Yosef chose to nullify it [Hashem's decree] when they sold him [Yosef]. For they thought it very unlikely that he [Yosef] would rule over them after they distanced him so far from them, in conjunction with the fact that he was sold to be a servant. And this [the sale of Yosef for a slave] was the instrument for Yosef attaining the throne and the rulership.

And this occurs often with one who endeavors to nullify the de-

cree of Hashem in this fashion. As is told to us of Remus and Romulus, whose father dreamt on the night of their birth that two torches left his nostrils, and they burned the city of his rule. And when he [their father] awoke, they informed him that his wife had already given birth to twins. And he judged that these were the "torches" that he dreamt of. And he decreed that they should be thrown into a forest, and they would die there. And it happened that a female bear found them and nursed them, as they [the Rabbis] said in the Midrash Talim. And when they grew up, they destroyed the city of their father, and they built Rome.

OVERVIEW OF TEXT

Yosef was held in an Egyptian prison, where he gained renown as an interpreter of dreams. Pharaoh dreamt of seven fat cows swallowed by seven lean cows and seven bountiful stalks of corn swallowed by seven lean stalks. He sought interpretation of these dreams from the various court "experts," but all were considered unacceptable. Pharaoh then learned of *Yosef* and his abilities to understand dreams. *Yosef* was promptly removed from the jail and brought before the king.

Yosef's interpretation was that seven years of plenty would soon commence, only to be followed by seven years of famine. *Yosef* then additionally recommended that the Egyptians organize themselves to store the abundance that would grow during the first seven years. They would thereby be saved during the ensuing years of famine. *Yosef* then further advised that a wise and competent individual be appointed to head this effort.

Pharaoh then proclaimed that a wiser and more capable individual than *Yosef* could not be found for the position. *Yosef* was summarily freed from jail and granted royal powers, instantly becoming the second most powerful man in all of Egypt. He was then given a wife who bore him two sons whom

Yosef named *Menashe* and *Ephraim*.

The *Ralbag* explains that *Yosef*'s spectacular salvation and rise to power teaches the fundamental truth that all good things in this world emanate from *Hashem*. The *Ralbag* adds that *Yosef* named his sons *Menashe* and *Ephraim*, for those names allude to this theme.

The *Ralbag* also writes that *Yosef*'s dramatic ascent to royalty teaches that one should not attempt to overturn a decree of *Hashem*. Earlier, *Yosef* had prophetically dreamt[1] that his brothers would bow down before him. A component of their intention in selling *Yosef* was to thwart this vision by preventing it from occurring. Nevertheless, *Yosef*'s dream eventually came to pass. The brothers later journeyed to Egypt to purchase grain during the famine and, not realizing who he was, bowed before *Yosef*.

The *Ralbag* (quoting a *Midrash*) describes a similar turn of events in the story of Romulus and Remus, the founders of Rome. Their father had dreamt that they would one day attack his city. He therefore attempted to kill them immediately after their birth, in order to protect himself. They were abandoned and left to die in an uninhabited forest. Through the miracle

---

1.   The *Ralbag* evidently felt that *Yosef*'s dream was a prophecy rather than a mere dream. It appears that the *Ramban* (on *Bereishis* 42:9) subscribes to the same interpretation, for the *Ramban* explains that *Yosef*'s reason for not immediately revealing himself to his brothers was to bring about the fulfillment of his dream. By not revealing himself suddenly, *Yosef* caused his brothers and his father a great deal of suffering. Seemingly, this proves that *Yosef* saw his dreams as part of a Divine plan. Otherwise it would appear hard to understand how *Yosef* had the right to cause them this torment.

of being nursed by a wild bear[2] their lives were spared. They grew to adulthood only to destroy their father's city as had been predicted in the dream. They later founded Rome.

---

2. The prevailing legend of the Western world is that they were nursed by a wolf. However, the *Midrash* quoted by the *Ralbag* states that the animal was a bear.

BASIC FAITH

Part I

The *Rambam* elucidates thirteen principles of faith that should be accepted by all observant Jews. The first of those principles is "I believe with complete faith that the Creator, blessed is His Name, creates and guides all of the creations and that He alone made, makes and will make all things."

Yaakov was known for his study of Torah (*Rashi* on *Bereishis* 25:27), and by age seventeen, *Yosef* had already been taught all of the Torah that *Yaakov* learned at the *yeshivah* of *Shem* and *Ever* (*Rashi* on ibid. 37:3). *Yosef* was also a prophet (*Rashi* on ibid. 45:14) and is referred to as *Yosef Hatzaddik.* As a *tzaddik* and one of the greatest Torah scholars to have ever walked the face of the earth, *Yosef* certainly believed in the *Rambam's* first principle that all events emanate from *Hashem.*

One could perhaps understand that the turn of events led *Yosef* to recognize some heretofore-unknown abstruse kabbalistic or philosophic insight into *Hashem* and His ways. In truth, it may have very well been that *Yosef* did deepen his insights into these issues. Yet, *Yosef's* stated response to the miracle was simply the reaffirmation that all good things came from *Hashem.* That reaffirmation was behind *Yosef's* choice of what to name his sons. Didn't *Yosef* already know and accept this elementary idea? Seemingly that concept is not a revelation — even to laymen of this age!

Apparently, belief in *Hashem* is not a black and white issue — something that either exists or doesn't exist. Rather, this faith is many-tiered, and one can continually advance (or regress) from level to level. One may truly believe in *Hashem* and see His hand in daily events. However, this recognition can always be deepened, and it continually grows stronger as one draws closer to G-dliness.

Even one so utterly spiritual as *Yosef* cannot be said to have reached the ultimate level of this basic faith. *Yosef*'s experience fostered yet a deeper acceptance of the credo that all good comes from *Hashem*. Accordingly, *Yosef* chose to mention that "revelation" as the most momentous insight gleaned from his dramatic ascent from slave to king of Egypt. Even a small upgrading in one's basic faith in *Hashem* is of enormous significance.

Part II

A similar idea, but in the converse, can also be gleaned from the *Ralbag*. The *Ralbag* describes another lesson contained in this story: *Hashem*'s will cannot be overturned and events will run their course as He decreed despite human intervention to change the outcome. The brothers attempted to alter the course of future occurrences that were prophesied in *Yosef*'s dreams. Notwithstanding their efforts, all that had been forecasted came to pass, and their endeavors were proven futile.

The *Ralbag*'s analogy is to all those who attempt to change that which *Hashem* is about to do. *Yosef*'s brothers were then further compared to the father of Romulus and Remus who also attempted to elude a prophetic forecast (see foreword, part IV).

Just as *Yosef* was a great and pious individual, the same can be said of his brothers (see chapter 22, note 1). Did such *tzaddikim* really think that they could defy and change *Hashem*'s plans for the future as did the father of Romulus and Remus? They too certainly believed in the first of the *Rambam*'s Thirteen Principles.

Evidently, there are also infinite levels in one's basic conviction that he cannot defy *Hashem*. There may be a slight in-

Defining Humanity

finitesimal residual belief, albeit subconscious, that one can defy *Hashem, chalilah.* This remains true even in the case of *tzaddikim* and prophets of the highest caliber, such as *Yosef* and his brothers. According to the *Ralbag,* it was this subliminal thought within the brothers that was a pivotal factor in their decision to sell *Yosef.*

POSSIBLE APPLICATIONS

A basic component of R. *Yisrael Salanter*'s teachings in *mussar* was the necessity to continually focus on one's basic belief in *Hashem* and His punishments for wrongdoing. One might assume that one who has attained a higher level of Torah scholarship need not further develop this basic belief; it is already known and accepted.

When one thinks of people whose closeness to *Hashem* was renowned, one name that frequently comes to mind is that of the *Arizal.* Although he lived over four hundred years ago, stories still abound about his miracles and his interactions with the Heavens. This example is equally true of any other legendary *tzaddik* of any age.

According to the *Ralbag,* the Torah meant to teach all Jews that all things come from *Hashem.* Even a most sacred personality such as the *Arizal* had to continue to deepen and expand this basic lesson of faith when studying the story of *Yosef*'s rise to power.

Furthermore, even the *Arizal* could have further assimilated the notion that one cannot overturn *Hashem*'s decrees. Even *Yosef*'s brothers (who were far greater than the *Arizal*) erred because of a minuscule deficiency in this basic belief.

Certainly then, the peril posed by a small lack of faith is even greater to lesser people of later generations. People must constantly deepen the commitment to the elementary tenets of basic belief in *Hashem.*

CHAPTER 25

בראשית, מקץ מב:א,ב

א. וירא יעקב כי יש שבר במצרים ויאמר יעקב לבניו למה תתראו:
ב. ויאמר הנה שמעתי כי יש שבר במצרים רדו שמה ושברו־לנו
משם ונחיה ולא נמות:

ספורנו

למה תתראו: למה תביטו זה אל זה, וכל אחד מכם מצפה שילך
חבירו ויתור, כאמרם ז"ל "קדרא דבי שותפי לא חמימא ולא
קרירא".
ונחיה: אף על פי שלא יהיה לשובע נשיג די מחיתנו ובאופן זה -
לא נמות: ברעב.

BEREISHIS, MEKETZ 42:1,2

1. And Yaakov saw that there was food in Egypt, and Yaakov said to
his sons, "Why do you look upon each other?"
2. And he said, "Behold, I have heard that there is food in Egypt; go
down there and purchase for us there, and we will live and we will
not die."

SFORNO

Why do you look upon each other? Why do you look upon each other with each one of you expecting that your peer will undertake the journey? [This is] in keeping with their [the Rabbis of the Talmud, Eruvin 3a] saying that "A pot owned by partners neither becomes cold nor does it cook."

And we will live: Even though it will not be fully satisfying, we will acquire enough for our sustenance, and in this fashion we will not perish in the famine.

OVERVIEW OF TEXT

Yosef's interpretation of Pharaoh's dream was realized. Egypt enjoyed seven years of abundant harvests, followed by severe famine. During the period of plenty, Egypt stored the surplus food under the direction of *Yosef*. Once the famine began, there were widespread food shortages, and people began buying their grain from the storehouses of Pharaoh.

The famine also affected *Yaakov* and his family who were then living in *Eretz Yisrael*. According to the *Sforno*, it became apparent that to avoid hunger and possible death from starvation they too would have to purchase provisions in Egypt. Nevertheless, time passed, but not one member of *Yaakov's* family actually took steps to travel to Egypt. Finally, *Yaakov* came forward and commanded his children to journey to Egypt to procure food, warning them that without this purchase, they all could perish.

The *Sforno* explains that their inaction was due to the Talmudic dictum: "A pot owned by partners neither becomes cold nor does it cook."[1] *Yaakov* and all his sons were partners — members of a group that was collectively faced with the need to procure foodstuffs.

---

1.   The *Maharsha* (*Eruvin* 3a) explains the example of the pot as follows: The pot neither cooks when the partners prefer cooking, nor is it chilled when that is what they desire. The reason for the inaction is that each partner assumes that another partner will attend to the matter.

JOINT UNDERTAKINGS

The Talmud's words regarding the "pot of partners" describe a basic characteristic of group dynamics: a task placed before a body of people will tend to remain undone.

In the actual Talmudic example of the pot, the issue at hand is generally benign; whether or not a given food item is served in its optimal state is normally immaterial. But would a joint responsibility for something more crucial elicit a different outcome? What if the situation is potentially life threatening? What if the people of the group were extremely high-minded and capable? Could one expect a different response from the group? Would people then overcome their collective inertia and rise to immediate action?

The task before *Yaakov* and his sons concerned a life-and-death situation. And although all human life is precious, their lives were especially important. *Yaakov* is referred to in rabbinic literature as the chosen (most perfect) of the forefathers; his great and distinguished family was the Jewish nation of the future. If food were not procured in Egypt, they could have all died of starvation.

Why didn't they act sooner? Inaction would have endangered the lives of *Yaakov*, his sons and the Jewish people of the future. One can hardly imagine a more urgent yet doable task being placed before a more virtuous and capable group of individuals. Could there ever be a greater likelihood that a group would overcome its inertia and act? Yet they did not take action and only journeyed to Egypt after the explicit command of *Yaakov*.

The *Sforno* is teaching that the paralysis of the "pot of partners" can incapacitate people in any situation, notwithstanding the uprightness and wisdom of those involved and the gravity of the situation.

The following is illustrative: What if the lives of a group of ten extraordinary and talented people were suddenly endangered? In one scenario, those of the group had to save themselves; in a second case, their salvation was delegated to another individual of average intelligence and ability. Seemingly, three factors would render the group of people the one more likely to save themselves:

- ten people were working at the task rather than one,

- each of the ten was of greater capability and intelligence than the single other individual, and

- the ten were working to save their own lives, and their motivation was thus greater.

Nevertheless, according to the *Sforno*, the single outsider might have a greater chance of success. The dynamic of the "pot of partners" mummifies communal response, irrespective of the talents of those involved and the seriousness of the situation.[2]

From the response of *Yaakov*, one can also discern the method for overcoming this phenomenon of collective inaction. *Yaakov* understood that as an entity, the group itself would do little or nothing to save itself, mortal danger notwithstanding. *Yaakov* therefore stepped into the breach and person-

---

2.   My *rebbe* once quipped that, in fact, there really is no such thing as an organization. Every enterprise, from the smallest to the very largest, is in truth an entity for which one individual is ultimately responsible. The other members of the grouping are followers who take their cues from the leader. The same principle applies whether it is a *yeshivah* or, *lehavdil*, a business; whether it is the smallest or the largest of entities.

ally assumed control of the situation, thereby averting disaster.

A group can best realize an objective when one of its members assumes leadership and acts with cooperation and assistance from the others.

POSSIBLE APPLICATIONS

. Twentieth century Jewry endured two great holocausts. One was the German destruction of European Jewry. Another catastrophe, currently ongoing, is that Jews themselves have abandoned their own traditions. Millions are assimilating, intermarrying and being absorbed into the gentile population. The first holocaust may have been all but impossible to prevent. However, the second can be somewhat impeded by human intervention in the form of *kiruv*.

Presumably, a factor that diminishes the sense of emergency among Torah-observant Jews is the psychology of the "pot of partners." People assume that the job of outreach is being handled adequately by others, particularly by the so-called outreach professionals. In truth, despite the great accomplishments of these "professionals," much more remains to be done. The participation of all Jews is required.[3]

---

3.   A prominent *rav* recently declared that, in his opinion, it would be relatively easy to significantly change the assimilation rate among Jews. Every Torah-observant family, he argued, should make themselves a *kiruv* project of one family at a time. The outreach activity need not involve anything terribly complex. Developing respectful and friendly relationships with members of the target family together with invitations to *Shabbos* meals and some time devoted to Torah study can often gradually accomplish a complete changeover. Almost every observant family has the connection with at least one other Jewish family with whom this can be done. (There would

. . . .

Any bureaucracy, especially government, certainly falls under the category of a "pot of partners." As such, according to the Sforno, the following is veritably guaranteed: The extent of government involvement in the operation of almost any entity will likely correlate with its inefficiency and demise. The recent spectacular collapse of the Communist governments in Russia and Eastern Europe was almost entirely due to economic factors. The communist collectivization of private business that was then run by government was the ultimate "pot of partners."

---

also be a significant benefit to the host family. It is a learning experience to intelligently explain everyday observances such as those at a *Shabbos* meal. Explaining common Torah practices to an intelligent person is almost always an adventure in learning for the teacher as well.)

CHAPTER 26

בראשית, מקץ מב:כז,כח

כז. ויפתח האחד את שקו לתת מספוא לחמרו במלון וירא את
כספו והנה הוא בפי אמתחתו:
כח. ויאמר אל אחיו הושב כספי וגם הנה באמתחתי ויצא לבם
ויחרדו איש אל־אחיו לאמר מה־זאת עשה אלהים לנו:

בראשית רבה צא:ט

כד דמך ר' סימון בר זביד עאל ר' אלעא ופתח עלוהי (איוב כח)
והחכמה מאין תמצא וגו' ונעלמה מעיני כל חי וגו'... ת"ח שמת אין
אנו מוצאין תמורתו. א"ר לוי שבטים מציאה מצאו כתיב ויצא לבם
ואנו שאבדנו את ר' סימון עאכ"ו:

פירוש עץ יוסף על המדרש רבה צא:ט

שבטים מציאה מצאו: שעכשיו היה המציאה לפניהם ועכ"ז היו
דואגים וכואבים על העלילה והאבידה שאפשר לבא אח"כ ע"י
מציאה זו. אנו שהאבידה לפנינו שאבדנו את רבי סימון עאכ"ו
שנדאוג על זה. שאף שאם נמצא אח"כ צדיק אחר כדדרשו חז"ל על
פסוק וזרח השמש ובא השמש. מכל מקום להאבידה לא תשלים
המציאה.

BEREISHIS, MEKETZ 42:27,28

27. When one of them opened his sack to feed his donkey at the inn, he saw his money and, behold, it was at the mouth of his sack. 28. And he said to his brothers, "My money has been returned, and behold, it too is in my sack!" Their hearts sank, and they turned trembling one to another saying, "What is it that Hashem has done to us?"

MIDRASH RABBAH 91:9

When R. Siman bar Zvid passed away, R. Ilaya rose and began [speaking] concerning him [with the pasukim from Iyov 28:12, 13], "And from where will the wisdom be found...And it is hidden from the eyes of all living." .... A scholar who dies, we cannot find one who will replace him. R. Levi said, The tribes [the brothers of Yosef] found something [the money in the mouth of their sacks], and yet it is written that their hearts went out [they were fearful]. We who lost R. Siman, how much more so [should we be fearful]!

ETZ YOSEF on the Midrash Rabbah 91:9

The tribes found something: *For now, the thing [money] which they found was before them. Nevertheless [despite the joy of finding this large sum of money], they were very fearful and pained over the transgression and the loss that could possibly come [to them] later through this which was found. We who have this loss in front of us, that we lost R. Siman, how much more so should we be fearful of this. For even if we will later find another tzaddik, as our Rabbis learned from the pasuk, "The sun rises and the sun sets" (Koheles 1:5), nevertheless, that which is found later will not completely substitute for that which was lost.*

OVERVIEW OF TEXT

The great famine was raging, and the sons of *Yaakov* traveled to Egypt to procure food. They had difficulties with the viceroy of Egypt who, unbeknownst to them, was their brother *Yosef.* Before they left, *Yosef* had the money they paid secretly inserted in the sacks of grain they had purchased. While returning home, the brothers opened their bags and found the money that they had paid. In one respect, this was a favorable development, for they were once again in possession of a considerable sum. However, their overwhelming response was one of angst. The brothers understood that grave calamities might ensue as a result of this newfound money.[1]

The *Midrash* relates that when R. *Siman bar Zvid* passed away, the comparison was made to this incident of *Yaakov's* sons. The brothers feared what could ultimately evolve. In a similar vein, the loss of the great leader created anxiety over the future. The *Midrash* mentions but one difference between the two losses: The discovery of the money had the positive aspect of the brothers being enriched. R. *Siman's* passing, however, was totally negative.

The *Etz Yosef* asks the following: In *Koheles* (1:5) it is written: "The sun rises and the sun sets." The Talmud (*Kiddushin* 72b) interprets this to mean that "A *tzaddik* does not depart from the world until another *tzaddik* who is his equal is created." If so, why was R. Siman's demise so devastating? *Hashem's* pledge was that another Torah scholar would surely rise up to replace him.

The *Etz Yosef* answers that the words of the Talmud in *Kiddushin* ("who is his equal") must be somewhat qualified. Although there is a guarantee of a comparable replacement, the substitute will not quite measure up to the deceased scholar. R. *Ilaya* was thus bemoaning the fact that a person the exact equal of R. *Siman's* stature would never again arise.

---

1. Evidently, Torah law did not oblige them to return what was found. Nevertheless, they were fearful. Their quandary was possibly something of this nature: They were not sure if the lost money would be traced to them. If not, the money would be best left unreturned; its return, albeit voluntary, could invite questioning and antagonism. If it were not returned and later eventually traced to them, the money could cause even greater difficulty. Their protestations of innocence might not suffice.

TORAH LEADERSHIP

What were the possible long-term problems that fright-
ened the brothers? They suspected that the Egyptian (who, in
fact, was *Yosef*) might seize *Binyamin* during their next trip,
which would cause untold suffering to their father *Yaakov*. Another possibility was that he could kill, or at least forever enslave, their brother *Shimon* who was already being held hos-
tage. They also feared that this viceroy could refuse to sell
them food in the future, causing them all to possibly die of
starvation. That, in turn, would spell the end of the Jewish
people. There was thus a very grave foreboding that gripped
them when they saw their money returned.

The *Midrash* compares this situation to the problems faced
by the Jews upon the death of R. *Siman*. Only one difference is
mentioned. The tragedy faced by the brothers was somewhat
mitigated by the discovery of the money; they were personally
enriched. Otherwise, both misfortunes were comparable.

How could the loss of R. *Siman* be compared to the problem faced by the brothers? The very lives of *Yaakov*'s family
were hanging in the balance, while R. *Siman*'s death in no way
endangered life. Furthermore, it was guaranteed by *Hashem*
that R. *Siman* would be replaced by someone comparable, albeit not quite the equal of R. *Siman*.

The following historical example may place the difference
between R. *Siman* and his replacement in perspective. Thirteenth-century Spanish Jewry was led for years by R. *Moshe ben
Nachman* — the *Ramban*. Their next leader was R. *Shlomo ben
Aderes* — the *Rashba*. Both were Torah giants whose writings

have been studied continuously over the centuries. However, the *Ramban* was somewhat greater than his student, the *Rashba*. The generation that lost R. *Siman* was akin to the world of Spanish Jewry suddenly being led by the *Rashba* in place of the *Ramban*. One might argue that a community headed by the *Rashba* hardly suffers from a tragic dearth of rabbinic leadership. The difference between the two was no doubt indiscernible to all but the most learned. Nonetheless, the leadership of the post-*Ramban* world lacked a certain additional measure of Torah scholarship. The *Midrash* likens this loss to the potentially life-threatening disaster faced by the brothers when they· came upon their money. This highlights the enormous significance of every nuance of a leader's stature in Torah.

Leadership of the Jewish people by an outstanding *talmid chacham* is crucial; the substitution of a lesser scholar is catastrophic; it could physically endanger the very existence of the Jewish people.[2] This remains true even when the second leader is an outstanding, world-class Torah scholar who only falls short when compared to his predecessor.

If so, it is infinitely more disastrous when a group of Jews is headed by one who is not an accomplished *talmid chacham* by any standard.[3] A yet far greater tragedy is communal leader-

---

2. One might ask: By definition, every generation loses its leaders. Thus, if the loss of the greater *talmid chacham* is so tragic, how is it that we have always survived, seemingly without automatic ensuing tragedy? Presumably the answer is that *Hashem* helps to offset the hazard, just as He helps with other catastrophes. But if people do not do their best to protect themselves from this peril, then *Hashem* may not offer His full measure of protection.

3. When R. *Dovid Leibowitz* came to America in the 1920's he saw it as one of his responsibilities to train rabbis and educators to serve in the country's far-flung communities were Jews

ship by unobservant secular Jews who are almost altogether ignorant of Torah.[4]

lived and were terribly ignorant of Torah (see Chapter 11, Note 1). However, he established as a criteria for ordination that his students first spend a fairly long period of time in the yeshiva to imbibe the depths of Torah and *mussar* to the extent of their capacity. Only then did he see them as being adequately prepared for that task.

4.   Some seek to justify this type of leadership with the argument that rabbis should be heeded in spiritual issues, while the laity (however ignorant of Torah) is more qualified to lead in temporal matters. That reasoning is flawed, for in truth, all issues have a right and a wrong according to the Torah. Sincerity notwithstanding, one who is not steeped in Torah will surely trample upon those rights and wrongs. (The wife of a great *gadol* once revealed that when they were married they agreed that he would decide on all matters spiritual, while her view would be followed on all other issues. However, she said, the issue never arose that wasn't spiritual.)

CHAPTER 27

בראשית, ויגש מה:ד,ה,ז,ט,יא

ד. ויאמר יוסף אל־אחיו גשו־נא אלי ויגשו ויאמר אני יוסף אחיכם
אשר־מכרתם אתי מצרימה:
ה. ועתה אל תעצבו ואל־יחר בעיניכם כי־מכרתם אתי הנה כי
למחיה שלחני אלהים לפניכם:
ז. וישלחני אלהים לפניכם לשום לכם שארית בארץ ולהחיות לכם
לפליטה גדלה:
ט. מהרו ועלו אל־אבי ואמרתם אליו כה אמר בנך יוסף שמני
אלהים לאדון לכל מצרים רדה אלי אל־תעמד:
יא. וכלכלתי אתך שם כי־עוד חמש שנים רעב פן־תורש אתה וביתך
וכל־אשר־לך:

רמב"ן מה:יא

ואמר פן תורש אתה וביתך: דרך כבוד, כי לאחיו אמר כי למחיה
שלחני אלהים לפניכם, ולשום לכם שארית, שהיו מתים ולא ישאר
להם שארית, אבל לאביו לא רצה לאמר כן ואמר שאם תתעכב
בארץ כנען תורש, כי אני לא אוכל לשלוח לך לארץ כנען לחם רב
מגנזי המלך, כי יחשדו אותי שאני מוכרו שם לעשות לי שם אוצרות
כסף ולשוב אל ארצי ואל מולדתי, ובבואכם וידעו כי אתם אבי
ואחי יתן לי המלך רשות:

BEREISHIS, VAYIGASH 45:4, 5, 7, 9, 11

4. And Yosef said to his brothers: Please come near to me, and they came neaR. And he said: I am Yosef your brother, whom you sold into Egypt.

5. And now, do not be grieved nor angry with yourselves that you sold me here; for it was to keep you alive that Hashem sent me ahead of you.

7. And Hashem sent me ahead of you to insure your survival on the earth, and to sustain you alive for a great deliverance.

9. Hasten and go up to my father, and say to him: So said your son Yosef: Hashem has made me master of all Egypt; come down to me; do not tarry.

11. And I will provide for you there; for there are yet five years of famine; lest you become destitute, you and your household and all that you possess.

RAMBAN 45:11

Lest you become destitute, you and your household: *Yosef said this respectfully [out of honor to his father]. For to his brothers he said, "For it was to keep you alive that Hashem sent me ahead of you... to insure your survival," and none would survive [if they did not move to Egypt]. But he did not want to say this to his father. And [instead] he said, "If you will delay in the land of Canaan you will become impoverished." For I cannot send you abundant food from the royal storehouse as they [the Egyptians] will suspect me of selling it there [in Israel] so as to accumulate treasures of money there and to [then] return to my land and my birthplace. But when you come here [to Egypt], and they will know that you are my father and brothers, the king will give me permission [to sustain you].*

OVERVIEW OF TEXT

The great famine predicted in Pharaoh's dreams, as interpreted by *Yosef*, persisted. As a result, *Yaakov's* sons had to undertake a scond journey to Egypt in order to purchase food necessary for survival. Unbeknownst to them, the viceroy of Egypt who oversaw these transactions was, in fact, their brother *Yosef* whom they had sold into slavery years earlier.

Yosef finally revealed his true identity and then attempted to assuage his brothers' embarrassment over what they had done to him. *Yosef* explained that *Hashem's* prophetic plan was that he should rise to an influential position in order to save his entire family from death by starvation. *Yosef* then went on to urge his brothers to journey homeward and to then return, bringing *Yaakov* and the entire family. Once in Egypt, they could live with honor in the area of *Goshen* while being sustained by *Yosef*.

The message that *Yosef* relayed to his father was somewhat different from what he communicated to his brothers. To his brothers *Yosef* said that *Hashem* sent him to save their lives (*pasuk* 5). To his father (*pasuk* 11) he spoke of being sent by *Hashem* to prevent their becoming destitute (if they had to remain in *Eretz Yisrael* and spend their entire fortune on food).

The *Ramban* explains that *Yosef's* shift in language was very deliberate. The actual truth was the message he conveyed to his brothers: ignoring *Yosef's* offer of help could result in their demise. However, openly confronting *Yaakov* with this reality involved a certain departure from the respect due *Yaakov*. It would be tantamount to saying that the very life of the father was in the hands of the son. *Yosef* therefore understated the urgency and sent a different message to *Yaakov*: moving to Egypt was necessary to avoid poverty. This was more deferential for it stated only that the son would help the father retain his wealth.

RESPECT

It is apparent from the *Ramban* that it was only the special *derech eretz* due *Yaakov* as a parent that prevented *Yosef*
from speaking more directly. Wouldn't *Yosef* speak most respectfully even without these special considerations? Furthermore, when addressing his brothers, *Yosef* opted for the less respectful approach, and he spoke more directly. Why didn't he
also accord them the respect of speaking more indirectly?

In truth, there was a good reason to speak directly. From
the fact that *Yosef* launched into these arguments it is apparent that *Yaakov* and his sons had to be convinced to move. As
such, a more forceful message provided greater assurances
that *Yaakov* and his family would be saved.

Thus, in acting with respect, *Yosef* was somewhat compromising his attempts to save his father (and the Jewish nation of the future). Why then was *Yosef's* approach proper at
all? Was the deference of more delicate speech appropriate if it
heightened the danger to *Yaakov's* life?

Evidently, the protocols of *derech eretz* largely define the
parameters within which a person must function. Words that
transgress upon that propriety are malapropos — even those
that are of vital importance. *Yaakov's* interests would have
been best served by a jolting and brutally honest message.
However, since that direct approach violated *derech eretz*, it
was deemed unacceptable. More respectful words were utilized despite the possible consequences.[1]

---

1.   A similar idea can be found in the *Ramban* in *Bereishis* 39:12.

In a case of immediate mortal danger, the *halachic* imperative to save that life preempts all other prohibitions of the Torah, save three exceptions. Accordingly, if rescuing a life entails disrespect, one must do so regardless. Why then did *Yosef* diminish his efforts to save *Yaakov* due to the factor of respect?

In truth, the situation facing *Yosef* was different from typical danger to life for at least two reasons: (1) The threat was not immediate, for it involved a future danger; perhaps the morrow would bring *Yaakov* a different salvation. (2) *Yosef* did partially discuss the urgency at hand, and *Yaakov* could have surmised that it was his life and not just his money that was endangered. Therefore, this was not a case of a *halachic* imperative to save a life. As such, *Yosef*'s communication to *Yaakov* was bound by the conventions of *derech eretz.*

(Similarly, in the case of *Yosef* (see note 1), there was no certainty that leaving his garment with *Potifar*'s wife would prove dangerous; perhaps she would ignore the incident and continue her attempts to seduce him. Hence, it was not a case

---

The Torah there describes the attempts of the wife of *Potifar* to seduce *Yosef* (see chapter 23). On a day when they were alone in her house, she grabbed his clothing, at which point he fled, leaving the garment in her hand. The *Ramban* explains that *Yosef* had the strength to easily wrest the item from her hand, but refrained from doing so out of respect toward his master's wife.

How much *derech eretz* was due to one who was ceaselessly enticing him to adultery? Additionally, *Yosef* must have realized that his garment might be used as false evidence against him, as it eventually was. Therefore, leaving it in her hands could have possibly endangered his life (see *Ibn Ezra* 39:19). Nevertheless, the imperative to act with *derech eretz* was deemed a higher priority.

of a *halachic* threat to his life. Consequently, *Yosef* was duty-bound by *derech eretz* to refrain from seizing his garment.)

POSSIBLE APPLICATIONS

The idea and ethic of the *Ramban* can impact upon virtually every human conversation. It was more important to address *Yaakov* with the *derech eretz* that was his due than to have a somewhat better chance at saving his life. Certainly then, there is an obligation to always address others with honor when there is no such imperative for disrespect.

. . . .

To one extent or another, most people attempt to impress upon others the mores they deem proper. Parents seek to raise their children with their own value system. Rabbis and teachers attempt the same with congregants and students.

As the passion of these attempts grows, the peril of a corresponding breakdown of *derech eretz* may also increase. For example, a burning drive to promulgate ideas of the Torah is certainly praiseworthy. However, that intense drive can result in a disregard for the Torah's obligation to communicate respectfully. One may mistakenly consider the cause too urgent to be hampered by the niceties of respect. The *Ramban* is teaching that, notwithstanding their urgency, disrespectful words should normally be modified or left unsaid.[2]

---

2.   R. *Moshe Feinstein, z"l*, once answered a questioner in a manner that reflects this idea. A young man had left his small town to study at a large *yeshivah*, and returned home for holidays. While away, he adopted the *yeshivah*'s custom of taking a fairly long time to recite the *Shemoneh Esreh*. Doing so in his hometown *shul* would mean finishing *Shemoneh Esreh* long

after the local *rav*. The locals, who had never attended a *yeshivah*, could misconstrue that as being somewhat disrepectful and disparaging to the rabbi.

R. *Moshe* was asked: Should the young man finish *Shemoneh Esreh* after the *rav*? R. *Moshe* answered, *Chalilah*! The young man should not in any way even appear to be lessening the honor of the *rav*. Rather, he should observe *derech eretz* and *daven* more quickly, and he would still be capable of devout prayer.

A fairly distressing sight is that of the hometown rabbi speaking from the pulpit when a *yeshivah* student is at home. Thinking the content beneath him, the student begins studying Torah from a *sefer*, in plain view of all, while the rabbi is speaking. That is likely a flagrant violation of the *Ramban's* definition of *derech eretz*. That is because his Torah study at that time entails acting with enormous disrespect for the *rav*.

CHAPTER 28

בראשית, ויגש מו:לד

ואמרתם אנשי מקנה היו עבדיך מנעורינו ועד־עתה גם־ אנחנו גם־
אבתינו בעבור תשבו בארץ גשן כי־תועבת מצרים כל־רעה צאן:

רש"י

בעבור תשבו בארץ גשן: והיא צריכה לכם שהיא ארץ מרעה,
וכשתאמרו לו שאין אתם בקיאין במלאכה אחרת, ירחיקכם מעליו
ויושיבכם שם.
כי תועבת מצרים וגו': לפי שהם להם אלהות:

שפתי חכמים על רש"י

לפי שהם יודעים שהרועים רועי הצאן יודעין הוויתן לפי שהם
תמיד אצלן הלכך יודעין שאין בהם ממש, הלכך שונאים כל רועי
צאן.

BEREISHIS, VAYIGASH 46:34

And you will say, Your servants were cattlemen from our youth until

now, both we and our forefathers, so that you should dwell in the
land of Goshen, for all shepherds are abhorrent to the Egyptians.

RASHI

So that you should dwell in the land of Goshen: *And you re-*
quire that, for it is a land of grazing. And when you tell him [Pha-
raoh] that you know no other craft, he will move you away from him
and settle you there [in the land of Goshen].

For all shepherds are abhorrent to the Egyptians: *For they*
[sheep] are a god to them [the Egyptians].

SIFSEI CHACHAMIM on Rashi

For they [sheep] are a god to them [the Egyptians]: *For they*
[the Egyptians] know that shepherds who herd sheep know the real-
ity [of sheep], for they are always with them [sheep]. Therefore, they
[shepherds] know that there is nothing at all [godly] to them.
Therefore, they [the Egyptians] hate all shepherds.

OVERVIEW OF TEXT

Yosef and his brothers, who were about to settle in Egypt,
were discussing their upcoming encounter with Pharaoh. It
was anticipated that Pharaoh would question the brothers
about their occupation. Yosef advised them to emphasize that
they were shepherds who really knew no other trade. This was
so that Pharaoh would agree to have them dwell in the land of
Goshen that was well suited to grazing.

Yosef then added that the Egyptians hated shepherds.
Rashi explains that the reason for this hatred was because
sheep were Egyptian gods. Why did the Egyptian worship of
sheep engender their hatred of shepherds? The Sifsei
Chachamim explains that shepherds who spend a great deal of
time with sheep see firsthand that there is no divinity to these
animals. It was that cognition of shepherds that earned them
the enmity of the Egyptians.

DEFENDING FALSE BELIEFS

Yosef's brothers, as shepherds who spent time with sheep, had an "insider's view" of those animals. As such, their conception of the true nature of sheep differed from the widely held Egyptian view. They realized the folly of investing these very earthy creatures with godly characteristics.

On a purely rational level, people shown the errors of their religious beliefs would recant and change their belief system. The new but truthful wisdom could prevent their widespread worship of a sham. The sheep-worshiping Egyptians should thus have abandoned their idol-worship and then gratefully lauded and thanked the shepherds for their deeper insight. Instead, the Egyptians reacted by abhorring all shepherds.

Certainly, in a typical scenario, a person does not automatically detest anyone who differs on a given issue. There are probably no two people who agree fully on all subjects, and yet, these differences typically do not lead to mutual hatred. Why did the Egyptians react so negatively?

The language of the *Sifsei Chachamim* is: "They [shepherds] know that there is nothing at all [godly] to them [sheep]. Therefore, they [the Egyptians] hate all shepherds." The Egyptians did not react because the shepherds had a different view of the sheep. Rather, it was because the Egyptians themselves sensed that the shepherds were the ones who had the truthful perception of the sheep; they clearly understood that the Egyptian religious belief (that attributed divinity to sheep) was based on a foolish and false assumption.

Apparently, on some, possibly subconscious, level, the Egyptians recognized the absurdity of their own belief system.[1] Nonetheless, they chose to perpetuate their practices and live with the fraud. But the awareness that others perceive one's irrationality and inconsistency is highly unsettling. Rather than to simply stand corrected, the Egyptian reaction was to persist in their foolish notion and "kill the bearer of bad tidings" — they despised the shepherds who understood their folly.[2]

Bogus expressions of religion with legions of followers, workers and contributors have always been a classic component of society. Seemingly, those adherents are absolutely certain that their beliefs are correct without a shred of doubt! Nevertheless, the *Sifsei Chachamim* implies that on some level, that same person may be aware of the underlying inconsistencies and falsehoods of his own belief system. He must therefore erect a defense mechanism to remove the nagging dis-

---

1.   That the Egyptians were aware of the foolishness of their beliefs is borne out by the language of the *Sifsei Chachamim*. "They [shepherds] *know* that there is nothing at all [godly] to them [sheep]." In acknowledging that the view of the shepherds was correct, the Egyptians were also in effect stating that their own position was incorrect. Yet, the Egyptians clung to their own false religion while hating those who discerned the truth.

2.   One might ask, Perhaps the Egyptians feared being mocked by the shepherds and they responded out of the instinct of self-protection. That is not likely because the brothers were hardly in a position to mock the Egyptian populace and their Pharaoh; they were guests who were forced to flee their land because of famine. Furthermore, the text does not indicate anything that suggests that the fear of censure or ridicule was behind the Egyptian reaction. Rather, it was simply that the Egyptians despised those who recognized their foolishness.

comfort that accompanies the subliminal cognition of his own folly.

One subconscious defense mechanism is to irrationally cling to false beliefs and to then harbor a loathing for those who discern the truth. This subconscious response is certainly full of illogic. Hatred for those who recognize folly will not rectify one's own false belief system. Nevertheless, this is how people often respond in order to protect their beliefs. That loathing evidently brings them a measure of psychic relief. Deep sincerity and honesty is required to first recognize and then successfully deal with one's own mistaken ideas (see chapter 32, note 4).

POSSIBLE APPLICATIONS

A person who has adopted a mistaken belief may suddenly find himself personally disliking upstanding individuals who do not agree with his flawed thinking. This is the subconscious reaction described by the *Sifsei Chachamim*. However, one may then gravitate to an entirely different social circle where others are more in step with one's misguided doctrine. This new group of friends will in turn further enforce the error in thought. The consequences can affect generations.

. . . .

Even within the camp of traditional Judaism, there are groups of Jews whose practices may have drifted somewhat from Torah. On the right there are extremist types whose Torah zeal may, upon occasion, encroach on principles of that same Torah; on the left there are some who take liberties with normative *halachah* and time-honored *hashkafah*.

Very often, there is a fairly observable warning flag waving atop both camps. That flag is a prevalent attitude of personal animosity, characterized by constant criticism, directed at other Jews who do not subscribe to their views. Yet, although in most disputes between people both parties participate equally, this almost personal hostility is typically not reciprocal. The words of the *Sifsei Chachamim* explain the paradox. The hostility is not part of a fued in which case it would be reciprocal; rather it is the function of a defense mechanism.

Another sadly common phenomenon of current times is the more overt and public antagonism of many of the non-Orthodox camp to their Orthodox Jewish brethren, both in and out of Israel. Once again, the antagonism is generally not mutual, and again, the words of the *Sifsei Chachamim* help explain the phenomenon.

It could almost be said that it is a tellingly negative sign if incessant criticism and ill will characterize a person's conversation regarding other groups of Jews and members of those other groups. Based on the *Sifsei Chachamim* one wonders, "Why does he have the need to constantly berate those others? Perhaps it is his own defective belief system that begets this enmity?"

CHAPTER 29

בראשית, ויגש מז:כ,כא

כ. ויקן יוסף את כל אדמת מצרים לפרעה כי מכרו מצרים איש שדהו כי חזק עליהם הרעב ותהי הארץ לפרעה:
כא. ואת־העם העביר אתו לערים מקצה גבול־מצרים ועד־קצהו:

רש"י

כא. ואת העם העביר: יוסף מעיר לעיר, לזכרון שאין להם עוד חלק בארץ, והושיב של עיר זו בחברתה, ולא הוצרך הכתוב לכתוב זאת, אלא, להודעיך שבחו של יוסף, שנתכוין להסיר חרפה מעל אחיו שלא יהו קורין אותם גולים (חולין ס:):

רש"י על חולין ס-ב
כי היכי דלא ליקרו: מצרים לאחיו לאחר זמן גולים בני גולים לכך הגלם.

נחלת יעקב על רש"י

בפ' אלו טרפות (דף ס') ופרש"י שם כי היכי דלא ליקרו מצרים
לאחיו לאחר זמן גולים בני גולים לכך הגלם ע"כ... ועוד הוקשה לו
דאיך יעלה על דעת מצרים לזלזלם ולקרותם גולים בהיות יוסף
המושל עליהם ובלעדו לא ירים דקדק לאחר זמן כלומר לאחר
מיתת יוסף ולפי זה הוקשה לו דמסתמא כשימות יוסף ימות כל
הדור וא"כ למי יקראו גולים לכן דקדק בני גולים שיקראו אותם
בני גולים ודברים אלו נאים הם לו וכאן קיצר במובן.

בכור שור

ואת העם העביר אותו לערים: שהיה מיישב אנשי עיר אחת
בעיר אחרת ומחליף את יושבי עיר בעיר לפי שקנה אדמתם, שלא
יחזרו ויחזיקו בארץ לאחר זמן, לומר כל אחד על שדהו: זה של
אבותי היה מעולם, וירושתי מעולם ויחזיק כל אחד בשלו, ולפיכך
העבירם שלא יהיה להם טענה במה שבידו, ותהא מוחזקת ביד
פרעה.

BEREISHIS, VAYIGASH 47:20,21

20. And Yosef bought all of the land of Egypt for Pharaoh, for the Egyptians sold, every man his field, for the famine had overwhelmed them; and the land became Pharaoh's.

21. And the people he [Yosef] transferred into cities from one end of the border of Egypt to the other end.

RASHI

21. And the people he [Yosef] transferred: Yosef [moved them] from city to city as a reminder that they no longer had any portion in the land. And he settled [the people] of one city into another. And it was not necessary for the pasuk to write this, only to let you know the praise of Yosef, that he intended [thereby] to remove the stigma from his brothers, so that [the Egyptians] should not call them exiles (Chullin 60b).

RASHI on Chullin 60b

So that after some time the Egyptians would not call his brothers *"exiles, the sons of exiles."*

NACHALAS YAAKOV on Rashi

In perek Eilu Treifus [a chapter in tractate Chullin] Rashi explains that it was so that the Egyptians would not call his brothers in later times "exiles, the sons of exiles." Therefore, he [Yosef] exiled them [the Egyptians]... And he [Rashi] had another difficulty: How could the Egyptians possibly abuse them and call them exiles with Yosef being the ruler over all of them? And [it is written] "Without you [Yosef] no man will raise his arm?" (Bereishis 41:44). Therefore, he surmised that it was a reference to later times, meaning after the death of Yosef. Consequently, what he [Rashi] found difficult was that, probably, when Yosef would die, all of that generation would [also] perish. And if so who would they refer to as exiles? Therefore, he [Rashi] deduced "sons of exiles," that they [the Egyptians] would call them [the Jews] "sons of exiles."

And these words are beautifully appropriate to him [Rashi] but here [in the Chumash] he wrote cryptically.

BECHOR SHOR

And the people he [Yosef] transferred into cities *He [Yosef] settled the people of one city into another city and exchanged the residents of one city with another, for he had acquired their land. [And this was done] so that they should not return and take hold of their own land at a later time, each man saying about his field, "This always belonged to my forefathers, and it always was my inheritance." And they would each grab onto their own. Therefore, he moved them so that they should not have [such] a claim regarding that which was theirs, and [it would therefore] remain secured in the hands of the Pharaoh.*

OVERVIEW OF TEXT

The effects of the great famine predicted by *Yosef* intensified. The Egyptians were forced to purchase their food from *Yosef*, who represented Pharaoh. After exhausting their capital, the Egyptians had to sell their lands to pay for their food.

Eventually, Pharaoh owned all of the land in Egypt.

Yosef then relocated the entire Egyptian populace from one area of the country to another. *Rashi* (quoting the Talmud, *Chullin* 60b) explains that *Yosef* instituted the forced migration to prevent the Egyptians from referring to *Yosef's* brethren as exiles. *Rashi* in *Chullin* writes that the epithet would be "exiles, the sons of exiles." The commentary of the *Nachalas Yaakov* asks and answers several questions on *Rashi*. The *Nachalas Yaakov* concludes by explaining *Rashi* to mean that *Yosef* acted to prevent subsequent generations of Egyptians from invoking this insult toward the Jews of their time.

NACHALAS YAAKOV: *A Partial Synopsis*

If *Yosef* was the most powerful individual in Egypt aside from Pharaoh, why did he fear that the Egyptians would mock his family? The *Nachalas Yaakov* answers that during *Yosef's* lifetime, the ridicule of his family would not occur. However, there was fear of the family being maligned after *Yosef's* death. By that time, *Yosef's* immediate family members would have likewise died. So who then would be mocked? The answer given is that the Egyptians would ridicule the next generation — the descendants of the original exiles. That is why *Rashi* on *Chullin* wrote that the slur would be "exiles, the sons of exiles." The *Nachalas Yaakov* concludes that both *Rashi*s are in agreement. *Rashi* on *Vayigash*, however, was written more cryptically.

The *Bechor Shor* has an entirely different explanation of why *Yosef* uprooted and transplanted the Egyptians. The *Bechor Shor* explains that *Yosef* acted to prevent the Egyptians from one day arguing that their homes were their ancestral property. This claim would allow them to illegally contest Pharaoh's legitimate ownership of their former properties. By moving all of them elsewhere, *Yosef* prevented them from ever posing this challenge. (The Chizkuni has a similar interpretation.)

A) EMBARRASSMENT

The Talmud (*Bava Metzia* 59A) writes "He who embarrasses a friend has no portion in the World to Come...Better to throw oneself into a fiery furnace and [thereby] not embarrass a friend in public." Quoting *Dovid Hamelech*, the Talmud continues: "An adulterer is executed by *chenek* and has a portion in the World to Come. But he who embarrasses someone publicly loses his portion [earned through other meritorious deeds] of the World to Come." Publicly embarrassing a fellow Jew is a terrible sin.

Bava Metzia deals with the sin of the one who actually embarrasses someone else. However, in this case, it was not *Yosef* himself who would be dishonoring the Jews; furthermore, the embarrassment wouldn't occur during *Yosef*'s lifetime. Rather, *Yosef* acted to make certain that Egyptians of a later generation would not embarrass the descendants of his family.

It should also be noted that being called "exiles, the sons of exiles" was not excessively derogatory. In *Bereishis* 46:3,4, *Hashem* assured *Yaakov* that He would one day redeem him (his family). *Avraham* had received similar guarantees (*Bereishis* 15:14). *Yaakov*, no doubt, transmitted these basic promises of redemption to his children.[1] The knowledge that their exile status was not a permanent condition must have somewhat inured the Jews to the taunts of the Egyptians. Furthermore, since *Yaakov* himself was also exiled, these "exiles, the sons of exiles" were among distinguished company. Yet, *Yosef* went to such great lengths to prevent this embarrassment, however slight, from occurring.

This teaches that it is not enough to merely refrain from personally embarrassing a fellow Jew. Even others who were not involved in the activity have the obligation to go to great lengths, if necessary, to prevent that embarrassment from ever occurring. This is why *Yosef* uprooted the entire Egyptian nation.

Another consideration facing *Yosef* was the Torah's ethic of not inconveniencing a community. Even causing a group of people to wait a few seconds is significant.[2] Yet, to accomplish his goal, and despite the factor of only "minimal" future embarrassment to the Jews, *Yosef* did far more than ask the Egyptians to wait for a few moments. He uprooted the entire nation, forcing them to move from one end of the country to another.

Whether this ethic applies in its full measure to relation-

1.　There is another indication that the Jews were aware of their eventual redemption from Egypt. When the *mishkan* was subsequently built in the desert, the Jews used materials that *Yaakov* had brought with him when moving to Egypt (*Midrash Tanchuma, Terumah,* 9. *Yaakov* instructed his family to care for these items so that they would be available for the construction of the *mishkan* following their redemption.

2.　In the laws of Torah reading (*Orach Chaim* 139:4) there is a striking example of this ethic. Ideally, when a person is called for an *aliyah* to the Torah, the following order should be observed: (a) One should first look at the opened page of the Torah and then (b) roll the Torah closed, and then (c) recite the blessing and then (d) open the Torah again so that it can be read. However, this would necessitate causing the congregation to wait for the Torah to be rolled closed and then opened. It is therefore *halachically* preferable to keep the Torah open and recite the blessing while closing one's eyes. To avert the one or two second imposition on the public, the *halachah* opts for the otherwise less optimal method of reciting the *berachos* with one's eyes closed.

ships with Egyptians is questionable. However, in a general sense, the great people of that era acted with enormous kindness to gentiles. For example, *Avraham* welcomed his idol-worshiping guests with unrivaled magnanimity (see chapter 8). Presumably, *Yosef* was bound by the same ideology, at least to the extent that he should not have seriously troubled so many people, unless for very urgent reasons.

Furthermore, *Yosef* had the additional factor of gratitude defining his relationship with the Egyptians. At that point, the Egyptians had just saved the lives of *Yaakov's* family and had not yet begun to enslave them. *Yosef* was obligated to show them gratitude and respect. From the *Ramban, Devarim* 23:7, it is evident that, notwithstanding the slavery that ensued, Jews still bear a debt of gratitude to the Egyptians for welcoming *Yaakov* and his family and sparing them from starvation. Certainly at that time, which was before the slavery commenced, gratitude was a factor preventing *Yosef* from so inconveniencing the entire Egyptian nation.

Yosef went to such enormous lengths to prevent the minimal embarrassment that would take place, during a later generation, at the hands of other individuals. If so, one is certainly required to avoid personally dishonoring or shaming a fellow Jew in the here and now!

POSSIBLE APPLICATIONS

There are those who wrongly believe that, under certain conditions, one may embarrass others. For example:

- At certain types of social gatherings, there is a roast, featuring "good-natured" ridicule.
- Some groups have the practice of presenting a *Purim* play, during which time fun is often poked at individuals very

publicly.

• Occasionally, a person may do something drastically
  wrong. Some may then feel the need to make a statement,
  by publicly refusing to speak to him or to even remain in a
  room when he is present.[3]

All of the above examples involve publicly embarrassing a
fellow Jew. Unless sanctioned by explicit *halachic* mandate,
they are all forbidden. *Rashi* and the *Nachalas Yaakov* teach that
even individuals uninvolved in the wrongful activity must go
to great lengths to see that this embarrassment does not occur,
even if it will take place only in a later era. Certainly, those actually perpetuating this sin are most blameworthy; they are also
endangering their entire portion in the World to Come.

---

3.   In truth, one is permitted to embarrass a person labeled by
      halachah as a sinner. The laws of the Torah that protect him are
      waived. Regarding this concept, my *rebbe* has often quoted the
      Chofetz Chaim's commentary to *Mishpatim* 23:4. The *Chofetz
      Chaim* wrote that in his time, most out-and-out "sinners" were
      not really rebellious against *Hashem*. To truly defy *Hashem*, one
      must first know a great deal about Him. The *Chofetz Chaim* felt
      that this level of knowledge was almost nonexistent in his gen-
      eration. He considered the people of his era to be misled rather
      than true sinners. Therefore, the protections of the Torah re-
      mained intact in their cases.
          This was written with regard to late-nineteenth- or early-twentieth-
      century east European Jewry. If so, certainly in this day and
      age, few if any could be labeled sinners. Thus, there is almost
      never a dispensation that allows one Jew to embarrass another
      publicly, claiming him to be a sinner. Doing so involves the
      possible forfeiture of one's place in the World to Come.

B) ENABLING WRONGDOING

In order to secure the land legally purchased by Pharaoh, *Yosef* relocated the Egyptians. The *Bechor Shor* explains this would prevent the Egyptians from one day claiming that the land they had sold was their ancestral property, and was therefore still theirs.

Actually, this argument alone is almost meaningless, for even ancestral land could have been sold. It must be that the Egyptians also meant to imply that the sale of the land was not legal. But this begs the question — why was their claim presented in such a roundabout and logically vulnerable fashion? Instead, they should have simply stated that either they had never sold their land or that the sale was invalid. Evidently, they could never overtly deny that a legal sale had occurred; that was obvious to all. But if so, what was achieved by the specious argument that invoked the issue of ancestral land?

This "peculiar" Egyptian response that *Yosef* sought to preclude illuminates a most unusual yet prevalent tendency within the human personality. The Egyptian focus on the factor of ancestral land was not solely for the purpose of deluding *Yosef*. Rather, it was their own internal rationalization process that was needed to pave the way for the illegal land grab that would ensue.

In fact, this is an everyday phenomenon. Proponents of society's most depraved behavior tend to cloak their beliefs in high-sounding terms. For example, the Torah forbids abortion in most cases, but proponents of that right speak of "freedom to choose" (rather than freedom to kill a fetus). Adulterers speak of "open marriage," male homosexuals are "gay," and cowardly cutthroats that bomb women in supermarkets are "radicals." Even the murderous Germans had the need to becloud their evil carnage in World War II with self-justifying verbiage (i.e., talk of racial *purity* or the final *solution*).

On a more personal level as well, one constantly hears many unusual ideas that justify improper behavior as it is happening.

However, it is unfortunately far easier to perceive the unusual in the thinking of others than it is in one's own self. Man has the capacity to be unaware of his improprieties and equally blind to the illogic of the rationale that allows these deeds to be committed. Great sagacity and integrity are needed to overcome the distortions of this ubiquitous bias (see chapter 32, note 4).

CHAPTER 30

בראשית, ויחי מט:כא

נפתלי אילה שלחה הנתן אמרי־שפר:

רש"י

...ורבותינו דרשוהו על יום קבורת יעקב, כשערער עשו על המערה, במסכת סוטה (יג).

סוטה יג-א

כיון שהגיעו למערת המכפלה אתא עשו וקא מעכב וכו' אמרו ליה זבינתה וכו' אמר להו הבו לי איגרת אמרו ליה איגרתא בארעא דמצרים היא ומאן ניזיל ניזיל נפתלי דקליל כאילתא וכו', חושים בן דן תמן הוה ויקירן ליה אודניה אמר להו מאי האי אמרי ליה קא מעכב האי עד דייתי נפתלי מארעא דמצרים אמר להו ועד דאתי נפתלי מארעא דמצרים יהא אבי אבא מוטל בבזיון שקל קולפא מחייה ארישיה וכו'.

מהר"ל על סוטה יג-א

חושים בן דן תמן הוה ויקירן ליה אדנא: ומה שלא עשה א' מן
השבטים האחרים, זהו מפני כי לא היו חושבים מתחלת המעשה
שיהיו צריכים לדבר זה, וכאשר התחיל עשו לחלוק לא היה נמצא
אצלם ההתעוררות, שאין כח ההתעוררות נמצא בתחלה רק כאשר
הדבר ההוא (בכח) [חדוש לו] מאוד כאשר נודע, ואז הוא מתעורר
בכח לעשות מעשה, וחושים בן דן שלא ידע מתחלה המעשה כלום,
וכאשר כבר היו במחלוקת והוצרכו לשלוח אחר הראיה, ואז נאמר
לו לחושים בן דן ואז היה מתעורר בכח להרוג את עשו.

BEREISHIS, VAYECHI 49:21

Naftali is a hind let loose who delivers beautiful sayings.

RASHI

...And our Rabbis interpreted it in reference to the day of Yaakov's burial, when Eisav contested the ownership of the cave [of Machpelah], as explained in the Talmud [Sotah 13a].

TALMUD SOTAH 13a

When they arrived at the Cave of Machpelah, Eisav came and prevented them [from proceeding with the burial]. They [the brothers] said to him, "He [Yaakov] bought it [the grave]." He [Eisav] said to them, "Although I sold my birthright, this [the burial plot] I did not sell. Bring me written proof of this sale." They said to him, "We have a letter [written proof] in the land of Egypt. Who should go to fetch it? Let Naftali, who is light-footed like a hind, go."

Chushim ben Dan [one of Yaakov's grandsons], who was hard of hearing, was there [at the graveside]. He said to them, "What is this [discussion with Eisav about]?" They said to him, "He is preventing [the burial] until Naftali returns from the land of Egypt." He [Chushim] said to them, "And until Naftali comes from the land of Egypt will my father's father be lying in shame?" He took a lance and struck him [Eisav] on the head.

MAHARAL on Talmud Sotah 13a

And [concerning the fact] that none of the other tribes did this [striking of Eisav until Chushim finally did it], it is because they did not think from the start of the incident that they would be required to do this. And when Eisav began to dispute [their course of action], they did not have the emotional arousal [to perform the act], for the power of emotional arousal begins only when the matter is very new to him when it first becomes known. Then, he can be powerfully incited to perform an act.

And Chushim ben Dan, who did not know anything from the beginning of the incident, and it was only after they were involved in dispute [with Eisav] and were required to send [Naftali] for the proof, and [subsequently] it was told to Chushim ben Dan, then he was emotionally aroused with the strength to kill Eisav.

OVERVIEW OF TEXT

The body of Yaakov was brought from Egypt to be interred in the Cave of Machpelah in the city of Chevron in Eretz Yisrael. Upon arrival at their destination, Eisav appeared and confronted Yaakov's family. He claimed that as the eldest son, he was the owner of the cave's one remaining grave, and the funeral should therefore not proceed.

The brothers countered that Eisav had sold Yaakov his rights to the burial place (see Rashi, Bereishis 50:5). When Eisav asked for written proof, the brothers replied that the supporting documents had been left in Egypt. Eisav persisted, so Naftali was dispatched to Egypt to return with the paperwork. Until his return, Yaakov's body would have remained unburied.

Chushim ben Dan, a grandson of Yaakov, did not follow the discussion because he was hard of hearing. Sensing a problem, Chushim inquired as to why the burial was being postponed. His relatives explained that Eisav had compelled them to delay the funeral until Naftali could fetch documents from

Egypt. Enraged over the indignity to the body of his grandfather, *Chushim* struck *Eisav's* head with a lance. *Eisav* was killed,[1] and the burial was promptly concluded.

Chushim's reaction is considered by the Torah to have been proper and appropriate. The *Maharal* therefore asks why *Yaakov's* sons didn't kill *Eisav* themselves. The *Maharal* answers that because the others heard *Eisav's* arguments as they were being presented, they only realized in stages that *Eisav* was seriously impeding their plans. Thus, they had time to acclimatize themselves to *Eisav's* words and their ramifications. Accordingly, their ire was not suddenly aroused at any one

---

1.   The sin of delaying a funeral is certainly not a capital offense. Nevertheless, the commentaries seem unconcerned with the justification for slaying *Eisav*. To the contrary, the *Maharal* questioned why someone other than *Chushim* didn't kill *Eisav* sooner. Why indeed was it permissible to execute *Eisav*?

Perhaps the answer is that *Eisav* was governed by the law of a *rodef* (*Choshen Mishpat* 425:1). Person A becomes a *rodef* if he is attempting to murder person B. The *halachah* states that all are commanded to kill A, if that is what is necessary to save B.

On at least two previous occasions *Eisav* had taken steps to kill *Yaakov*. After being blessed by his father, *Yaakov* fled to *Charan* because *Eisav* was plotting to kill him. When *Yaakov* returned home with his family, *Eisav* and four hundred armed men accosted him. It was only a last-minute change of heart that prevented *Eisav* from carrying out his murderous plan. Presumably, his basically bloodthirsty designs had not changed. Furthermore, according to the *Eitz Yosef* (on *Ein Yaakov* in *Sotah*), *Eisav's* real scheme in delaying the burial was to initiate a battle and murder *Yaakov's* family. And they may have sensed his true intent.

Eisav was thus likely considered a *rodef* whom they were all required to eliminate. However, it was only *Chushim* who was actually capable of the act.

given point. *Chushim*, however, was apprised at once of the entire incident. When incitement occurs suddenly, emotional intensity is at its greatest. *Chushim* was therefore "aroused with the strength to kill *Eisav*."

DEPTH OF FEELING

The *halachah* (*Yoreh Deah* 357) considers it an indignity if a body isn't promptly buried. Normally, burial is only delayed for such reasons as arranging a more prestigious funeral. *Eisav*, who certainly knew that he had sold his rights to the site, was deliberately delaying the interment. The children were forced to stand idly by as the body of their illustrious father lay unburied before them. Presiding over this painful delay, no doubt, agitated and enraged them all to the extreme. However, because of the gradual unfolding of the scene, they were, to a minute degree, less inflamed than *Chushim*. That small extra measure of passion led *Chushim* to react when the others did not.

There is, however, a question. If it was proper to kill *Eisav* (see note 2) why didn't they do so, even if their emotions were at a slightly less intense pitch? Evidently, the brothers felt physically incapable of overcoming *Eisav*. They surely called to the fore every ounce of their capacity: physical, intellectual and spiritual. But they were unequal to the task. Proof of such is that the Torah does not criticize them for their inaction.

Chushim was different. His additional surge of emotional arousal infused him with an extra measure of strength. Consequently, the same task that was impossible for *Yaakov's* sons became doable for this newcomer on the scene. This understanding of the source of *Chushim's* additional capacity is borne out by the language of the *Maharal*: "And then, he [*Chushim*, unlike *Yaakov's* sons] was emotionally aroused with the *strength* to kill *Eisav*."

The fact that *Chushim* had the strength to act when the others did not underscores the significance of the emotional

component of one's personality. One may be absolutely incapable of a given task. However, attaining a deeper emotional
commitment to the goal may invigorate and strengthen a person. The absolute outer limit of one's physical capacity is expanded, and heretofore impossible goals become attainable.[2]

---

2.   Classically speaking, the progression of one's Torah learning follows a prescribed order. One begins with the study of the revealed
Torah; in some groups, those who have attained a comprehensive
knowledge of the entire revealed Torah may then go on to the study
of the hidden secrets of *kabbalah*. There are now elements within the
Jewish community who advocate study of *kabbalah*, even by those
who lack a thorough knowledge of the revealed Torah.

This is not an attempt to comment on the matter as a whole, but
rather to touch on one aspect of the issue as it pertains to this chapter.

One argument cited in favor of this study is that *kabbalah* can
often touch the emotions of the soul in a manner that purely
rational Torah thought cannot. Seemingly, the *Maharal* of this
chapter might be viewed as a support for this argument, for it
demonstrates the enormous significance of emotionalism.

In fact, upon closer inspection, it is apparent that the idea of the
Maharal is irrelevant to the debate over the possibly premature
study of *kabbalah*. The objection to such study is that a person
with limited Torah knowledge will not understand the *kabbalah*
that he studies.

What confronted the burial party was something eminently
understandable — the indignity to *Yaakov's* body. *Chushim* acted
differently because he emotionalized that understandable matter
more deeply, and he was thus energized with the enthusiasm to
accomplish what the others could not. But this does not necessarily prove that pure emotionalism that is mostly disconnected from
rational thought confers any significant gain. Such might not
have helped *Chushim* at all. (In fact, my *rebbe* once remarked that
emotionalism that is not linked to logical thought will tend to dis-
sipate without leaving any enduring benefit in its wake.)

(For further discussion of how one's limits are expanded, see chapter 22, section A.) Whether or not a highly significant event will transpire may lie in the balance. The consummate service of *Hashem* is not a purely intellectual excercise.

POSSIBLE APPLICATIONS

This insight can be used as a tool to accomplish more. One should take advantage of the numerous opportunities to upgrade one's emotional connection to *Hashem*. For example: Deep inspiration can constantly occur during the daily recitation of the various prayers. An uplifting of spirit can result from visits to *tzaddikim* or holy places. The heartfelt singing of *Shabbos* and holiday *zemiros* inspires many.

Within the *mussar* movement, great stress is placed on continually reviewing in a singsong manner words of the Torah that speak of already accepted beliefs. This exercise emotionalizes basic concepts, so they become more firmly embedded into one's personality (see chapter 24). Otherwise, the heavy traffic of life can cause one to overlook that which he may have already assimilated intellectually.

The text demonstrates that attaining even the slightest additional measure of feeling (the very slight difference in emotional outrage between *Chushim* and the others) can prove critical in a matter of major significance.

CHAPTER 31

בראשית, ויחי נ:ו

ו. ויאמר פרעה עלה וקבר את־אביך כאשר השביעך:

רש"י

כאשר השביעך: ואם לא בשביל השבועה לא הייתי מניחך אבל ירא לומר עבור על השבועה שלא יאמר א"כ אעבור על השבועה שנשבעתי לך שלא אגלה על לה"ק שאני מכיר עודף על שבעים ל' ואתה אינך מכיר בו כדאי' במס' סוטה (דף לו):

ט"ז על רש"י

קשה וכי בשביל שיעבור על שבועה אחת הותר לו לעבור על כל שאר שבועות שלו. ונראה דהיה מקום לומר שאין עונש על שבועה אלא אם נשבע מעצמו אבל לא כשאחר משביעו, דאז אין לבו שלם מצד עצמו באותה שבועה, ומשום הכי מה שהשביעו יעקב ליוסף אין עונש אם יעבור עליה, ע"כ אמר א"כ גם השבועה שהשביעו פרעה לא יהיה על יוסף עונש אם יעבור עליה:

BEREISHIS VAYECHI 50:6

And Pharaoh said, "Go up and bury your father, as he made you swear."

RASHI

As he made you swear: And if not because of the oath, I would not allow you [to go out of Egypt to bury your father]. But he [Pharaoh] was afraid to say "Violate the oath" so that he [Yosef] should not say, "If so, I will violate the oath that I swore to you not to reveal [the secret] regarding the holy language [Hebrew], that I know it and also the seventy languages, and you do not know it," as it says in tractate Sotah [36b].

TAZ on Rashi

It [Rashi] is difficult [to understand]. Is it true that because he [Yosef] violated one oath it was permissible for him to violate all of his other oaths? And it would appear that there was place to argue that there is no punishment regarding [violating] an oath except in cases where one swears out of his own volition. But not when another person makes him swear, for then it is not a wholehearted oath. And therefore, there would not be a punishment for what Yaakov made Yosef swear, if he [Yosef] violated it. Therefore, he [Pharaoh] said, If so, [Yosef might say that] for the other oath that Pharaoh made him swear [regarding the seventy languages], punishment will likewise not befall Yosef if he violates it.

OVERVIEW OF TEXT

Pharaoh faced a predicament. In those times, it was considered critical that leaders speak all of the world's languages. Yosef was fluent in Hebrew, the one language that Pharaoh did not understand. If this information were to become public knowledge, it would be a humiliation to Pharaoh (and even a possible threat to his throne; see commentary of Maharshal on Rashi). Pharaoh therefore had Yosef swear never to disclose Pharaoh's ignorance of this particular extra language.

When *Yaakov*'s death approached, *Yaakov* asked of *Yosef* that he bury him in Israel. He then had *Yosef* swear to fulfill this request. Upon *Yaakov*'s death, *Yosef* entreated Pharaoh to allow the burial in Israel. Pharaoh acquiesced "As he made you swear."

Rashi explains that Pharaoh consented only because *Yosef* had sworn to *Yaakov* that he would fulfill his request. Pharaoh feared that compelling *Yosef* to break the oath to *Yaakov* could lead *Yosef* to break his prior oath regarding the languages to Pharaoh. If not for that fear, the permission to bury *Yaakov* in *Eretz Yisrael* would have been denied.

The *Taz* asks, why was there a fear that *Yosef* would break his pledge to Pharaoh? Does being made to breach one oath confer a sweeping dispensation to violate all of one's other oaths? *Yosef*'s other vows should have remained binding.

The *Taz* answers that were *Yosef* forced to break his vow to *Yaakov*, he might have then rationalized that a promise made under the duress of an outside party is not valid, for then it is not a wholehearted oath. *Yosef* could have then seen both his oaths as being non-binding, prompting him to break his pledge to Pharaoh. It was this fear that prompted Pharaoh to allow the burial in *Eretz Yisrael*.

ONE BROKEN PROMISE

The *Taz* explains what Pharaoh feared could ensue if he forced *Yosef* to break his vow to *Yaakov*. *Yosef* might reason that an oath demanded by an outside party is not truly binding. Thus, the promise not to disclose Pharaoh's ignorance of the Hebrew language could therefore be broken.

One issue should be clarified. Was this rationale to violate both oaths (that Pharaoh feared) correct and legal, or was it not?

Apparently, the fact that *Yaakov* had *Yosef* swear to carry out the burial means that both parties (who certainly knew the *halachos* of swearing) assumed the oath to be valid and binding, notwithstanding the fact that *Yaakov* all but forced it upon *Yosef*. If so, how did the *Taz* answer his basic question? If the oath was indeed valid, why would coercing *Yosef* to break one promise suddenly predispose him to break other similar promises as well (such as the promise to Pharaoh)?

The explanation of the *Taz* requires mention of the following idea:

It is an axiomatic concept of Torah that man is endowed with a G-dly *neshamah* and *tzelem Elokim* (see chapter 15, section B). This lofty *neshamah* has an agenda and an expectation: it calls upon every man to act in a G-dlike manner and to avoid wrongdoing. Therefore, when one sins, his *neshamah* is pained, for its call to nobility of deed has been violated.

The correct response to a transgression is *teshuvah*. However, upon failure to pursue *teshuvah*, there is an internal discomfort, and conflict over one's wrongdoing remains and festers.

In order to ease this conflict, the subconscious mind may

begin to reassess whether or not the act was indeed truly sinful. An ostensibly rational theory that nothing improper was done may soon miraculously emerge. The newly formulated philosophy that the sin was permissible is, in truth, a result of having sinned; it is a defense mechanism that relieves one's lingering psychic pain.

Adopting this new belief system places one upon the proverbial slippery slope. The new justification will likely give rise to more sins of the type that have been theorized away as being proper. This further sinning (and the consequent additional pain to the *neshamah*), will then beget even more perverse rationalizations that in turn bring about yet more sinning, and so forth. A sequence of this type might be launched upon the heels of any transgression not quickly rectified by *teshuvah*.

This mental process is clearly at work when pledges are broken. The inner angst of confronting one's own duplicity can beget the rationale that behavior of this kind is permissible, thus inspiring further dishonesty of the same type. Ultimately, the person may become a habitual liar who sincerely believes that his behavior is allowable.

Pharaoh thus feared that forcing *Yosef* to break his word might lead *Yosef* to posit that oaths of the type made to *Yaakov* (prompted by others) are really not binding. Therefore, *Yosef*'s other oaths of the same character (i.e., to Pharaoh) could be broken as well. This incorrect rationalization could be formulated and adopted even by a *tzaddik* of *Yosef*'s stature (see preface, section G).

It is evident that *Yosef*'s justification would have been of this type. Proof is from the *Taz* who writes that *Yosef*'s rationale would have occurred only *after* his being forced to break his vow to *Yaakov*. Were he not forced to break the first oath, *Yosef* would have never theorized that such oaths could be violated.

There are two additional factors that are worthy of note. One factor is that violating an oath is an extremely grave transgression.[1] Yet this tendency to rationalize past misdeeds might have led even *Yosef Hatzaddik* to reason incorrectly and then proceed to commit the reprehensible sin of breaking a vow. That is how insidious and powerful this process can be.

Furthermore, without Pharaoh's permission, *Yosef* simply could not have kept his vow to *Yaakov*, and he thus would not have been in violation of Torah; he would have had no choice. Nevertheless, if coerced into "transgressing" that vow, *Yosef* might have one day violated his pledge to Pharaoh as well.

Apparently, a broken promise is a psychologically devastating occurrence. Even a single unavoidable incident of breaking of one's word can ultimately beget a sequence of mistaken justifications that in turn lead to further and greater falsehoods. It can transform the greatest *tzaddik* into one who violates his oaths, one of the greatest of sins. Certainly then, a far greater deterioration of one's moral fiber could occur in the case where one who is less righteous than *Yosef* unjustifiably breaks even one pledge.[2]

---

1.   The following underscores the seriousness of breaking an oath: The Talmud (*Shavuos* 39a) writes that the entire world shook when *Hashem* spoke the words of the Ten Commandments regarding the sin of swearing falsely. The Talmud continues that one can become cleansed from all other sins, but not from a false oath; moreover, (though this may be difficult to understand) with other sins only the perpetrator is punished, whereas one person's false oath might bring punishment upon his family and even the entire world.

2.   Both this chapter and chapter 17, section A discuss falsehoods and misrepresentations that are unavoidable or mandated. However, the *Taz* deals with the possible repercussions of promises not kept. Chapter 17, section A deals with the extent to which one should attempt to distance himself from the utterance of anything less than absolutely honest,

. . . .

In truth, the phenomenon of "rationally" formulating new concepts to justify wrongful deeds already committed is not limited to the instance of a broken pledge. Logic dictates that the syndrome is universal; any wrongdoing can soon beget the new idea that such behavior is indeed proper. And ever greater rationalizations may soon follow (see chapter 32 note 4).[3]

---

      notwithstanding the fact that such may be called for.

3.   There is a well-known story of R. *Chaim Volozhin* that is reflective of this idea. A student of R. *Chaim* joined the *haskalah* and became unobservant. Years later R. *Chaim* met his former student and asked him, in effect, "What happened?" The student proceeded to enumerate several of his theoretical difficulties with traditional *Yiddishkeit.*

      R. *Chaim* replied by asking: "Did these problems trouble you before you abandoned your traditions or only afterward?" The student answered that the questions began to trouble him after he had already changed his ways. R. *Chaim* then replied that if so, they were not questions at all; rather, they were answers (justifications to explain sins already committed).

      The story involving R. *Chaim* demonstrates the basic notion that one's past deeds impact upon subsequent thinking. The *Taz* illustrates the absolutely incredible power of this bias to undermine one's reasoning. Even...

    • that which was not a technical violation of the Torah (as in the case of *Yosef,* where breaking the promise would have been absolutely unavoidable)

    • can give rise to the abrogating of an oath (a terrible sin)

    • by one of *Yosef*'s piety and wisdom

    • through creating a newly formed false rationale that can distort even that which was so surely correct (for both *Yaakov* and *Yosef* had originally agreed to its veracity).

      In situations involving outright falsehoods committed by people of lesser piety than *Yosef,* the possibility for distorted thinking

POSSIBLE APPLICATIONS

The everyday conduct of business, professions and politics is often rife with falsehoods and broken promises (see chapter 20, note 2). Some might conjecture that "business is business; it is to be expected. But home is home!" They presume that although a certain measure of dishonesty is tolerated or even expected at the workplace, that is because such is the modus operandi of contemporary business. However, upon returning home, one can then revert to upstanding and ethical behavior.

The *Taz* soundly refutes this notion. Even violations of integrity that are Torah-mandated (usually not the case in the conduct of business), committed by history's most righteous people, can give rise to false rationalizations that transform future untruths into imagined honesty. Ultimately, one who utters untruths at work will likely soon lie as convenient, even to his family and closest friends. Furthermore, he will probably see his own conduct as being truly righteous.

Speaking more generally, this chapter explains why it can be extremely difficult for one to recognize the error within his own past actions. He may have already intellectualized the utterly profane that he committed as being the utterly permissible.[4] Similarly, this is why it is often surprisingly difficult to

---

brought on by this psychodynamic is obviously far greater.

4.   A similar point can be deduced from the opening lines of the second chapter of the *Mesillas Yesharim*, which begins: "The issue of watchfulness [avoiding sin] is for man to exercise caution in his actions and general issues, **meaning** (emphasis mine) that he should contemplate his deeds and accustomed ways to determine whether they are good or not." The third chapter of the *Mesillas Yesharim* opens with a similar idea.

Seemingly, the concept of avoiding sin connotes distancing

make another person aware of even his glaring improprieties. He could be seeing acts of obvious wrongdoing as an outright *mitzvah*.

---

oneself from two domains of human transgression. One is quite obvious, while the other is more subtle.
• One must surely repent from unquestionable wrongdoing that he is aware of.
• A second, more subtle issue involves instances of uncertainty as to whether or not a given activity was sinful. There too, a conscientious individual would presumably examine those areas carefully — perhaps a deed was sinful and repentance is thus required.

The *Mesillas Yesharim* begins with the general idea that one must desist from wrongdoing. He then immediately describes avoiding sin only in terms of the second area — the process of determining whether his deeds were truly sinful or not. Why is there no mention of *teshuvah* for one's areas of acknowledged violations?

Apparently, the *Mesillas Yesharim* is saying that there is no such thing as one's own recognized wrongdoing; if it truly is wrongdoing (from which one did not quickly repent), man will tend not to recognize it. While one certainly would not deny that he habitually violates certain areas, his admission is not really heartfelt. Deep down that person does not see himself as a wrongdoer — he could even be rationalizing that his improper behavior is, in truth, out-and-out piety. That is why all of one's actions require examination — even those that appear to be *mitzvos*. One will likely abandon his wrongful behavior only after recognizing its true nature. That recognition can be attained only through intense introspection that ascertained that the said deed was sinful rather than praiseworthy.

The idea of the *Mesillas Yesharim* mirrors the concept of the *Taz*. The *Taz*, however, is discussing the instance of a broken promise; the *Mesillas Yesharim* applies the concept of blindness to one's past wrongdoing to virtually every human failing.

CHAPTER 32

בראשית, ויחי נ:טו-יז

טו. ויראו אחי־יוסף כי־מת אביהם ויאמרו לו ישטמנו יוסף והשב
ישיב לנו את כל־הרעה אשר גמלנו אתו:
טז. ויצוו אל־יוסף לאמר אביך צוה לפני מותו לאמר:
יז. כה־תאמרו ליוסף אנא שא נא פשע אחיך וחטאתם כי־רעה גמלוך
ועתה שא נא לפשע עבדי אלהי אביך ויבך יוסף בדברם אליו:

מדרש רבה בראשית ק:ח

ר' לוי אמר שלא זימנן לסעודה. א"ר תנחומא הוא לא נתכוון אלא
לשם שמים אמר לשעבר אבא מושיב לי למעלה מיהודה שהוא מלך
ולמעלה מראובן שהוא בכור עכשיו אינו בדין שאשב למעלה מהן.
והן לא אמרו כן אלא לו ישטמנו יוסף.

עץ יוסף על המדרש

א"ר תנחומא שחשדוהו שלא כדין כי הוא לא נתכוון אלא לשם
שמים כי אמר לשעבר אבא היה מושיב לי למעלה כו' ואז עשיתי כן
בע"כ מפני מצות אבי ולא הייתי רשאי לסרב כנגדו. אבל עכשיו
אינו בדין שאשב למעלה כו' כי לא רצה כלל לנהוג שררה עליהם
והוא ידע כי גם הם לא יקבלו עליהם הדבר לישב למעלה ממנו
לשנות סדר הנהוג בחיי אביהם:

חזקוני

טו. ויאמרו לו ישטמנו יוסף: כששב מקבורת אביו עבר על בור שהשליכוהו בו אחיו וברך עליו שעשה לי נסים במקום הזה, והם שמעו, על כן יראו פן תתחדש עליו כל הרעה שעשה לו (תנחומא ויחי יז):

ספורנו

טז. ציוו אל יוסף: וו לעבדי יעקב או זולתם על אודות יוסף כמו ויצום אל בני ישראל: **לאמר אביך צוה**: צוה שיאמרו ליוסף אביך צוה לנו שנאמר אליך מאלינו לא מצדו שאינו חושד אותך כלל אבל שאם ייראו אחיך נאמר אליך אלה הדברים: **יז. ויבך יוסף**: בהזכירם את אביו ואת חבתו שלא חשדו:

BEREISHIS, VAYECHI 50:15,16,17

15. And Yosef's brothers saw that their father was dead, and they said, "Perhaps Yosef will nurse hatred against us and then he will surely repay us all the evil that we did to him."

16. And they commanded that Yosef be told, Your father commanded before his death, saying:

17. Thus shall you say to Yosef: "Please kindly forgive the spiteful deed of your brothers and their sin, for they have done you evil; so now, please forgive the spiteful deed of the servants of your father's G-d." And Yosef wept when they spoke to him.

MIDRASH RABBAH 100:8

Rabbi Levi said [what aroused the fear of the brothers was] that he [Yosef] did not invite them to dine with him. R. Tanchuma said, His [Yosef's] intention was only for the sake of Heaven. He [Yosef] said, "In the past, Father sat me ahead of Yehudah, who is a king, and *ahead of Reuvain, who is the firstborn. Now it is not proper for me to sit ahead of them." And they [the brothers] did not say so [attribute a noble motive to Yosef] but said instead, "It may be that Yosef will hate us."*

ETZ YOSEF on the Midrash

R. *Tanchuma said that they suspected him improperly, for he meant [to act] only for the sake of Heaven. For he said, "In the past Father sat me ahead of [them]..., and then I complied against my will because of the commandment of my father, and I was not permitted to oppose him. But now it is not proper for me to sit ahead of them" For he did not at all wish to conduct himself with any form of lordship over them.*

And he [Yosef] knew that they as well would not accept upon themselves to sit ahead of him and change the order that was practiced during the lifetime of their father.

CHIZKUNI

15. ...And they said, "perhaps Yosef will nurse hatred against us:" *When he [Yosef] returned from the burial of his father, he passed the pit where his brothers cast him, and he [Yosef] blessed [Hashem] over it [saying, Blessed is the One] that performed miracles for me in this place. And they heard [Yosef's blessing]. Therefore they feared that all of the evil they had done to him would be reawakened [in Yosef's mind].*

SFORNO

16. Your father commanded: *He commanded that they should say to Yosef "Your father commanded us [regarding] what we should say to you on our own [initiative], not on his part, for he does not suspect you at all. But [Yaakov said] should your brothers be fearful, we should say these words to you."*

17. And Yosef wept: *When they mentioned his father and his love,* *that he did not suspect him.*

OVERVIEW OF TEXT

Yaakov and his eleven sons resided in Egypt under the protection of *Yosef,* who was viceroy of the country. As his death approached, *Yaakov* formulated a request to be presented posthumously to *Yosef,* should the need arise. In that request, *Yaakov* implored *Yosef* to forgive his brothers for selling him into slavery.

The *Sforno* explains that the brothers might one day become fearful of *Yosef's* reprisal. It was to allay those ungrounded fears, if necessary, that *Yaakov* left this appeal for possible presentation to *Yosef.* However, *Yaakov* himself deeply loved *Yosef* and therefore firmly believed that he would never act with vengeance toward his brothers. *Yosef* understood the origin of *Yaakov's* lack of suspicion and therefore wept over the extent of *Yaakov's* love for him.

After *Yaakov's* burial in *Eretz Yisrael, Yaakov's* suspicions were realized. The brothers suddenly became fearful that *Yosef* still hated them and that his retribution could soon follow. They therefore presented *Yaakov's* request to *Yosef.* The brothers then went even further, offering themselves to *Yosef* as slaves.

Why did the brothers suddenly suspect that *Yosef* harbored feelings of hatred and revenge? The *Midrash* explains that when *Yaakov* was alive they would often all dine together at *Yosef's* request. Upon *Yaakov's* death, *Yosef* suddenly discontinued the invitations. This caused them to wrongly presume that *Yosef* still bore a profound grudge against them.

The *Midrash* clarifies that *Yosef's* discontinuance of the invitations was in response to an inescapable predicament. When they all dined together, *Yaakov* would always command *Yosef* to sit at the head of the table — an honor that *Yosef* only grudgingly accepted. With *Yaakov* no longer present, *Yosef* would not assume that honor on his own, for he refused to take precedence over two of his brothers, *Reuvain*, who was the eldest, and *Yehudah* who was treated deferentially as royalty. (King David and his royal dynasty would descend from *Yehudah*.)

The *Etz Yosef* explains further that *Yosef* himself would have gladly ceded the front seat. However, that would have been contrary to *Yaakov's* seating protocol, and *Yosef* realized that his brothers would never agree to defy *Yaakov's* wishes.

Yosef thus found himself in an intractable quandary. He himself would not consent to sit at their head, nor would they agree to any other arrangement. With no acceptable solution available, *Yosef* simply discontinued the mealtime invitations. The commentaries do not criticize *Yosef* for this decision.

. . . .

The *Chizkuni* explains the brothers' sudden fear altogether differently from the *Midrash*. When returning from *Yaakov's* burial, they passed the very pit where *Yosef's* brothers had left him to die. *Yosef* paused at that spot and uttered blessings of gratitude to *Hashem* for his miraculous salvation that had occurred there. The brothers feared that this experience might rekindle *Yosef's* hatred toward them and a subsequent desire for revenge. They therefore sought to protect themselves by conveying *Yaakov's* appeal and additionally offering themselves as slaves.

INTRODUCTION TO IDEAS A) & B)

Yaakov's positioning of *Yosef* at the head of the table (because he was the local sovereign) no doubt represented what was proper according to the Torah. The brothers felt that the ruling remained in effect even after *Yaakov's* demise, and they would thus never agree to any other seating order. *Yosef* presumably understood their rationale, for he apparently did not argue the matter theoretically. (The following argument would seem to further bolster the position of the brothers: While *Yaakov* lived, *Yose* at not only ahead of his two brothers, but ahead of *Yaakov* himself as well. After *Yaakov's* death, *Yosef* would only be taking precedence over his brothers.)

Yet *Yosef's* desire to avoid his rightful front seat resonates throughout the entire story. When *Yaakov* was alive, *Yosef* would always go most reluctantly to the table's head, and only at his father's command. After *Yaakov's* death, *Yosef* seemingly disregarded *Yaakov's* edict altogether by categorically refusing to sit ahead of *Reuvain* and *Yehudah*.

This reveals the unique paradox that exists in the matter of accepting and bestowing honor. One might be required to bestow a specific honor upon another; yet that other person's imperative may be to refuse that very same honor. After *Yaakov's* passing, the brothers continued to abide by their father's ruling and accorded the front seat to *Yosef*. *Yosef*, however, refused to sit ahead of *Reuvain* and *Yehudah* since he was no longer being specifically commanded by *Yaakov*. *Yosef* rightfully fled from the same honor that they were obligated to bestow.

Parts A and B provide greater clarification of this theme.

A) ACCEPTING HONOR

Yosef avoided the same honor that his family was required to proffer. Apparently, there are special guidelines when it comes to accepting honor from others. One should always be extremely reluctant to be honored over others, notwithstanding the most valid of reasons for accepting the acclaim. What could be more justified than honor being accorded at the specific command of *Yaakov*? Nevertheless, regarding that honor *Yosef* said (see *Etz Yosef*): "In the past Father sat me ahead of [them]..., and then I complied against my will because of the commandment of my father, and I was not permitted to oppose him." *Yosef* always accepted his rightful honor with that recalcitrant attitude.

What changed upon the death of *Yaakov*? Why did *Yosef* then ignore his father's edict and absolutely refuse the honor after *Yaakov*'s passing?

A closer analysis reveals that the situations before and after *Yaakov*'s death were somewhat different. *Yaakov* had indeed positioned *Yosef* ahead of his brothers. However, *Yaakov*'s example only demonstrated that *Yosef* had to accept that honor after being instructed to comply by someone else of greater authority and stature, such as *Yaakov*. *Yaakov* never ruled that *Yosef*, from his perspective, should, in effect, seat himself at the head of the table. In the absence of that directive, *Yosef* correctly declined the honor.

When honor cannot be refused (*Yosef*'s situation before *Yaakov*'s death), it should be accepted but with an attitude of extreme reluctance. However, when honor can be declined outright (*Yosef's* situation after *Yaakov's* death), it should often be refused.[1]

It goes without saying that in instances (unlike that of *Yosef*) where the real justification for a given honor is dubious, accepting the tribute is certainly ill advised. Asking for or demanding the front seat in such cases can be an outrage.

---

1.   There are numerous instances where one is required to accept honor. Parents and teachers must train their charges to act with deference by accepting the respect offered. In a similar vein, the *halachah* (*Yoreh Deah* 242) enumerates ways in which a student must honor his *rebbe* and states: "Anyone who prevents his student from serving him, is withholding kindness from the student" (ibid., 20). The *rebbe* should not decline the appropriate veneration of his student.

Another common scenario is that of a charitable organization beseeching someone to be honored at a fundraising event. Oftentimes, his accepting the tribute generates contributions that could not be raised otherwise. It may then be obligatory to accommodate the *tzedakah* organization. However, the honoree's attitude throughout should be one of aversion and discomfort; he should genuinely feel that what is being done is against his personal wishes. That is how *Yosef* responded when seated at the head of the table by *Yaakov*.

B) BESTOWING HONOR

There is another aspect to *Yosef*'s response that requires further clarification. A common rabbinic saying is that "One honors a person by conforming to his wishes" (*Sefer Chassidim* 152). Thus, *Yosef*'s acceptance of his brothers' wishes to sit at their head was seemingly the ultimate deference to them. Why then did *Yosef* demur, claiming he was according honor to *Reuvain* and *Yehudah*?

Yosef's actions reveal a fundamental concept pertaining to the subject of bestowing honor. Honor must often be accorded even when absolutely contrary to the wishes of the honoree. *Yosef* felt compelled to honor *Reuvain* and *Yehudah*, notwithstanding their adamant refusals (and the idea of the *Sefer Chassidim*). *Yosef*'s commitment to according this honor was extreme; once he realized that he could not so honor them, he discontinued the invitations altogether.

The advancement of honor to another cannot be likened to the payment of a personal debt. Debt, once truly forgiven by the lender, is nullified. Certainly, when the lender objects strenuously to being paid, the debt no longer exists. Honor is different, for it must often be given despite the objections of the recipient.

In summation, part A makes the point that the honoree should often decline the accord even when the Torah requires others to bestow the said honor. And in instances where the honor must be accepted, it should be received with an attitude of great aversion. Part B explicates that an obligation to bestow honor may exist notwithstanding the genuine discomfort and strenuous objections of the recipient.[3]

POSSIBLE APPLICATIONS

The general level of parental honor practiced by children has declined in recent decades. In a general sense, the Torah seems to support the more traditional approach. Two telling examples found in *halachah* are: "One should not contradict his parent [even when not in the presence of the parent — *Shach* 2]...one should stand up when a parent enters the room" (*Yoreh Deah* 240).

As a practical matter, in most contemporary situations, not conforming to that classical *halachic* standard is likely not a

---

3.   The following is reflective of these two ideas: When *Yaakov* journeyed with his family to Egypt and was about to arrive, it is written (*Bereishis* 46:28) "And he sent *Yehudah* ahead of him to *Yosef* to show [the way] before him to *Goshen.*" One interpretation in *Rashi* (based on the *Midrash* 95:2) is that *Yehudah* was sent to prepare a dwelling place for the family in *Goshen* that would be ready upon their arrival.

The *Etz Yosef* further explains that *Yaakov* feared being honored by *Yosef* with interim lodging in the royal palace while a dwelling place was readied in *Goshen*. To avoid that acclaim, *Yaakov* sought to facilitate his immediate move to the land of *Goshen*. *Yehudah* was therefore asked to enable *Yaakov* to move directly to *Goshen.*

Yosef, who knew his father's piety and modesty, must have realized that *Yaakov* would have strongly disliked the tribute of residence in the royal palace. Yet, he might have so hosted *Yaakov* had *Yehudah* not been sent to specifically preclude that possibility.

Thus, regarding the hosting of *Yaakov* in the royal palace, it was correct for *Yosef* to confer an honor that *Yaakov*, in turn, was called upon by the Torah to avoid.

technical violation. That is because the Talmud (*Kiddushin* 32a) writes that a parent may forgo his right to parental honor. In an age when very few children stand when parents enter a room, one can likely presume that, unless otherwise specified, a parent does not expect such; he is forgiving his due.

However, although not technically binding, the Torah's standard nevertheless remains the exemplar of befitting conduct. And *Yosef*'s behavior demonstrates that the ethical imperative to bestow honor may even supersede the expectations and preferences of the honoree. As such, children should perhaps adopt a standard of parental respect somewhat more akin to the model of the Torah, and not necessarily be limited by what others expect.

C) DORMANT FEELINGS

The *Chizkuni* explains that the brothers suddenly feared *Yosef's* vengeance because of an incident that occurred. When returning to Egypt from *Yaakov's* burial, they passed the pit where the brothers had left *Yosef* to die years earlier. *Yosef* paused there to utter blessings of gratitude to *Hashem* for his salvation. As a result, the brothers suddenly feared that *Yosef's* hatred of them for what they had done to him could be rekindled, and that *Yosef's* lethal reprisal might be imminent. It would appear from the story in the *Chumash* that the brothers were never truly in danger. However, if they harbored this fear of what *Yosef* might do, such was at least theoretically possible (see preface, section H).

What did those blessings of *Yosef* to *Hashem* reveal? Seemingly, if *Yosef* thanked *Hashem* for his salvation, such was proper, and to do otherwise would have been considered a failing. In fact, *halachah* obliges one to utter a special blessing when passing a spot where a miracle had occurred to him (*Orach Chaim* 218:4). Why then was this prayer or blessing seen as a possible harbinger of *Yosef's* renewed hatred?

The *Chizkuni* indicates that it was the stop-off itself that could have resuscitated *Yosef's* animosity. Had *Yosef* not paused to utter the blessing at that spot there would have been no fear of his murderous revenge. This is apparent in the *Chizkuni's* words: "They feared that all of the evil they had done to him would be reawakened [in *Yosef's* mind]."

The *Chizkuni* is revealing that in some instances where utter forgiveness has seemingly occurred, it is not necessarily so.

Beneath the surface of the apparent act of forgiving, the old resentment may be very much alive, but in a latent state. A trigger or an incident can unexpectedly reawaken it. Even when history's most righteous of people (e.g., *Yosef Hatzaddik*) sincerely grant complete forgiveness, it may not be as it appears. A suddenly rekindled thirst for vengeance that could even turn physically deadly could appear in one so consummately righteous as *Yosef Hatzaddik* for something that occurred thirty years earlier (the sale of *Yosef* occurred thirty years prior to *Yaakov's* death).

Presumably, this psychodynamic applies not only to latent feelings of vengeance, but to other strong drives as well. Physical lusts, paralyzing phobias or destructive behavior could also appear to be conquered, only to unexpectedly reappear later with the proper stimulus. Once a person has experienced a powerful urge within him, he presumably must always be on guard. Even after lying dormant for many years, the drive could abruptly reappear.

The *Mesillas Yesharim* (chapter 11) writes that when one person truly harms another, the Torah forbids revenge of any sort and requires absolute forgiveness devoid of any lingering inner resentment. However, the *Mesillas Yesharim* continues that only the angels of *Hashem* can easily fulfill these precepts.

The *Mesillas Yesharim* is saying that it is theoretically possible to completely rid oneself of all traces of a desire for revenge, both conscious and subconscious. The *Chizkuni*, however, teaches that some cases are not as they appear. Although the urge for retribution may appear to be conquered, it may still be lurking beneath the surface of one's personality, and it could suddenly emerge in all its devastating power. Seemingly, it is hard for a person to ever be certain that he has been completely internally cleansed of every vestige of a destructive internal drive.[4]

---

4.   The syndrome revealed by the *Chizkuni* is recognized in the field of substance abuse treatment. Former alcoholics are taught to forever see themselves as "recovering" rather than "recovered" alcoholics. Underlying that approach is the belief that the addiction can never be completely eliminated. Even after years of total abstinence, it is possible for one to quickly revert to his former alcoholism as a result of imbibing just one drink.

The Torah's approach, *lehavdil*, is that it may be true in some cases that even after years of "recovery," a dormant alcoholism may indeed be lurking just beneath the surface. However, it is also possible to entirely rid oneself of alcoholism. If a person can totally purify himself from all vestiges of the inner desire for revenge (something easy only for angels), he can also presumably completely rid himself of the desire for ruinous alcohol consumption.

R. *Yisrael Salanter* provided further clarification on this issue. In *Even Yisrael, Maamar B'inyan Chizuk Lomdei Torah*, R. *Yisrael* makes the distinction between two types of human drives. There are drives that, to varying degrees, are universal to all mankind, such as the desire to eat or the love for one's own natural child. Other drives such as jealousy and hatred are not harbored by all people.

R. *Yisrael* taught that man can only somewhat control the first type of drive, but he can never fully rid himself of it. However, one can completely purify his personality of the second category of drive, even in instances where the trait was innate in that person from birth. This further supports the notion that man can totally eliminate an excessive lust for alcohol. That urge is certainly not universal to all mankind.

D) LOVE AND SUSPICION

Before dying, *Yaakov* bequeathed an appeal; he beseeched *Yosef* to refrain from vengeance against his brothers. According to the *Sforno*, *Yaakov* knew that *Yosef* would never act in a vengeful manner. Rather, *Yaakov's* intention was to assuage the brothers' unfounded fears. When *Yosef* heard that *Yaakov* himself had no such suspicions, he wept. He cried in the knowledge that *Yaakov's* love for him was so intense that he did not suspect him of harboring vengeance.

At first glance, it would appear that *Yaakov* understood *Yosef's* piety, and therefore realized that he would not take revenge. How did *Yaakov's* love of *Yosef* prevent *Yaakov* from having these suspicions? Despite being loved by *Yaakov*, *Yosef* may still have been willing to harm his brothers.

The *Sforno* is revealing a novel consequence of love of humanity. There is a direct correlation between a dearth of love for another individual and the tendency to be unjustifiably suspicious of that person's motives and activities. As the affection grows, there is a corresponding decrease of unwarranted suspicion. This does not mean that one cannot see the genuine flaws in a loved one. What the *Sforno* means is that one's unfounded suspicion of another will diminish as love increases.[5]

---

5.   There are several chapters in this book that touch upon the unseen but mind-bending effects of subconscious bias. Furthermore, it has been shown how even the greatest of *tzaddikim* are vulnerable to this influence, despite the fact that enormously weighty consequences may be at hand. In this book, the concept is dealt with most fully in chapter 22, section B. Following is a very brief summation of the bias-related

POSSIBLE APPLICATIONS

Unfounded suspicions lie behind many disputes and mis-understandings among people. What is in fact a truly inno-cent act or statement may be presumed by others to be nefari-ous and treacherous. Discord may then follow.

The *Sforno's* insight provides another impetus for the *mitzvah* of loving a fellow Jew. As one's love for people increases, he will be less likely to improperly suspect others of ignoble motives and intentions. And he will thus be less prone to the strife that can occur when others are falsely suspected. (In truth, it is a *mitzvah* to judge people favor-ably [*Sefer Hamitzvos* 177] — if unsure whether another person acted improperly, one is obliged to give him the benefit of the doubt.)

---

ideas of those chapters and the differences between them:

• A person sees others as having his own personal faults (chap-ter 3, section B).

• One tends to adhere to and defend decisions already made even when, if facing that same quandary for the first time, he would have decided otherwise (chapter 10, section B).

• Social pressure causes one to see the societal norm as being proper, and that in general, one's thinking is altered by his de-ficient character traits (chapter 22, section B).

• A person's false belief system gives rise to a hatred for those who recognize the falsehood of the said belief system (chapter 28).

• The desire to do something improper could cause a person to hide the wrongdoing of a given deed from himself and others in order to embark upon that said deed (chapter 29, section B).

• An improper deed already committed can give rise to a newly created theory that such behavior is indeed proper (chapter 31).

This chapter shows how a lack of love of people goes hand-in-hand with an increased likelihood of harboring un-grounded suspicions of others; and that as love increases, those suspicions will tend to abate.

GLOSSARY

aggadah: the parts of the Torah that deal with human and ethical issues.

Ahron: Aaron the high priest, brother of *Moshe*.

ah tsenter: Yiddish for "a tenth" (man)

R. Ahron Kotler: an east European rabbi who escaped the Holocaust and emigrated to America; founder and head of the *Beth Midrash Gevohah* in Lakewood, NJ; student of the *Slobodka Yeshivah*.

R. Akiva Eiger: 1761–1837, one of the greatest eighteenth- and nineteenth-century commentators on the Talmud; Rabbi of Posen.

Alter of Slabodka: R. *Nosson Tzvi Finkel*, 1847 - 1927, one of the greatest figures of the *Mussar* Movement; headed the yeshiva in *Slabodka* for many years; later headed the yeshiva in *Chevron*; rebbe to many students who themselves became great Torah leaders.

am haaretz: one who is ignorant of Torah.

Amrafel: a king against whom *Avraham* waged war.

Aner, Eshkol and Mamreh: three contemporaries of *Avraham* with whom he had a friendly relationship.

Antoninus: a benign Roman ruler who maintained a close friendship with *Rebbe*.

Arizal: R. Yitzchak Luria, a sixteenth-century rabbi who lived first in Egypt and later in Safed, Israel, who did much to popularize the study of *kabbalah*.

Avodah Zara: a tractate of the Talmud.

Avos D'R. Nosson: a section within the Talmud devoted almost entirely to ethical teachings.

Avraham: the patriarch Abraham.

R. Avraham Trop: an east European rabbi who escaped the Holocaust and emigrated to America.

baal chessed: one steeped in the trait of kindness.

baal(ei) mussar: one(s) steeped in the ideas and practices of *mussar.*

baal(ei) teshuvah: one(s) who has (have) repented (colloquially, a reference to one who has undertaken the observance of *kashrus, Shabbos* and other *mitzvos*).

baalei battim: laymen; also lay leaders.

Beitzah: a tractate of the Talmud.

Bemidbar: the fourth of the Five Books of Moses.

Bava Basra: a tractate of the Talmud.

Bava Kama: a tractate of the Talmud.

Bava Metzia: a tractate of the Talmud.

Be'er Mayim Chaim: a commentary on *Rashi* by R. *Chaim ben Betzalel,* brother of the *Maharal* of Prague.

bein adam laMakom: (usually referring to *mitzvos*) between man and *Hashem.*

bein adam l'chavero: (usually referring to *mitzvos*) between man and his fellow man.

beis din: rabbinical court.

benching: the Grace after Meals; the recitation of the Grace after Meals.

Ben Yehoyada: a commentary on the *aggadah* of the Talmud by R. *Yosef Chaim* of Baghdad, 1834-1909, author of the *Ben Ish Chai.*

Bereishis: the first of the Five Books of Moses.

Bilam: a gentile prophet who was engaged to curse the Jewish people.

Binyamin: the youngest of *Yaakov's* twelve sons.

Bisuel: the father of *Rivkah*.

bitachon: trust in *Hashem*.

bnei Torah: people living the Torah's way of life.

Canaan: the fourth son of *Cham*; also a biblical name for the land of Israel.

R. Chaim Brisker: R. *Chaim Soloveitchik*, a teacher of great students who was first a *rosh yeshivah* in *Volozhin* and later the rabbi of the city of Brisk.

R. Chaim Ozer Grodzensky: a pre-World War II Torah leader of eastern Europe; head of the rabbinical court of the city of Vilna.

chalilah: an idiomatic expression meaning something on the order of "G-d forbid!"

Cham: the second son of *Noach*.

Chasam Sofer: R. *Moshe Sofer*, an east European rabbi of the eighteenth and nineteenth century.

chassid: one who has attained extreme piety and saintliness; also a member of the *Chassidic* movement.

chassidim: members of the movement of *Chassidus*; also plural of *chassid*.

Chassidus: a movement within traditional Judaism, founded by R. *Yisrael Baal Shem Tov*.

chassidus: extreme piety; saintliness.

Chavah: Eve, the wife of Adam.

Chazon Ish: R. *Avraham Yeshaya Karelitz*, a great Torah scholar who emmigrated from Eastern Europe to Israel prior to World War II.

chenek: a form of execution.

cherem: excommunication.

Cheshbon Hanefesh: a work of *mussar* by R. *Mendel ben Yehudah Leib Zbaraz*; first printed 1845.

chessed: kindness.

Chevron: Hebron.

Chiddushei Halev: a book in Hebrew of some the *mussar* talks of my *rebbe*, R. *Alter Chanoch Henach Leibowitz, shlita*, compiled by a student.

chillul Hashem: desecration of *Hashem*'s Name.

chinuch: upbringing and/or Torah education.

Chizkuni: a thirteenth-century commentary on the Torah by R. *Chizkiya ben Manoach*; first printed 1549.

chochmas hamussar: within the *mussar* movement, the theoretical study of ethics and character traits.

Chofetz Chaim: R. *Yisrael Meir Hakohen*, 1840-1933, an east European rabbi who authored many famous works of *halachah* and ethics.

Chovas Halvavos: a classical wide-ranging work of *mussar* by R. *Bachya Ibn Pekudah*, early eleventh century.

Chulda: a prophetess who lived at the time of the destruction of the First Temple.

Chumash: the Five Books of Moses.

Chushim ben Dan: a grandson of *Yaakov*.

Daas Zekeinim MiBaalei HaTosafos: a commentary on *Chumash* by the authors of the commentary of *Tosafos* on the Talmud.

daven: pray.

davening: praying, prayers.

derech eretz: respect.

Devarim: the fifth of the Five Books of Moses.

Divrei Hayamim: the Book of Chronicles.

Divrei Shaul: a commentary on *Chumash* by R. *Yosef Shaul Halevi Natanson*.

Dovid Hamelech: King David.

R. Dovid Leibowitz: an east European rabbi who emigrated to America; founder of *Yeshivas Chofetz Chaim*; a close disciple of the *Alter* of *Slobodka* and my *rebbe*'s father and *rebbe*.

drash: an exposition upon a text that is definitely not *pshat*.

Edom: *Eisav*.

Ein Yaakov: a compilation of the *aggadic* material found in the Talmud by R. *Yaakov ibn Chaviv*, 1445-1516.

Eisav: Esau, brother of *Yaakov*.

Eliezer: the trusted servant of *Avraham*.

Eretz Yisrael: the Land of Israel.

Etz Yosef: commentary on the Midrash and Ein Yaakov by R. Chanoch Zundel ben Yosef.

Even Haezel: a commentary on *Rambam* by R. *Isser Zalman MeltzeR*.

even shisia: the large stone that was in the holiest section of the Temple, presently covered by the Mosque of Omar.

frum: religious; G-d-fearing; devout.

frumkeit: the state of being *frum*.

gadol: a leader or a great person.

gadol hador: a great person of the generation.

R. Gamliel: a rabbi of the *Mishnah*, mentioned frequently in the Talmud and *Midrash*.

Gan Eden: Garden of Eden.

Gemara: the Talmud.

Givonim: a biblical nation (see chapter 3, note 1).

Gog and Magog: two nations who will engage in cataclysmic warfare shortly before the coming of *Moshiach*.

Gur Aryeh: a commentary on *Rashi* by R. *Yehudah Loewy*, the *Maharal* of Prague, 1526-1607; first printed 1578.

Hagar: Sarah's maidservant whom *Avraham* later took as a wife/concubine.

hakaras hatov: gratitude.

halachah: Torah law.

halachic: pertaining to *halachah*.

R. Hama: a rabbi mentioned in the Talmud.

R. Hama bar Hanina: a rabbi mentioned in the Talmud.

hashkafah: outlook, usually connoting a specific view of some issues within Torah.

haskalah: the Enlightenment.

R. Henach Leibowitz: present head of *Yeshivas Chofetz Chaim* of Forest Hills, NY, usually referred to in this book as "my *rebbe*."

Hilchos Shecheinim: laws of neighbors.

Imrei Shefer: a commentary on *Rashi* by R. *Nosson Nata Shapira* (d. 1577); printed 1597.

R. Isaac Sher: one of the great disciples of the *Alter* of *Slobodka*.

R. Isser Zalman Meltzer: an east European rabbi who emigrated to Israel prior to World War II.

Iyov: the Book of Job.

Iyun Yaakov: a commentary on *Ein Yaakov* by R. *Yaakov Reisher*.

kabbalah: the hidden (mystical) part of the Torah.

kabbalistic: pertaining to *kabbalah*.

kashrus: keeping kosher.

Kav Hayashar: a classical work of *mussar* by R. *Tzvi Hirsch Kaidenover*;

first printed 1705.

kavyachol: "as if it could be"; a qualifier utilized when anthropomorphizing about *Hashem*.

Kesubos: a tractate of the Talmud.

Kiddushin: a tractate of the Talmud.

kiruv: drawing people close to *Yiddishkeit*.

Klal Yisrael: the nation of Israel.

Koheles: the Book of Ecclesiastes.

kohen: a male patrilineal descendant of *Ahron*.

kollel(im): institution(s) where married students study Torah while being supported financially.

Korach: an individual who unsuccessfully challenged the authority of *Moshe*.

Lavan: Laban, the nephew of *Avraham*.

lehavdil: a caveat or form of separation employed when something (or someone) exceedingly righteous is mentioned together with the profane.

R. Levi: a rabbi mentioned in the Talmud.

lifnim mishuras hadin: beyond the letter of the law.

Mishulchan Gavoha: a collection of brief Torah insights on *Chumash*.

Maayano shel Torah: a collection of brief Torah insights on *Chumash*.

(Cave of) Machpelah: the burial place of four couples — Adam and *Chavah*, *Avraham* and Sarah, *Yitzchak* and *Rivkah* and *Yaakov* and Leah.

Maggid Mishnah: a major commentary on the *Rambam's* massive work on Torah law.

maggid shiur: one who teaches Torah, usually referring to

higher-level dissertations in a *yeshivah*.

Maharsha: a commentary on the Talmud by *R. Shmuel Eidels*, 1555-1632.

Maharshal: *R. Shlomo Luria*, 1510-1573, a commentator on the Torah and a leader of Polish Jewry.

Maharzu: a commentary on the *Midrash Rabbah* by *R. Zev Volf Einhorn*.

Makkos: a tractate of the Talmud.

mamzer(im): one(s) born of an illegitimate relationship.

marbitz Torah: one who spreads and/or teaches Torah.

masis: one who incites others to sin, especially when that sin is idolatry.

Maskil L'Dovid: a commentary on *Rashi* by *R. Dovid Pardo*; first printed in 1761.

Matnas Kehunah: a clasical commentary on the *Midrash Rabbah*.

Megillah: a tractate of the Talmud.

Melachim I and II: the Books of Kings.

Mesillas Yesharim: one of the greatest classical works of *mussar* by R. *Moshe Chaim Luzzatto*.

mesorah: tradition; often used to describe a specific concept or a general approach to Torah received from one's *rebbe* who received the same from his *rebbe*, and so on.

Midrash: a general name for several works dating from the times of the Talmud and *Mishnah* that deal primarily with the homiletical and ethical aspects of the Torah.

Midrash Rabbah: one of the principal works of *Midrash* that remain extant.

Midrash Tanchuma: one of the principal works of *Midrash* that remain extant.

Midrash Yalkut Shimoni: an anthology of different texts of the *Midrash* compiled by *R. Shimon Hadarshan*, late ninth / early tenth century; first complete printing 1527.

Minchas Yehudah: a commentary on *Rashi* on *Chumash* by R. *Yehudah Leib ben Ovadia*, printed in 1609.

minyan: a quorum of ten.

mishkan: the Tabernacle.

Mishlei: the Book of Proverbs.

Mishnah Brurah: A seminal work of *halachah* authored by the *Chofetz Chaim*.

Mishpatim: a section of the Book of Exodus.

Misnagdim: those who opposed *Chassidim*.

mitzvah(-vos): commandment(s) of the Torah.

Mizrachi: a monumental commentary on *Rashi* on *Chumash* by R. *Eliyahu Mizrachi*; first printed in 1627.

Moreshes Avos: an anthology of insights into the *Chumash*.

Moshe: Moses.

R. Moshe Chait: present head of *Yeshivas Chofetz Chaim* in Jerusalem; student of R. *Dovid Leibowitz*.

R. Moshe Feinstein: an eastern European rabbi who emigrated to America and who for many years was widely recognized as the world's preeminent authority in matters of *halachah*.

Moshiach: the Messiah.

mussar: the subject/study/practice of ethical behavior.

mussar seder: an emotion-laden session of *mussar* study.

mussar shmuess: a lecture on a *mussar*-related topic.

Nachalas Yaakov: a commentary on *Rashi* by R. *Yaakov Yekel Solnick*; first printed in 1642.

Nadav and Avihu: the two righteous sons of *Ahron* who lost their lives for improperly conducting the service in the *mishkan*.

Naftali: one of *Yaakov's* sons.

Neilah: the final service of *Yom Kippur*.

neshamah: soul.

Nimrod: A king who attempted to kill *Avraham* by throwing him into a fiery furnace.

Noach: Noah.

R. Nosson bar R. Abba: a rabbi mentioned in the Talmud.

R. Nosson Tzvi Finkel: the *Alter* of *Slobodka*.

Orach Chaim: the section of the *Shulchan Aruch* that deals with daily observances, *Shabbos* and holidays.

Orchos Tzaddikim: an early (probably twelfth- or thirteenth-century) and classic work of *mussar*; author unknown.

Or Hatzafun: a book containing several *mussar schmuessen* of the *Alter* of *Slobodka*.

pasuk(im): verse(es) from the Torah.

Pekudei: the last of the weekly portions of the Book of Exodus.

Pirkei Avos: *Ethics of Our Fathers*; a tractate of the *Mishnah* that deals entirely with ethics.

Pnei Yehoshua: an eighteenth-century commentary on the Talmud.

pshat: the straightforward meaning of a text.

rabbanim: rabbis.

Rabbeinu Bachya: one of the classical commentaries on the Torah which bears the name of its author.

Rama: R. Moshe Isserles of Cracow, 1530-1572, a preeminent *halachic* authority for Ashkenazic Jewry.

Rambam: R. *Moshe ben Maimon*, Maimonides; twelfth-century codifier of *halachah* and author of several major works, 1135-1204.

Ramban: R. *Moshe ben Nachman*; Nachmanides, thirteenth-century head of Spanish Jewry and author of commentary on much of the Torah, 1194-1270.

rasha: an evil person.

Rashba: R. *Shlomo ben Aderes*, thirteenth- and fourteenth-century head of Spanish Jewry, 1235-1310.

Rashi: *R. Shlomo Yitzchaki*, author of a seminal commentary on most areas of the Torah, 1040-1105.

Rav: a rabbi mentioned frequently in the Talmud.

rav: a rabbi.

Rebbe: R. *Yehudah Hanasi*, compiler of the *Mishnah*.

rebbe: teacher of Torah; also used to refer to one's primary teacher of Torah.

rebbetzin: the wife of a rabbi.

Reuvain: Reuben, the eldest of *Yaakov's* twelve sons.

Rivkah: Rebecca, the wife of our forefather *Yitzchak*.

rosh(ei) yeshivah: head(s) of a *yeshivah*; often, one who simply teaches Torah in a *yeshivah*.

ruchnius: spirituality.

Sanhedrin: a tractate of the Talmud.

Sarah: the wife of *Avraham* and mother of *Yitzchak*.

sefer: a book, particularly of Torah writings.

Sefer Chassidim: a book on ethics and *halachah* by *R. Yehudah Hachassid*.

Sefer Hamitzvos: a work by the *Rambam* enumerating the 613 mitzvos of the Torah.

seudah: meal or feast

Sforno: a commentary on the *Chumash*, authored by R. *Ovadia Sforno* (1470-1550); first printed in 1567.

Shaarei Teshuvah: a classical work of *mussar* dealing with *teshuvah* by *R. Yonah* of Gerona, 1180 - 1263.

Shabbos: the Sabbath; also, a tractate of the Talmud.

Shach: a major commentary on the *Shulchan Aruch*, authored by R. *Shabsi Hakohen* of *Vilna*, 1622 – 1663.

Shaul: King Saul.

Shekalim: a tractate of the *Mishnah*.

Shemoneh Esreh: a major section within the daily prayer service.

Shemos: the second of the Five Books of Moses.

shidduch: a mate in marriage; also a proposed partner for marriage.

Shimon: Simon, the second son of *Yaakov*.

shiva: the seven-day period of mourning over the death of a close relative.

shlita: a form of blessing and respect, typically inserted after mention of the name of a *talmid chacham*.

Shmuel: Samuel the prophet; also a rabbi mentioned frequently in the Talmud.

shmuess(en): lecture(s) on a *mussar*-related topic.

shul: synagogue.

Shulchan Aruch: the compilation of Torah law for Jews living during the exile.

sichah: a *shmuess*.

sidra: a portion of the Torah, e.g., *VayEtzei*, *Vayishlach*, etc.

Sifsei Chachamim: a widely used commentary on *Rashi* by R. *Shabsi Mishorer*; first printed in 1680.

R. Siman: a rabbi mentioned in the *Midrash*.

R. Simcha Zisel of Kelm: one of the great personalities of the *mussar* movement and a student of R. *Yisrael Salanter.*

simchos: celebrations such as weddings, bar mitzvos.

Slobodka: a small Lithuanian town that became famous for its great *yeshivah*.

Slobodka mussar: the approach to *mussar* taught by the *Alter* of *Slobodka*.

Sotah: a tractate of the Talmud.

Steipler Gaon: R. *Yaakov Yisrael Kanievsky,* a pre and post-World War II Torah scholar.

Sukkah: a tractate of the Talmud.

talmid(ei) chacham(im): Torah scholar(s).

Tanach: the written Torah; the Old Testament.

Targum Onkeles: an Aramaic translation/interpretation of the *Chumash* written in the period of the *Mishnah,* by *Onkeles* the convert.

Taz: a commentary on *Rashi* by R. *Dovid ben Shmuel Halevi* (author of the *Taz,* on *Shulchan Aruch*), d. 1667; first printed in 1689.

tefillin: phylacteries.

teshuvah: repentence.

tichyeh: a form of blessing for long life, typically inserted after mention of someone's name.

tikkun hamiddos: improvement of one's character traits.

Tisha B'Av: a day of mourning and fasting, a day when, among other things, both Temples in Jerusalem were destroyed.

toeles: benefit; in the commentary of the *Ralbag* an incident related in the Torah is often first discussed and explained. The points that can be learned from the story are then listed as *Toeles* 1, *Toeles* 2, and so forth.

Tomer Dvorah: a sixteenth-century work of *mussar* and *kabbalah* by R. *Moshe Cordevero.*

Tosafos: a massive commentary on the Talmud by a group of twelfth and thirteenth century French rabbis.

tzaddekes: an exceedingly righteous woman.

tzaddik(im): exceedingly righteous man(men).

tzedakah: charity.

Tzedah Laderech: a commentary on *Rashi* by R. *Yissachar Ber*

Eilenberg; first printed in 1623.

tzelem Elokim: the form of the Almighty; normally a referrence to the G-dliness with which man is endowed as a condition of his *neshamah*.

tznius: modesty, usually of dress.

ushpizin: seven guests who each visit the *sukkah* on one of the seven days of *Sukkos*. They are *Avraham, Yitzchak, Yaakov, Yosef, Moshe, Ahron* and *Dovid*.

Vayikra: the third of the Five Books of Moses.

Vilna Gaon: R. *Eliyau ben Shlomo Kramer* of *Vilna*, 1720-1797; one of the most outstanding scholars of Torah, relative to his peers, to have ever lived among the Jewish people.

Volozhin: a small Lithuanian town that became world famous because of its great *yeshivah*.

Yaakov: the patriarch Jacob.

R. Yaakov Kamenetsky: an eastern European rabbi who emigrated to America; student of the *Slobodka Yeshivah*.

yb"l: abbreviation for *yebadel l'chaim*, "may he or she be separated for life"; typically inserted when juxtaposing one who is deceased with one who is alive.

Yefe Toar: the abridged version of *Yefe Toar Haaruch*, printed in many versions of the *Midrash Rabbah*.

Yefe Toar Haaruch: the unabridged commentary on the *Midrash Rabbah* by R. *Shmuel Yafe*, 1525-1595. (In fact both the unabridged and abridged version of the commentary are simply titled *Yefe Toar*. However, to distinguish between the two, this volume has coined the term *Yefe Toar Haaruch*, the "long" *Yefe Toar*, to denote the original and unabridged version.)

Yehoshua: the prophet Joshua.

R. Yehoshua: a rabbi of the   *Mishnah*, mentioned frequently in

Talmud and *Midrash*.

Yehudah: Judah, the son of *Yaakov*.

yeshivah(-vos): school(s) for the study of Torah.

yetzer hara: the evil inclination.

Yevamos: a tractate of the Talmud.

Yiddishkeit: Judaism.

Yisro: Jethro, the father-in-law of *Moshe*.

Yisrael: Israel, the nation; also a name of the patriarch *Yaakov*.

R. Yisrael Baal Shem Tov: eighteenth-century east European rabbi; founder of the *Chassidic* movement.

R. Yisrael Salanter: nineteenth-century founder of the *mussar* movement.

Yitzchak: the patriarch Isaac.

R. Yitzchak Hamburg: R. *Yitzchak ben Yaakov Yekel Halevi Horowitz*, 1715-1767; rabbi of the combined communities of Hamburg, Altona and Wandsbeck.

R. Yochanan ben Zakai: student of *Hillel*, leader of the Torah faithful in Jerusalem at the time of the destruction of the Second Temple by the Romans.

Yoma: a tractate of the Talmud.

Yom Kippur: the Day of Atonement.

R. Yonason Eibeschutz: late seventeenth- and early eighteenth-century leader; rabbi of Prague.

Yoreh Deah: a section of the *Shulchan Aruch*.

Yosef: Joseph, the son of *Yaakov*.

zemiros: words or poetry containing praises to *Hashem* that are set to melody and are typically sung at the *Shabbos* or festival table.

z"l: abbreviation for *zichrono* (or *zichronah* or *zichronam) livrachah* "may his (or her or their) memory be a blessing"; typically inserted when referring to those who are deceased.